Policy and Politics of the Syrian Refugee Crisis in Eastern Mediterranean States

National and Institutional Perspectives

EDITED BY

MAX O. STEPHENSON JR. & YANNIS A. STIVACHTIS

E-INTERNATIONAL RELATIONS PUBLISHING

E-International Relations
Bristol, England
2023

ISBN: 978-1-910814-69-7

Production: Michael Tang
Cover Image: Photobank.kiev.ua/Shutterstock

A catalogue record for this book is available from the British Library.

BREATHE IN AND SMELL THE... IS IT CHEMICALS?
By Beth Greer

Source:

1. https://www.ncbi.nlm.nih.gov/pmc/articles/PMC5093181/

2. https://www.nrdc.org/stories/9-ways-avoid-hormone-disrupting-chemicals

3. https://www.ncbi.nlm.nih.gov/pmc/articles/PMC1892134/

4. https://greatergood.berkeley.edu/article/item/how_to_protect_kids_from_nature_deficit_disorder

5. https://www.epa.gov/report-environment/indoor-air-quality

THE ART OF BREATHING – AS IMPORTANT TODAY AS IT WAS IN ANCIENT CHINA
Dr. Erlene Chiang

References:

1. https://www.ncbi.nlm.nih.gov/pmc/articles/PMC3085832/

* 9 7 8 1 7 3 2 4 4 9 4 5 9 *

E-International Relations

Editor-in-Chief and Publisher: Stephen McGlinchey
Books Editor: Bill Kakenmaster
Editorial assistance: Farah Saleem Düzakman, Qi Zhang, Sam Noble

E-International Relations is the world's leading International Relations website and publisher. Our daily publications feature expert articles, reviews, podcasts and interviews – as well as student learning resources. The website is run by a non-profit organisation based in Bristol, England and staffed by an all-volunteer team. In addition to our website content, E-International Relations publishes a range of books.

As E-International Relations is committed to open access in the fullest sense, free versions of our books are available on our website: https://www.e-ir.info

For Jessica

Whose Joy and Wonder Provided
An Enduring Example to All
Who Encountered Her

Editors

Max O. Stephenson, Jr. serves as a Professor of Public and International Affairs and the Director of the Institute for Policy and Governance at Virginia Tech (VTIPG). His research and teaching interests include human rights and refugees; civil society and democratic theory, especially as pertaining to conceptions of political agency and social change processes; NGOs and international development; and peacebuilding. He is the author or editor of 11 books and more than 80 refereed articles and book chapters. He has taught graduate and undergraduate courses related to community change and development both domestically and internationally for nearly three decades. Stephenson has also led the VTIPG Community Change Collaborative (CCC), an interdisciplinary graduate student group with academic and professional interests in community change dynamics and praxis in the United States and abroad, for more than a decade. His commentaries concerning American and international politics and democracy can be accessed at the following links: https://ipg.vt.edu/tags.resource.html/ipg_vt_edu:Soundings https://ipg.vt.edu/tags.resource.html/ipg_vt_edu:Tidings

Yannis A. Stivachtis is Professor of Political Science and holder of the Jean Monnet Chair at Virginia Tech. He also serves as Director of the Center for European Union, Transatlantic & Trans-European Space Studies (CEUTTSS) – *A Jean Monnet Center of Excellence*; Director of the International Studies Program; and University Coordinator of the Diplomacy Lab. His research and teaching interests include International Relations theory (English School), security/strategic studies, and European Studies. He is currently the editor of the *Critical European Studies* book series (Routledge) and co-editor of the *Athens Journal of Mediterranean Studies* (AJMS). His most recent books include: *The Routledge Handbook of Critical European Studies* (Routledge, 2021; co-editor); *Regional Security in the Middle East: Sectors, Variables and Issues* (E-International Relations Publishing, 2019; co-editor); *Conflict and Diplomacy in the Middle East: External Actors and Regional Rivalries* (E-International Relations Publishing, 2018; editor); *The State/Society Relationship in Security Analysis* (U.S. Army War College Press, 2015). *Revisiting the Idea of the European Union as Empire* (Routledge, 2015; co-editor); *Europe after Enlargement* (Routledge, 2014; co-editor); *The European Union and Peace-building* (special issue, *Review of European* Studies, 5(3), 2013; co-editor); *EUrope and the World* (special issue, *Review of European* Studies, 4(3), 2012; editor); *Human and State (In)Security in a Globalized World*, 2nd edition (Kendall Hunt, 2011); and *The Economic Dimension of Turkey's Accession to the European Union* (Brussels University Press, 2011; co-editor). He has also published several book chapters and articles in peer-reviewed journals.

Abstract

The large and continuing refugee stream that arose from the long-lived Syrian Civil War that began in 2011 has deeply affected the politics and demography of the countries of the eastern Mediterranean. This edited volume assesses the politics of that recent refugee crisis from the vantage point of those nations shaped by it or whose leaders have explicitly sought to ameliorate it or use it otherwise to mobilize support.

First, and overall, the book employs the Copenhagen School theoretical framework to analyze how Syrian refugees have been securitized and de-securitized by national governments as well as political and social groups operating in the eastern Mediterranean countries. Second, and relatedly, it explores whether and to what extent the nations of that region have sought to integrate Syrian refugees into their societies. To that end, its chapters examine the policies that receiving states have enacted and the actions that they have undertaken to address that challenge. A share of the contributors also analyze the roles that international actors, including the European Union (EU), the United Nations High Commissioner for Refugees (UNHCR) and non-governmental organizations (NGOs), have played in the process of Syrian refugee integration in the east Mediterranean region.

To investigate these overarching concerns, the chapters address four basic questions for the nations or organizations they treat. First, how the still unfolding refugee crisis has affected the institution or country under examination; that is, what policies and processes were pursued, crafted or adopted to address the effects of the crisis and how government leaders and advocates framed, justified or rationalized those strategies. Second, how relevant governmental or institutional policy has evolved as the Syrian Civil War and its displacing effects have continued and why. Third, what the implications of evolving national or organizational choices have been for the security and humane treatment (conduct in accord with existing human rights conventions) of refugees. Finally, what broader significance the Syrian crisis appears to portend for policy and law governing refugees in the relevant states and institutions analyzed.

Taken together, this book's chapters suggest that several cross-cutting themes or phenomena have played vital, if varying, roles in east Mediterranean government and popular responses to the mass displacement and migration prompted by the Syrian Civil War. First, these essays highlight the problem of alterity or othering as a central feature of these nations' reactions to the Syrian mass migration challenge. Second, human tendencies to xenophobia and fear of difference and change have played a key role in producing broad popular ill-will and government opposition to assisting Syria's displaced. Finally, these currents merged in each of the countries under examination, although at varying speeds and to changing degrees during the decade of the Syrian migration, to generate calls by many individuals within them that migrants and refugees constituted a security threat to be met with demonization and removal and/or with efforts to ensure they were kept 'at bay' at all costs. The comprehensive security approach employed in this study helps analysts identify salient forces and concerns crucial to such public movements and, at least indirectly, can help government leaders marshal efforts to prevent or mitigate their exacerbation or recurrence.

Acknowledgements

One truism of all scholarship, indeed, of all writing, is that authors accumulate a list of debts to those who assist and support them as they develop their work. This volume is no exception to that well-worn rule. We wish to thank our participating contributors who exhibited both patience and persistence as this book came together during the travails of a world pandemic. We have worked with each appreciatively and commend and thank them for their dedication and professionalism as they honed their efforts during a difficult time. We have each also relied on family as we developed this volume. We sincerely appreciate their support. Yannis A. Stivachtis wishes to thank Max Stephenson Jr. for his excellent editorial work. Max Stephenson Jr. wishes to thank Yannis Stivachtis for reaching out concerning this project possibility, for his enduring good will and for his always balanced perspective and judgment. Finally, we each wish to thank Cathy Grimes for her superb editorial assistance.

Max O. Stephenson Jr. & Yannis A. Stivachtis

Blacksburg, VA

4 February 2023

Contents

Contributors

Renad Abbadi serves as Professor of Linguistics and Translation at Al-Hussein Bin Talal University (AHU), Jordan. She has served at (AHU) as Director of the Language Center, Head of the Department of English Language and Literature, and Dean of the College of Arts.

Fatima Alzyoud is an Assistant Professor at the University of Massachusetts Dartmouth, College of Nursing and Health Sciences.

Sukaina Alzyoud serves as Dean of Academic Development and International Outreach at Hashemite University, Jordan. She has also served as Head of Faculty at the Department of Community and Mental Health Nursing, Faculty of Nursing.

Evanthia Balla is an Assistant Professor at the University of Évora, Department of Economics, *Escola de Ciências Sociais* (Portugal). She directs the MA in International Relations and European Studies.

Emma Casey serves as a Research Assistant at the Virginia Tech Department of Political Science specializing in conflict studies and non-governmental organizations.

Muddather Abu Karaki serves as Professor of Political Science at Al-Hussein Bin Talal University (AHU), Jordan. He has also served as head of the Department of Strategic Studies and International Relations as well as Dean of the College of Arts at AHU.

Erica Martin serves as a Research Assistant at the Virginia Tech Department of Political Science specializing in National Security and Foreign Affairs, Criminology, and Russian.

Zeynep S. Mencutek is a Senior Researcher at Bonn International Centre for Conflict Studies, Germany and Research Affiliate at Canadian Excellence Chair in Migration and Integration Programme, Ryerson University, Canada.

Neda Moayerian is an Assistant Professor at the University of Tehran School of Urban Planning and a Non-resident Research Associate at the Virginia Tech Institute for Policy and Governance.

Augusta Nannerini is a PhD candidate in International Relations and Political Science at the Geneva Graduate Institute for International and Development Studies and a Research Assistant at its Centre on Conflict, Development and Peacebuilding.

Ayat Nashwan is Head of the Department of Sociology at the University of Sharjah, United Arab Emirates as well as faculty member of the Department of Sociology and Social Work at Yarmouk University, Jordan.

Georgeta V. Pourchot is Associate Director for Strategic Initiatives and Partnerships at the Center for European Union, Transatlantic & Trans-European Space Studies (CEUTTSS) - *A Jean Monnet Center of Excellence* at Virginia Tech.

Alexandra Prodromidou is an Assistant Professor at the Business Administration and Economics Department of CITY College, University of York, Europe Campus and Research Associate at the Southeast European Research Centre (SEERC).

Dina Rashed serves as Associate Dean of the College for Academic Affairs, the University of Chicago. She is a political scientist specializing in Civil-Military Relations, state-society dynamics, violence against women, and Middle East politics.

Dania Shahin serves as a Research Assistant at the University of Jordan, School of Pharmacy.

Dimitris Tsarouhas is Associate Professor at the Department of International Relations, Bilkent University, Turkey and Research Fellow at Virginia Tech's Jean Monnet Center of Excellence for European Union, Transatlantic, and Trans-European Space Studies (CEUTTSS), USA. He is a Non-resident Senior Research Fellow at ELIAMEP and a Scientific Council Member of the Foundation for European Progressive Studies in Brussels.

Faye Ververidou is a Research Associate at the Southeast European Research Centre (SEERC).

Introduction

MAX O. STEPHENSON JR. AND YANNIS A. STIVACHTIS

The Syrian refugee crisis began in 2011, when the Arab Spring reached that nation and the Bashar al-Assad regime sought to counter protests demanding social justice and democracy. The first wave of 5,000 Syrians fled the ensuing conflict to seek asylum in Lebanon at the end of March 2011. Syria's civil war resulted in the forcible displacement of about 13.2 million people, including 6.6 million refugees, 6.2 million internally displaced people, and 140,000 asylum seekers, to various countries around the world. Over time, European Union (EU) member states took in a share of those Syrian refugees. In 2015 alone, more than 1 million Syrian and other refugees from the Middle East applied for asylum in the EU, and approximately 3,770 of that number died while trying to cross the Mediterranean Sea to possible refuge.

The Syrian refugee crisis continues to have a large impact on European societies today and has sparked a dangerous rise in exclusionary populism, right-wing nationalist movements, and national security concerns. Anti-immigration and anti-asylum seeker sentiments have escalated in Europe since the outset of the Syrian refugee crisis. This growth stems from two sources. First, it arises from concerns that the national security in affected nations is being threatened by 'outsiders'. Those fears have resulted in the 'otherization' of emigres by nationalistic groups, particularly. Second, it stems from a post-9/11 linkage in the popular mind between Islam and terrorism in many Western countries, which has resulted in the framing of refugees from the Middle East for many Europeans as possible 'terrorists'. Due to the salience of these sentiments, various far-right political parties and groups in Europe have gained political power and recognition during the past decade, adopting harsh immigration rhetoric and successfully 'othering' migrants and refugees, making it very difficult for EU member nation governments to enact and implement policies seeking the integration of Syrian refugees into their societies.

This edited volume explores whether and to what extent the countries of the Eastern Mediterranean especially have sought to integrate refugees of the Syrian conflict into their national societies. To this end, each chapter examines the rhetoric of various political actors operating in those countries as well as the practices of their governments. Specific chapters ask how those forces securitized and de-securitized Syrian refugee flows and how effective national governments have been in addressing the national security concerns their exodus and influx have created. A share of our authors analyze the roles that international actors, such as the EU, the United Nations High Commission of Refugees (UNHCR), and nongovernmental organizations (NGOs), have played in assisting the process of Syrian refugee integration into the societies of the Eastern Mediterranean countries.

The Geographical Context: Eastern Mediterranean

As we considered what nations to address in this volume, we first had to identify what constitutes the eastern Mediterranean. We have adopted Regional Security Complex Theory (RSCT) to help us address that challenge (Buzan 1983 and 1991; Buzan and Waever 2003).

Given the increasing significance of international relations in the eastern Mediterranean area during the past decade or so, scholars have taken it for granted that there exists an eastern Mediterranean regional security complex, but few have sought to demonstrate why that is so (Litsas and Tziambiris 2019). This is despite the fact that Buzan, the originator of this conceptualization, has rejected the idea that such a security complex exists and has instead placed the states of the south and eastern coast of the Mediterranean Sea in the Middle East security complex and those of the north shore within the European security complex (Buzan 1983 and 1991).

Stivachtis (2019) has attempted to tackle this challenge by pointing to the need to revisit Buzan's Regional Security Complex Theory. He (2021) has argued that there is a need to expand the range of factors that play an important role in defining a Mediterranean security complex and, as an extension, the Mediterranean region. Unlike Buzan, he suggests that security threats are not necessarily the product of enmity among states or the result of a state's foreign policy, but they can also arise from domestic political and economic instability. This assemblage of threats bind the Mediterranean countries together to such an extent that one may reasonably speak of a 'Common Security in the Mediterranean Region' (OSCE 2015). Such matters include, among other concerns that might be listed, violent extremism and radicalization that lead to terrorism and arms proliferation; cultural and religious intolerance that necessitates the undertaking of interfaith and intercultural dialogue; irregular migranti and refugee flows that require the regulation of migration and the protection of refugees; migrant smuggling and human trafficking that demands enhanced regional cooperation in criminal matters; and economic sluggishness and stagnation that requires new models of development and creates demand for regional economic cooperation. Taken together, these factors help to define a Mediterranean security complex.

Indeed, according to Stivachtis (2021), the Mediterranean security complex includes three security sub-complexes. The first is an eastern Mediterranean sub-complex centered on three conflicts: Greek-Turkish enmity, the Syrian Civil War, and the ongoing Israeli-Palestinian/Arab clash. This sub-complex includes Greece, Turkey, Cyprus, Israel, the Palestinians in the West Bank and Gaza Strip, Lebanon, Syria, Egypt, and Libya. The second group or sub-complex includes Italy, Libya, Albania, and Malta in the central Mediterranean. This security regime revolves mainly around migration, with Italy playing a dominant role due to its historical ties with Libya and Albania. The third sub-complex includes France, Algeria, Tunisia, Morocco, Spain, and Portugal in the western Mediterranean and revolves mainly around migration and its perceived associated threats (i.e., terrorism, radicalism, human trafficking, etc.). Due to its significant power capabilities and its traditional ties (political, cultural, and linguistic) with the countries of northwest Africa (Algeria, Tunisa, and Moroco), France is the dominant actor in this sub-complex.

However, nothing prevents the analyst from addressing a particular security sub-complex in its own right. Therefore, the character and dynamics of the eastern Mediterranean security sub-complex can surely be studied, reuslting in a focus on Greece, Turkey, Cyprus, Israel, Lebanon, Syria, Egypt, and the Palestinians in the West Bank and Gaza Strip.

But what about Libya, Malta, and Italy in the central Mediterranean? According to Buzan and Waever (2003), nothing prevents an analyst from investigating two security sub-complexes at once, provided that they exhibit shared concerns that suggest the utility of considering them as a single security complex. There are two factors that bring Libya, Malta, and Italy within the eastern Mediterranean complex: the Syrian refugee flow of the past decade and the need for all ten coastal states to regulate their affairs and to manage potential or actual conflicts that have arisen due to the New International Law of the Sea, which has necessitated the definition of the sea zones (especially the Exclusive Economic zones) of those states.

Moreover, the eastern Mediterranean region constitutes a high-level security complex, which also includes France, a Mediterranean country which has significant power capabilities that extend beyond its immediate western Mediterranean security sub-complex neighbors. The eastern Mediterranean security complex also experiences a significant degree of 'overlay' through its member nations' involvement in regional affairs with the great powers, including the United States, the United Kingdom, Russia, the EU, and lately, China, whose capabilities extend far beyond their immediate boundaries and whose power is sufficient to influence actors in the eastern Mediterranean region. Finally, as far as its essential structure is concerned, the eastern Mediterranean security complex is anarchic in character, as no state dominates it. Within the complex moreover, certain patterns of amity and enmity have remained relatively constant, while the distribution of power favors states such as France, Turkey, and Israel. Nevertheless, it is important to underscore the fact that, the Mediterranean security complex is very dynamic as there are states (i.e., Turkey) that seem eager and capable of challenging the *status quo* thereby contributing to a measure of fluidity in the complex's patterns of integration and organization.

We turn next to a discussion of the theoretical framework that has guided us as we have sought to understand and describe the rhetoric of various political actors operating in this volume's targeted countries regarding the Syrian refugees as well as the resulting constraints that the governments of those nations have encountered in efforts to integrate those individuals into their societies.

The Theoretical Framework: Comprehensive Security and Securitization

To understand how the issue of refugee flows can be perceived as a security issue, we need first to note that a perceived concern becomes a security issue to government actors and advocates alike when it is defined as posing an existential threat that requires immediate and extraordinary measures to address it. We employ the comprehensive approach to security associated with the Copenhagen School to help us explore this dynamic here.

Comprehensive Security

This security approach developed in the early 1980s and called for a redefinition of the concept of security, arguing that non-military issues may also constitute security matters and consequently should be considered part of the international security agenda. Thereafter, the concept of security came to include an array of political, societal, economic, and environmental dimensions (Buzan 1983).

In the military sector, the referent object of security is the state and military action usually threatens its territorial integrity and the function of various national institutions (Buzan 1991, 116–118). This is so because military action can repress the idea of state, subject its physical base to strain and damage, destroy its various institutions, diminish its basic protective functions, and damage the layers of social and individual interest that underlie its superstructure. Therefore, military threats, which mainly arise from the external environment, are traditionally accorded the highest priority in national security consideration.

In the political sector, relevant security threats influence or are perceived as potentially affecting, the organizational stability of the state. For example, such concerns may result from governmental actions that pose major threats to individuals or groups. In turn, resistance to the government, efforts to overthrow it or movements aimed at autonomy or independence may all threaten state stability and security (Buzan 1991, 119–122). Very often, political threats may result from actors and forces in both the domestic and external environments of a state and thus, it can become quite difficult to distinguish those from military threats. Consequently, state actors may fear political threats as much as overtly military ones.

In the societal sector, the referent object of security is collective identities that can function independent of the state, such as religions and ethnicities (Buzan 1991, 122–123). In relations between states, significant external threats are often part of a larger constellation of military and political threats. Such perceived threats can be difficult to disentangle from political or military ones.

The referent objects and existential threats in the economic sector are more difficult to identify. The main problem with the idea of economic security arises from the fact that the normal condition of actors in a market economy is one of risk, competition, and uncertainty. However, when the consequences of economic threat reach beyond the strictly economic into the military and political spheres, three potential national security issues may emerge. Those involve linkages between economic capability on the one hand, and military capacity, power, and socio-political stability, on the other hand (Schultz 1977).

In the environmental sector, the range of possible referent objects is large. The basic concern, however, is how human beings are relating to their physical environment. These threats do not operate in isolation, but interact in several and often contradictory ways. Environmental threats, including military and economic ones, can damage the physical base of the state, perhaps to a sufficient extent to threaten its animating idea and institutions. As a result of this salience, environmental issues have increasingly moved into the political arena.

According to the comprehensive security perspective, the military, political, economic, societal, and environmental sectors are interdependent with the result that 'spill-over' effects afoot in one sector have the potential to affect, positively or negatively, other sectors. For example, migration and refugee issues are often associated with societal and economic security, but they often also have implications for the political and environmental security sectors (Stivachtis 1999).

The comprehensive security approach addresses relevant factors at three levels: first, for whom is security intended to be provided (i.e., individual, group, community, state, etc.); second, from what kind of threats are they to be secured; and, finally, by what means is such security to be obtained. These are critical questions because this approach is often employed by government actors to devise and press specific policy prescriptions. In this sense, it is noteworthy that its use may raise significant political questions that invite resistance from an initially unknowable share of affected parties.

Securitization

Securitization is the process whereby various actors operating within the domestic environment of a state seek to transform subjects from political issues into matters of security, thus enabling extraordinary means to be implemented to address them. Issues that become securitized do not necessarily represent concerns essential to the objective survival of a state, but rather matters that one or more actors have successfully constructed as existential problem(s) (Waever 1993 and 1995; Buzan, Waever and de Wilde 1998; Williams 2003).

Securitization theorists assert that successfully securitized subjects receive disproportionate amounts of attention and resources compared to concerns that do not, regardless of the objective significance of each. Securitization studies aim to understand who securitizes (securitizing actor), on what bases (threats), for whom (referent object), why, with what results, and not least, under what conditions (Waever 1993 and 1995; Taureck 2006).

Securitization typically begins with a 'speech act' concerning a particular threat, by an authoritative national leader, institution, political party, or political group. Such efforts attempt to shift an issue from normal politics into a security concern, thereby legitimating extraordinary measures to address it. To be successful, the securitization act must be accepted by the audience, regardless of whether the concern constitutes a legitimate threat (Balzacq 2005). The audience may be technical, bureaucratic, policymakers or the public. Different audiences can perform different functions by accepting a securitizing claim (Roe 2008).

Securitization involves four components: first, a securitizing actor/agent (the entity that makes the securitizing statement); second, a proposed existential threat (the object or idea that has been identified as potentially harmful): third, a referent object (the object or idea that is purportedly under threat and needs protection); and finally, an audience (the target population that needs to be persuaded to accept the issue as a security threat) (Waever 1993; Taureck 2006).

That a given subject is securitized does not necessarily mean that such must occur for the survival of a given state, but merely means that someone has successfully constructed an object or concern as an existential problem. The ability to securitize a given subject is, however, highly dependent on the status of a given actor and whether similar issues are generally perceived as threats.

A subject that has been successfully securitized will receive disproportionate attention and resources in comparison with matters that have not been securitized, even when other concerns cause more harm. Successfully securitizing concerns makes it possible for leaders to legitimize extraordinary means to address that matter. Such could include declaring a state of emergency or mobilizing the military and/or the police force. Furthermore, when an issue is labelled as a security problem, it can then be considered an illegitimate subject for political or academic debate. Thus, securitization can easily be viewed as a negative process that undermines democratic processes and diminishes necessary scrutiny that would otherwise be focused on political elites (Roe 2012).

Securitization affects all five security sectors identified by the Copenhagen School. However, due to interdependence, a securitization could involve more than one of those domains. For example, immigration and refugee issues are readily securitized as concerns of terrorist infiltration and that argument is regularly employed as grounds for tight control of borders (Faist 2005; Huysmans 2006; Adamson 2006; Gerard 2014). Because it is now generally easier to securitize an issue in the aftermath of the 9/11 attacks, a concern for safety and security has frequently taken attention away from the economic factors that have always been at play in international migration. In addition, leaders can seek to securitize migrants' countries of origin, diaspora, emigration, and citizenship (Waever et al., 1993).

Since securitized subjects receive disproportionate attention and resources compared to other concerns, some political strategists suggest that existing public policy issues can gain more salience with the public when advocates succeed in promoting such status for them. Daniel Deudney (1990) has criticized securitization as being too liable to unleash the emotive power of nationalism in unhelpful ways. Relatedly, and regarding the securitization of migration and refugees, Ainhoa Ruiz Benedicto (2019, 5) has warned of the adverse effects of such processes for forcibly displaced persons and argued that 'In this context of securitization of border regions, population movement is understood and treated as a suspicious activity that needs to be controlled, monitored and registered, while the migration of often forcibly displaced people and refugees is seen as a security threat that must be intercepted'.

Book Structure

This book is divided into two parts and fourteen chapters. In Chapter 1, Max O. Stephenson Jr and Yannis A. Stivachtis focus on how refugees are securitized and what policies receiving states should enact and what actions they should undertake to integrate refugees into their national societies effectively.

In Chapter 2, Neda Moayerian and Max O. Stephenson Jr. analyze how Jordan and Lebanon, two major Syrian conflict refugee host countries, and the UN High Commissioner for Refugees (UNHCR) have responded to the Syrian Civil War and the refugee exodus it spawned. More particularly, the authors trace the changing strategies that the UNHCR has adopted – and how it has responded to shifting social, political, and economic conditions and relevant public policies in Lebanon and Jordan during the Syrian conflict. They argue that since the Syrian Civil War began in 2011, the ensuing refugee crisis has required many nations and international and nongovernmental institutions to craft new policies and processes and implement existing ones on a large scale to address its impacts. According to Moayerian and Stephenson, this has been true not only in absolute terms, but also within specific nations across time. For example, as the conflict continued, with no solution in sight and host countries confronted an overwhelming demand for public services, even those with historically welcoming policies toward refugees reduced their support to Syrian refugees to decrease the costs on their infrastructures, economies, and citizenries.

In Chapter 3, Evanthia Balla observes that the war in Afghanistan, the war in Iraq, and the turmoil of the Arab Spring all led to growing instability in Europe's neighborhood, creating the most severe refugee crisis in the region since World War II. Balla points out that the EU and its member states are the leading donors of international aid to Syrians inside that country and across the region and that the humanitarian drama that the nation's civil war has produced is far from over. Her chapter explores and analyzes the EU's response to the Syrian refugee crisis. She presents an overview of the Syrian refugee crisis, followed by an analysis of the European Union's response to that humanitarian and security calamity. She contends that internal malfunctions at the European level – in terms of policy and politics – have negatively affected the EU's response to the Syrian refugee crisis. She concludes that the crisis needs to be treated as an opportunity for further integration, rather than as an excuse by Union member states for further division and political deadlock.

Georgeta Pourchot offers an evaluation of the rise of civil society in the context of the 2011 Syrian civil conflict and the resulting refugee crisis in Chapter 4. Pourchot asks whether a civil society could function in Syria under conditions of government restrictions on freedom, and in the context of a civil uprising lasting more than a decade. She uses Western and Arabic concepts of civil society to identify whether the activities of specific Syrian groups amount to an emerging civil society. She argues that two types of civil group activities, advocacy and humanitarian relief, indicate that Syrians have indeed organized themselves outside of, and despite, government efforts to exert control, to provide support to people displaced by the conflict; a fact that demonstrates in her view that Syria is evidencing a nascent civil society.

Part II explores national responses to the Syrian refugee crisis.

In Chapter 5, Zeynep Mencutek and Ayat Nashwan draw on the conceptual debates concerning resilience to examine the Jordanian response to Syria's mass refugee migration. They focus on how Jordan's long-term refugee policy plans have adopted the vocabulary of resilience. Their document analysis demonstrates that the concept of resilience is widely used and now connotes several positive, but ambiguous, meanings. They suggest that national policy plans describe resilience as a pillar of refugee governance alongside humanitarian assistance, as a substitute for development objectives, as a characteristic of the system and a desired trait of refugees and host communities. Moreover, they argue that policymakers perceive resilience as a good value and aim in which to invest. According to Mencutek and Nashwan, resilience terminology potentially yields three benefits. First, it enables governments to claim ownership of refugee governance and to address the needs of affected host communities. Second, through perhaps overemphasizing resilience, Jordanian policymakers have appropriated a regional and global humanitarian policy shift towards a long-term self-reliance agenda. Third, the vocabulary has further legitimized development support by providing evidence that employed wording to which many donors often react favorably, including transparency, cost-effectiveness, crisis prevention, vulnerability assessment, and others. In these ways, they argue, resilience discourse may allow Jordanian government policymakers to build on their adoption of a moderate diplomatic tone concerning hosting refugees.

Sukaina Alzyoud, Fatima Alzyoud, and Dania Shahin describe the Lebanese government's response to the evolving Syrian refugee crisis in Chapter 6. They assess published reports, studies, and articles to chart the twists and turn of the Lebanese response and argue that the nation's government enacted policies to address health care, education, food security, housing, and employment. They contend that the economic and health care system elements assumed center stage in the government's efforts to manage the crisis. They conclude that the country's economy and health care system were hard hit by the crisis and that the government's response appeared to occur piecemeal rather than to be strategically planned. In contrast, they suggest, the governmental response appears to be based on the government's political agenda and availability of donor money.

Jameel Abu Muddather, Renad Abbadi Karaki, and Max Stephenson Jr. report in Chapter 7 on the results of an empirical study they conducted to explore the self-perception and awareness of human rights and agency of a sample of Syrian refugees employed as itinerant farmworkers near Ma'an in south-central Jordan, and in Ghor in that nation's Jordan River Valley. They found that those they interviewed were leading geographically and socially isolated lives and knew little about their rights and did not seek actively to express their agency. They situated their analysis of their interviewees' sense of agency within Arendt and Benhabib's conceptions of 'the right to have rights,' the paradoxical danger implicit in human freedom and the power of alterity as a motive force in human behavior.

Chapter 8 presents Dina Rashed's investigation of Egypt's policies toward the Syrian refugee crisis since 2011. Her analysis highlights the combination of challenges and opportunities facing Syrian refugees and their host communities in Egypt during that period. Rashed discusses the political context of the Syrian and Egyptian uprisings and how they have affected Syrians in the country. She argues that the Egyptian government's stance towards refugees has been shaped by considerations of domestic stability and economic capacity. She notes that like Syria, Egypt experienced mass protests in 2011 but the political paths of the two countries have since diverged significantly. She argues that while Egypt's political turmoil resulted in two mass protests and regime changes in 2011 and 2013, Syria has slipped into civil war with regional and international powers supporting the warring parties. Moreover, Rashed suggests that Egyptian leaders view potential violent spillover effects from neighboring conflicts as a serious security threat and that perception has shaped that government's policies regulating entry and treatment of Syrian refugees. She concludes that economically speaking, the Egyptian government has worked to restore macroeconomic stability and provide appropriate services to its citizens during the years she examined, yet the effects of following neoliberal international prescriptions as it has done so have affected living conditions for both citizens and Syrian refugees.

Yannis Stivachtis and Erica Martin examine the responses of the Israeli and Cypriot governments to the Syrian refugee crisis in Chapter 9. They focus on the nativist frameworks used to discriminate against asylum seekers in both nations. They argue that Israel and Cyprus have exhibited many similarities in their political and social responses to asylum seekers and refugees as both countries have mandated that these groups may only temporarily be granted asylum. In addition, each has created policies that make it difficult for them to gain access to the social services they need to survive. In both states, Stivachtis and Martin claim, asylum seekers and refugees have been 'othered' by local right-wing political actors to protect the identity of the dominant ethnic group. Those groups have employed negative terminology including, 'infiltrators' and 'barbarians,' alongside mass media sources to dehumanize and delegitimize these already marginalized individuals. Moreover, right-wing groups have blamed asylum seekers and refugees for social problems, such as rising crime rates and economic hiccups for which they are not responsible. Finally, asylees and refugees have been targeted and 'otherized' in the context of Israel's historical conflict with Palestine and Cyprus's long-standing conflict with Turkey in which, in fact, they have no role. As such, they have also been racialized, discriminated against, and cut off from civil society. As a result, neither state has engaged in any meaningful efforts at refugee integration. Instead, each has maintained their practice of ethnocentrism and nativism through exclusionary frameworks to protect what their leaders perceive to be cultural security in Israel and cultural and economic security in Cyprus.

In Chapter 10, Dimitris Tsarouhas discusses Turkey's critical role in the migration and refugee crisis that affected the EU in 2015–16. His main argument is that Turkey has sought to cope with the crisis in two distinct identifiable phases. According to Tsarouhas, during the first, which spanned roughly 2010 to 2015, Turkey sought to reap political benefits from the Syrian crisis. The nation did so by welcoming millions of Syrians and seeking to manage the situation by upgrading its domestic infrastructure to do so with the support of external actors, including especially, the European Union. Turkish government leaders believed that Assad's regime would soon collapse, placing Ankara in a prime position to influence Syria's future. For Tsarouhas, the fact that this expectation did not materialize weighed heavily in subsequent developments. In the second period, post-2015, and as the crisis became endemic, Turkey's government confronted a threat and an opportunity. On the one hand, Turkey's ability to manage the crisis declined, as the number of Syrians residing in the country remained very high and opposition parties began offering an effective political narrative that blamed the government for harboring large numbers of 'interlopers'. Finally, and as a result, during this second period, Tsarouhas argues, Turkey's government began losing control of the discourse regarding Syrian migrants and refugees, a fact that contributed to its electoral defeat in the 2019 municipal elections.

In Chapter 11, Alexandra Prodromidou and Faye Ververidou examine the evolution of the Greek legal framework of integration policy and analyze that nation's policy implementation gaps in its application. They note that the 2016 EU-Turkey agreement shifted Greece's role gradually from a transit country to a destination nation. In turn, that fact prompted a rise in the importance of integration policies in Greece. They point out that despite this change, strong securitization tendencies in policy formation, both at the EU and the national levels, resulted in the prioritisation of deterrence of irregular migration and border security over integration.

In Chapter 12, Augusta Nannerini shows that that there has not been a single or unified Italian response to the Syrian refugee crisis. Instead, she outlines three different ways refugees, including those fleeing the Syrian Civil War, have recently been received in Italy. To do so, she frames her analysis by referring to the dangerous routes by which Syrian refugees can reach the country, paying particular attention to the Central Mediterranean Route. Next, she discusses the safe pathways to reach Italy put in place by the Ministry of the Interior with its resettlement program and the initiative of the Humanitarian Corridors led by faith-based organizations and civil society groups. She argues that the refugees who arrive in Italy by these means constitute a category dubbed 'administrative arrivals,' which entails special rules and procedures to apply for asylum and to be part of programs to foster social integration. She suggests that the difference between the categories and related treatments of the 'spontaneous arrivals' and the 'administrative arrivals' demonstrates that *how* Syrian refugees arrive in Italy has played a critical role in determining the different responses they have confronted.

In Chapter 13, Yannis Stivachtis and Emma Casey focus on the treatment of Syrian refugees in Libya and Malta. They argue that the Syrian refugee flow has put great strain on the resources and institutions of the two countries, which have found themselves pressed hard in their efforts to address the crisis. Stivachtis and Casey point out that both countries' governments have faced pressures from internal and external sources, which have fostered an environment in which it has been difficult for policymakers to address the refugee issue coherently. They also note that the two nations have both permitted, and failed to address, the inhumane conditions and treatment of refugees at their detention centers. In Libya, they suggest, detention centers have become a hotspot for corruption, human trafficking, torture, and forced labor while Malta's detention centers have been criticized for their improper screening processes and inadequate living conditions. They also argue that the decentralized nature of Libyan society and complexity of power relationships make any reform extremely difficult. Malta's government, meanwhile, has confronted the reality of the country's small size, limited resources, and its population's broad disdain for migrants. Malta's migration challenges have been exacerbated by the lack of a coherent EU policy, which has encouraged the nation's policymakers in their decision to adopt an aggressive anti-migrant posture.

Finally, Stephenson and Stivachtis sketch the main themes of the book, and their implications, in Chapter 14.

References

Adamson, Fiona. 2006. Crossing Borders: International Migration and National Security. *International Security* 31(1), 165–199.

Balzacq, Thomas. 2005. The three Phases of Securitization: Political Agency, Audience and context. *European Journal of International Relations* 11(2), 171–201.

Benedicto, Ruiz Ainhoa. 2019. Guarding the fortress. *Transnational Institute. 2019-11-26*. https://www.tni.org/en/guarding-the-fortress

Buzan, Barry. 1991. *People, States and Fear. 2nd edition*. London: Harvester Wheatsheaf.

Buzan, Barry and Waever, Ole. 2003. *Regions and Powers: The Structure of International Security*. Cambridge: Cambridge University Press.

Buzan, Barry, Waever, Ole, and de Wilde, Jaap. 1998. *Security: A New Framework for Analysis*. Boulder: Lynne Rienner.

Deudney, Daniel. 1990. *The Case Against Linking Environmental Degradation and National Security. Millennium: Journal of International Studies* 19(3), 461–476.

Faist, Thomas. 2005. The Migration-Security Nexus: International Migration and Security. In: *Migration, Citizenship and Ethnos: Incorporation Regimes in Germany, Western Europe and North America*, edited by Y. Michal Bodemann and Gökce Yurdakul, pp. 103–120. New York: Palgrave Macmillan.

Gerard, Alison. 2014. *The Securitization of Migration and Refugee Women*. New York: Routledge.

Huysmans, Jef. 2006. *The Politics of Insecurity: Fear, Migration, and Asylum in the EU*. Routledge: London.

Litsas, Spiros and Tziampiris, Aristotelis (Eds.). 2019. *The New Eastern Mediterranean*. New York: Springer.

OSCE. 2015. Common Security in the Mediterranean Region: Challenges and Opportunities. https://www.csce.gov/international-impact/publications/security-mediterranean-region-challenges-and-opportunities

Roe, Paul. 2008. Actor, Audience(s), and Emergency Measures. *Security Dialogue* 39(6), 615–635.

Roe, Paul. 2012. Is securitization an 'negative' concept? Revisiting the normative debate over normal versus extraordinary politics. *Security Dialogue* 43(3), 249–266.

Schultz, Charles, L. 1977. The Economic Content of National Security Policy. *Foreign Affairs*, 51(3), 529–535.

Stivachtis, Yannis A. 1999. Kosovar Refugees and National Security. *Refuge*, Special Issue, August 1999, 41–46.

Stivachtis, Yannis A. 2019. Eastern Mediterranean: A New Region? Theoretical Considerations. In: S. Litsas & A. Tziampiris (Eds.), *The New Eastern Mediterranean*. New York: Springer, 45–59.

Stivachtis, Yannis A. 2021 A Mediterranean Region? Regional Security Complex Theory Revisited. *International Relations*, 21(3), 416–428.

Taureck, Rita. 2006. Securitization theory and securitization studies. *Journal of International Relations and Development* 9(1), 53–61.

Waever, Ole. 1993. Securitization and Desecuritization. In: On Security, edited by Ronnie. D. Lipschutz, pp. 46–86.

Waever, Ole, Buzan, Barry, Kelstrup, Morten, and Lemaitre, Pierre. 1993. *Identity, Migration and the New Security Agenda in Europe*. New York: St. Martin's Press.

Williams, Michael C. 2003. Words, images, enemies: Securitization and international politics. *International Studies Quarterly* 47(4), 511–531.

1

From Securitization to Integration

MAX O. STEPHENSON JR. AND YANNIS A. STIVACHTIS

The 1951 Geneva Convention defined a refugee as someone who has a 'fear of being persecuted for reasons of race, religion, nationality, membership of a particular social group or political opinion, is outside the country of his nationality and is unable or owing to such fear, is unwilling to avail himself of the protection of that country'. The same agreement defined asylum seekers as people who, 'left their country of origin, have sought international protection, have applied to be recognized as a refugee and are awaiting a decision from the host government' (UNHCR 2016, 4). As we observed in the introduction to this volume, to understand how the issue of refugee flows has become a security issue, one must focus attention on how those flows have routinely been presented as posing an existential threat to the receiving nations' societies and thus require immediate and extraordinary measures by those states to address them.

A plethora of previous studies have illustrated that the securitization of refugees has the capacity to unleash the emotive power of nationalism in unhelpful ways (Deudney 1990). Moreover, the securitization of refugees, often, finds governments treating such population movements as suspicious activities that must be controlled, monitored, and registered. That is, the migration of often forcibly displaced people and refugees is very frequently seen as a security threat that must be intercepted (Benedicto 2019). Refugee issues are unfortunately readily securitized as potential terrorist infiltrations and that argument is regularly employed by public leaders and advocates alike as grounds for tight control of borders (Faist 2005; Huysmans 2006; Adamson 2006; Gerard 2014). Because securitizing the refugee issue is now generally easier in the aftermath of the 9/11 attacks, that concern for recipient nation safety and security has frequently taken attention away from the economic factors that have always been at play in international migration (Waever et al., 1993).

This chapter first describes the processes by which refugees are securitized and thereafter outlines the policies that receiving states should enact and what actions they should undertake to integrate refugees into their national societies effectively. Our reasons for undertaking this analysis are twofold. First, understanding how refugees are often perceived as threats to military, economic, political, societal, and environmental security will help readers of this volume comprehend why and how eastern Mediterranean governments and political and social groups have securitized Syrian refugees. Second, we hope that a description of 'best practices' of refugee integration will provide readers a heuristic that will help them understand how successful the countries of the eastern Mediterranean have been in integrating Syrian refugees into their national societies.

The Securitization of Refugees

Securitization is the process whereby various actors operating within the domestic environment of a state transform concerns from political issues into matters of security, thus justifying extraordinary measures to be implemented to address them. That a given issue, such as the refugees, is securitized does not necessarily mean that such must occur for the survival of a given state, but instead suggests only that one or more actors have successfully constructed an object or concern as an existential problem (Waever 1993 and 1995; Buzan, Waever and de Wilde 1998; Williams 2003). In other words, refugees may not pose any factual danger to a receiving state, but government and popular leaders may nonetheless effectively securitize them as representing a threat. The ability to securitize a targeted subject depends on the status of a given actor and whether similar issues are generally perceived as threats by those the leaders wish to mobilize.

In this sense, security becomes a self-referential practice, because it is within such practices that a matter becomes a salient security issue and not necessarily because that concern constitutes a real risk. Moreover, because social and political groups within different states possess the power to declare an issue a security concern, security is best understood as a social construct that may carry different meanings in different societies at different times (Weiner 1992, 103). This fact implies two things. First, some populations may consider the existence of Syrian refugees per se as a threat to their security, while others may not. Second, Syrian refugees may not pose any risk to a receiving state, but particular social and political groups within that country may nonetheless prove successful in framing them as a 'security problem'. Thus, any attempt to classify types of dangers that may arise from refugee flows must distinguish between real and perceived threats. Such analyses must likewise also grapple with often 'paranoid notions of threat or mass anxieties that can best be described as xenophobic and racist' (Weiner 1992, 104).

Successfully securitized subjects receive disproportionate amounts of attention and resources compared to concerns that do not, regardless of their objective significance (Waever 1993 and 1995; Taureck 2006; Balzacq 2005). Thus, in order to understand how refugees are securitized, one must, among other things, focus on the reasons offered for why they should be perceived as threats to a country's security. As we noted above, successfully securitizing refugees makes it possible for leaders to legitimize extraordinary means to address the issue. Those steps could include declaring a state of emergency or mobilizing the military and/or the police force to address the purported 'usurpation'.

The securitization of refugee issues becomes a relatively simple process in many cases because the distinction between refugees and immigrants is unclear in the eyes of the citizens of many potential host countries. Refugees are generally not the only foreigners living within the boundaries of potential recipient states. Most often, those who have previously immigrated voluntarily and for economic reasons will already reside in a nation prior to the arrival of refugees. When those economic migrants are broadly perceived as having affected the security of their receiving states, any potential influx will automatically also be viewed as potential threats to that security, whether they share common ethnicity, language, culture, or religion with prior migrants. In such cases, migrants and refugees will be viewed as foreigners, whose presence and actions jeopardize citizen and state security. This analysis implies that the Syrian refugees were very likely to be seen as a potential threat to the national security of those countries that already had a considerable number of migrants living within their territory, including Greece, Italy, Cyprus, and Malta. Again, Syrian refugees need not have posed any actual security threat to these states, but the fact that other 'foreigners' living within them were already perceived in such terms made the populations of these nations skeptical about receiving additional 'outsiders,' irrespective of the causes of their displacement.

Securitization affects all five security sectors of a nation's political economy identified by the Copenhagen School, namely, military, political, societal, economic, and environmental security. The comprehensive security perspective suggests that all these sectors are interdependent, with the result that 'spill-over' effects from one sector have the potential to affect, positively or negatively, other sectors (Buzan 1991, 111). For example, migration and refugee issues are often popularly associated with societal and economic security, but they often also 'spill-over' into the political and military security sectors (Stivachtis 1999).

Refugees and Military Security

For the military sector, the referent object of security is territorial integrity and the function of various national institutions (Buzan 1991, 116–118). Military threats, which mainly arise from the external environment, are traditionally accorded highest priority in national security consideration. Refugees may be perceived as threatening the military security of receiving states in four ways (Stivachtis 1999, 42). The first may occur if some use the territory of the receiving state as a base from which to initiate military activities against their home country. The latter may hold the receiving state responsible for those actions, whether or not it supported them. Second, refugees may come to be perceived as constituting a military danger when large numbers seek to persuade the receiving state to undertake direct actions against their home country. Third, refugees may be 'militarized' in these terms if the receiving state has an interest in challenging the regime of the refugees' home country and uses them to that end. Finally, when refugees are perceived as posing a substantial economic burden, whether such is the case, they can be seen as diminishing their receiving states' financial capacity to support defense spending and social services.

Refugees and Political Security

Political threats undermine the organizational stability of the state by threatening its national identity and organizing ideology and the institutions that express those beliefs (Buzan 1991, 119–122). Political threats often may result from actors and forces in the domestic and external environments of a state and thus, it can become quite difficult to distinguish such risks from military ones. Consequently, public leaders may fear political threats as much as overtly military ones.

Perceived political threats pose an even greater danger to weak states (Buzan 1991, 122). Such allegations seek to re-orient the political behavior of the state by manipulating principal factional disputes within it. Thus, a state may not threaten another state in a simple, direct fashion. Instead, it may participate in domestic disputes among various factions, backing whichever one seems most likely to pursue policies it favors. There are countless possible variations in this style of political intervention. These range from providing support to legal parties in a relatively stable electoral system, to encouragement of, and military assistance to, armed struggle within a targeted state. Such interventions may be aimed at changing the ideological character of the target government, or at encouraging secessionist forces within that state. Voluntarily or not, refugees may be perceived as serving as instruments in such intervention.

Internal threats may arise as a result of governmental actions that pose threats or constraints to individuals or groups. Resistance to the government, perceived or real, efforts to change its policies or overthrow it, or movements aimed at autonomy or independence all threaten state stability and enhance state insecurity. Externally, a state can be threatened by the ideology of another state, such as nationalism, fundamentalism, liberal democracy or communism. Such perceived threats stem from the great diversity of ideas and traditions. Because contradictions in ideologies are basic, states of one persuasion may well feel threatened by the ideas represented by others. In this sense, when the originating nations of refugees and receiving states do not share similar ideas, emigres may be seen as posing political threats to the ideology of the refugees' host country. Public leaders perceive political threats as more serious when nationalist ideology prevails (Stivachtis 1999, 43).

An external political threat may be transformed to an internal one. For instance, threats to national identity may involve attempts to heighten the ethno-cultural identities of groups within a target state. In the present case, it may also happen that a host country's leaders believe they do not share a common ideology with Syrian refugees, and they may perceive that those individuals constitute an external threat. Either of these scenarios will likely result in refugees being labeled as a security 'problem' (Stivachtis 1999, 43).

Officials may also believe the political security of their states may be under threat when refugees are opposed to the regime of their home country and are involved in activities aimed at undermining that government in their host country, even as their host nations may actively be supporting the Syrian refugees to achieve unrelated political ends.

Refugees may also be perceived by government leaders as threatening the political security of their host country by providing financial and military assistance to rebel groups or by marshalling public opinion through publicity campaigns aimed at the international community and at specific international institutions. They may also be viewed as affecting the internal security of their host countries by initiating activities (terrorism, violent protests, etc.) against the governments of states that are not willing to take any actions against Syria or that are determined to maintain friendly relations with it. Moreover, some political parties and groups in some host countries have exhibited concern when they became alarmed that refugees are placing significant pressures and constraints on their governments by successfully influencing host country public opinion. Such refugee political activity may become a source of conflict between the home and host governments (Stivachtis 1999, 44).

A difficult challenge can confront government leaders who do not wish to target refugees. When adopting that more beneficent stance, it may heighten conflict among officials within their governments. This situation may become more acute if those individuals criticizing refugees obtain the support of significant numbers of citizens. This concern may become even more acute for officials when refugees obtain the support of a significant minority (racial, religious, or ethnic, for example) group within the receiving state. This scenario may create fears that such support may lead to a considerable social upheaval or even to secessionist movements. Apart from threats arising from domestic law-making, refugees may be threatened by regime administrative or political action and activities related to law and order enforcement. In turn, they may undertake certain activities to minimize the impact of such policies and actions. Whatever the scenario, the governments of the receiving states may be pressed toward adopting a less friendly stance towards refugees, even as anti-foreign sentiments may rise in the general population because of their presence and activities. This analysis suggests that when state leaders perceive that refugees are severely at odds with the prevailing ideology or beliefs or other characteristic claims in their nation, they may act on that perceived dissonance in ways that target refugees unfavorably (Stivachtis 1999, 44).

Because refugees tend to maintain strong connections with their home countries, even when a political settlement has been reached there, we suspect that any subsequent turbulence or instability in post-conflict Syria (not yet a reality) may find expression within Syrian communities abroad as well, a challenge for their host societies.

In sum, refugees can play significant political roles in international and national politics (Bali 1997). Their continued political involvement in states whose rules they are not subject to may be perceived by their host nation's leaders as a serious challenge to their ability to exercise independent control over the direction of their own foreign and domestic policy. Paradoxically, that risk may be heightened when a host country has previously armed refugees against their country of origin (Bali 1994, 214).

Refugees and Societal Security

The referent object of security in social terms is collective identities that can function independent of the state, such as religions and ethnicities (Buzan

1991, 122–123). Perceived military and political threats are often part of a larger constellation of concerns in relations between states. Such perceptions can be difficult to disentangle from actual political or military concerns. More generally, even the interplay of ideas and communication may produce what are perceived to be politically significant societal and cultural threats, as illustrated by the reaction of many Western state leaders to religious fundamentalism.

As in the political sector, threats in the societal sector may arise from the internal or external environment of the state, while an internal threat may be transformed into an external one and *vice versa* (Buzan 1991, 123). If it can be said that societal security is about the sustainability of traditional patterns of language, culture, and religious, and ethnic identity, then it may also be argued that threats to these values may arise more frequently from within states, rather than beyond them. This dynamic occurs because the state-nation building process often aims at suppressing, or at least homogenizing, sub-state social identities. As a result, perceived internal societal threats may precipitate conflict within states.

In the long term, the most obvious effect of refugee migration is often the creation of ethnic minorities in host countries. Admitting refugees has long-lasting social effects on receiving states. Admitting refugees may turn relatively homogeneous societies into multi-ethnic and multicultural ones by the introduction of ethnically and culturally different people (Weiner 1992, 110). In this sense, refugees often raise societal concerns because they are perceived as challenging traditional notions about membership in a state, including the meaning of nationality and citizenship, and the rights and duties of citizens towards their country and *vice versa*. The fact that very few states fit the idealized picture of the homogeneous nation-state, and that most nations are cultural and social products of earlier movements of people, often fails to register in the popular consciousness when populists or nationalists raise these matters as concerns (Bali 1994, 214).

By receiving asylum and becoming citizens of the receiving state, refugees are commonly viewed as creating or constituting a cultural, linguistic, religious, and possibly a racially distinct minority within the host country, thereby altering the nature of its society. Thus, the migration of refugees can be seen as threatening communal identity and culture by altering the ethnic, cultural, religious, and linguistic character of the population of the receiving state.

Refugees are also very often seen as threatening the cultural norms and value systems of receiving societies. If, in fact, refugees become widely perceived as violating these norms and values, citizens of receiving states may come to view them as a threat to national security. In such scenarios societies may emphasize their perceived differences from refugees (Waever, et al. 1993, 77).

Government officials of receiving states may also become concerned because of refugees' alleged or purported social behavior, typically offered by populists or nationalists, such as criminality and illegal forms of employ. These claims may generate local resentment which, in turn, may lead to xenophobic popular sentiments and the rise of anti-migrant political parties that may be viewed as threats to the government in power (Widgreen 1990, 757). Indeed, political parties often use anti-migrant slogans and rhetoric to mobilize supporters to increase their electoral power. This situation may prompt the governments of countries receiving refugees to adopt anti-migration policies to blunt public reaction and avoid possible electoral loss.

How and why refugees can be perceived as cultural threats is a complicated issue, involving initially how a host community's population defines itself. Cultures differ with respect to how they settle on who belongs to or can be admitted into their community. These norms govern who is granted admission and what rights and privileges are accorded those individuals. Thus, a plausible explanation for relative state willingness to accept or reject migrants is perceived ethnic, cultural and religious affinity with groups (Weiner 1999, 105). A government and its citizens are likely to be relatively more receptive to those who share their language, religion, or race, while populations might regard as threatening those with whom they do not share such characteristics. Nonetheless, it is important to keep in mind that what constitutes 'ethnic affinity' is a social construct that can change over time. Moreover, what comprises cultural affinity for one group in a multi-ethnic society may be perceived as a cultural, social, or economic threat to another.

Societies may also exhibit a limited threshold of tolerance for refugee migration if that flow begins to undermine the social and political cohesion of the receiving country. When such may occur is shaped by the economic, social, and cultural circumstances of the receiving society as well as by the refugees themselves (Weiner 1999, 106). Anti-immigrant feelings and xenophobia also rise during times of recession and high unemployment. Finally, tolerance levels are likely to be lower in countries without a tradition of immigration and higher in those that have such histories.

Refugees and Economic Security

Referent objects and perceived existential threats in the economic sector that may shape a nation's attitude toward refugees are more difficult to identify. One principal difficulty associated with making such judgments is the fact that the normal condition of actors in a market economy is one of risk, competition, and uncertainty. However, when the consequences of a perceived economic threat reach beyond the strictly economic into the military and political spheres, three potential national security issues may emerge. These involve linkages between economic capability, on the one hand, and military capacity, power, and socio-political stability, on the other hand (Schultz 1977; Buzan 1991, 126).

Refugees may be perceived as threatening the economic security of their receiving states by imposing limits on their financial capability. That is, refugees are usually seen as creating a substantial economic burden on their host societies by straining housing, education, sanitation, transportation, and communication facilities, while at the same time increasing consumption.

Societies, or specific social groups within them, may react to an influx of refugees first, because of the economic costs the latter impose on the receiving state; second, because of the refugees' purported behavior, such as welfare dependency, that may affect a host country's tax payers; and third, because refugees are perceived as potentially displacing some people from employment because they are willing to work for lower wages (Buzan 1991, 127–128).

These perceptions and claims, when pressed by advocacy groups and party members in efforts to gain voters, may encourage a considerable degree of social hostility not only against refugees, but against all foreigners living in a host country. Put more generally, popular fears regarding economic security may engender sufficient social hostility to threaten to undermine the socio-political cohesion of states, and thereby, their security.

Refugees and Environmental Security

In the environmental sector, the basic concern, is how residents are relating to their physical surroundings. These threats do not operate in isolation, but interact in multiple and often contradictory ways. Environmental threats, including military and economic ones, can damage the physical foundations of a state, perhaps sufficiently as to threaten its animating idea and institutions. This salience has increasingly moved environmental issues into the political arena (Buzan 1991, 133).

In the absence of relevant infrastructure in a receiving country, the presence of high numbers of refugees in a particular place and at a specific time runs a higher risk than would normally obtain and result in air, water, and solid waste pollution. That condition may then prompt host country citizens at the local and regional level to frame refugees as a threat to their environment.

Integrating Refugees into National Societies

Securing refugees' social integration into host societies is, formally, at least, high on the international agenda. Refugees' social integration is also in line with Sustainable Development Goal 16, which is, 'to promote peaceful and inclusive societies for sustainable development, provide access to justice for all, and build effective, accountable and inclusive institutions at all levels,' particularly target 16.10, which focuses on 'Ensur[ing] public access to information and protect[ing] fundamental freedoms, in accordance with national legislation and international agreements' (UN 2022).

The 1951 Convention relating to the Status of Refugees and its 1967 Protocol place considerable emphasis on refugee integration. The Convention enumerates social and economic rights designed to promote and further that process, and in its article 34 calls on states to facilitate the 'assimilation and naturalization' of refugees (UNHCR 2014, 1).

The rationale for integration of refugees into receiving state societies rests on the contention that refugee status is not permanent. In practice, this argument assumes that refugees will either return voluntarily to their home country when the conditions that forced them into exile have been substantially ameliorated or overcome, or they will have to find a permanent home in a new community either in their country of first refuge or in another nation. Meanwhile, according to the 1951 Convention, refugees should gradually enjoy a wider range of rights as their association and ties with their host states grow stronger. In this sense, the 1951 Convention at least nominally offers refugees a solid basis on which to restore the social and economic independence they need to get on with their lives.

Berry's conceptual framework of immigrants' acculturation to host societies has been used frequently to address immigrants' adaptation and integration in their new home nations. That model includes four strategies or forms: assimilation when individuals do not wish to maintain their cultural identity and seek daily interaction with their new host cultures; separation – when individuals hold on to their original cultures and wish to avoid interaction with others; marginalization – when there is little cultural maintenance and few relationships with others; and integration – when emigres maintain their original cultures while engaging in daily interactions with other groups (Berry, 1997).

The integration of refugees is a dynamic and multifaceted process that requires efforts by all parties concerned, including a preparedness on the part of refugees to adapt to their new host society without having to forego their own cultural identity, and a corresponding readiness on the part of host communities and public institutions to welcome their new residents and work to meet their needs (UNHCR 2014, 1). The process of integration is complex and gradual, comprising distinct but inter-related legal, economic, social, and cultural dimensions, all of which are important for successful outcomes.

According to Berry (1997), integration can only be successfully attained when host societies are open and inclusive in their orientation toward cultural diversity. Inclusiveness implies that refugees should be provided with equal access to housing, health care, education, training, and employment opportunities. For their part, refugees' level of integration and adaptation depends on a number of factors, including their pre-migration experiences, departure process, and post-arrival experiences and environment. Many refugees and asylum seekers experience severe pre-migration trauma, including mental and physical torture, mass violence and genocide, witnessing the killings of family members and friends, sexual abuse, kidnapping of children, destruction and looting of personal property, starvation, and a lack – sometimes prolonged – of adequate water and shelter (UNDESA 2018, 2).

Refugee departure is a complex endeavor often associated with life threatening risks. Although arrival in a safe place provides initial relief, frustration sometimes develops for refugees as new difficulties emerge that may include family separation, language barriers, uncertain legal status, unemployment, homelessness, or lack of access to education and healthcare services (UNDESA 2018, 3).

The circumstances and experiences of forced migration have profound effects on refugees' health and integration into host societies. Migrants who fled from armed conflicts and persecution in their countries, such as that which has occurred in Syria since 2011, report high rates of pre-migration trauma and evidence high frequencies of mental health problems, particularly post-traumatic stress disorders (PTSD) and depression (UNDESA 2018, 3).

Post-migration experiences also shape refugee health and adaptation. Research shows that asylum seekers present higher rates of PTSD and depression than other refugees, due to post-migratory stresses, delays in application processing, conflicts with immigration officials, denial of work permits, unemployment, and separation from families (UNDESA 2018, 3). Forced migrants often arrive in places where they have no contacts or knowledge of the local language. These factors very often lead to relative social isolation and limit the opportunities accorded to refugees.

Almost all countries in the eastern Mediterranean that have received significant refugee populations during the Syrian exodus of the past decade are likely to see a substantial share of those individuals remain in their midst. A good number of those who fled their homes are now doing well economically in their new societies, and many have become citizens in their new countries. But many others have not yet been integrated, economically or socially. Unemployment and underemployment among Syrian emigres are endemic, and many who wish to naturalize have encountered barriers to citizenship and persistent residential and social segregation.

Although refugees are entitled by law to the same socio-economic rights as nationals, several obstacles typically impede their integration efforts. These include insufficient subsidized housing and access to employment, challenges relating to recognition of their academic and professional qualifications for employment, restrictions on family reunification, and stringent criteria for naturalization (UNHCR 2014, 1).

All of this is to say that there is no 'one-size-fits-all' approach to refugee integration. The situation of refugees must be analyzed in the context of their respective host societies, and with full awareness of the living and working conditions of those already residing in those nations. However, it is also clear that international events, discourses, and frameworks have an important impact on the integration of refugees and policies at the national and local levels. UNHCR and relevant international agreements have articulated broad goals for integration, irrespective of the specific country involved. These include efforts to enable refugees to reach and develop their full potential, to protect their human rights, prevent their marginalization, and foster social cohesion and harmonious co-existence (UNHCR 2014, 2).

As one considers these aspirations, a key question arises: At what point should integration programs begin? Upon application for refugee status? After recognition of refugee status? Upon the granting of citizenship? Every refugee is first and foremost a possible asylum seeker. A good reception policy for those individuals is therefore vital to a would-be refugee's eventual integration into a new society in legal, psychological, and social terms. It is in the best interests of both the host society and would-be asylees and refugees to promote a reception policy guided by a long-term perspective. Refugees who begin their lives in a host country in detention, or isolated for several months in a state of enforced inactivity at a collective reception center are likely to be hampered when they later attempt to integrate (UNHCR 2014, 2).

The conditions in which asylum seekers find themselves during the immediate reception stage are therefore significant mediators of their future possibilities for integration. A reception policy that combines effective and adequate services (particularly skills training, access to gainful employment, and health care) with a swift asylum decision procedure that is based on providing petitioning individuals as much autonomy as possible increases the chances of successful integration in a host country (UNHCR 2014, 2).

Specifically, international organizations, such as OECD, IMF, IOM and UNHCR have identified a set of guidelines to facilitate effective integration of refugees into host societies (WEF 2016; UNHCR 2021). First, host states should provide integration services as soon as possible for those asylum seekers most likely to be allowed to remain. Time spent waiting around can damage refugees' chances of integrating, yet they often must wait months or even years before receiving language training and other social support, including skills assessments and civic integration courses.

Second, when dispersing humanitarian migrants across countries, governments should consider whether the jobs available in a region match asylee/refugee capabilities. Many governments disperse refugees to prevent segregation, ensure suitable housing and spread costs. Refugees should thus be matched to localities based on their overall profile, including their education level and work experience.

Third, refugees should be treated differently, depending on their backgrounds. Different refugees require distinct levels of support. For example, those with college degrees have very different training requirements than those lacking such qualifications. Moreover, gender and age require specific consideration in light of prevailing social norms.

Fourth, host governments should pay particular attention to unaccompanied minors who arrive past the age of compulsory schooling. Most unaccompanied minors arrive around the age at which compulsory schooling ends, but have little or no formal education, and therefore often demand specific, appropriate support to catch up. Relevant integration programs should provide intensive case management by social workers, educational support, language training, career and educational counselling, mental health care, and social integration support to these individuals.

Fifth, host countries should be able to provide or match refugees with employment opportunities and thus enable them to integrate more quickly into receiving societies. Many host-government officials are often reluctant to allow asylum seekers to work as they fear doing so will encourage abuse of the asylum mechanism. They frequently therefore demand that certain conditions, often including a prior waiting period, are met before asylum seekers can legally work. But not working can have detrimental effects on asylee's ability to integrate in the long run as their skills may decrease and because such periods create gaps in their employment history. Moreover, local employers often discount and dismiss foreign qualifications and work experience, with the result that humanitarian migrants often struggle to secure jobs appropriate to their levels of expertise and experience. This challenge is often compounded by the fact that many fled their homes with no proof of their qualifications. Receiving countries can help with this difficulty by carefully empirically assessing and documenting newcomers' education, skills, and experiences.

Sixth, poor health affects a refugee's ability to obtain a job, learn the local language, interact with public institutions, and do well in school – all steps that are critical to integrating successfully.

Seventh, governments should not be alone in their efforts to support refugees' integration: employers, charities, immigrant associations, community-based organizations and trade unions all have roles to play. They may assist, for example, by providing needed support services, developing mentorship programs, thoughtfully appraising refugees' skills and welcoming the newcomers to their new communities.

Eighth, refugees will need to navigate various practical tasks in unfamiliar environments, often with limited fluency in the language of their new home nations. Providing early social support can help reduce anxiety and aid resettled refugees in developing a sense of control and independence. Early positive relationships in the receiving community have other benefits, too, including restoring a refugee's sense of belonging. Such support can be facilitated by integration caseworkers, youth workers, and volunteers (i.e., buddies, mentors). Whenever possible, resettled refugees should be placed close to family members because the support provided by those individuals is a vital resource in the integration process. Supportive relationships with members of established refugee and diaspora communities can also help resettled refugees build connections within their new communities. Such ties can allow them to access other important integration resources such as employment, volunteer opportunities and a wider social network. Social connections among resettled refugees and members of diaspora communities are particularly important in this regard. Supporting refugees to reconnect with familiar cultural and religious institutions can assist them in maintaining their cultural integrity while building new identities. At the same time, it should be kept in mind that some refugees might not seek contact with other refugees from their country of origin, due either to personal circumstances, or as a result of the specific reasons for their flight.

Finally, while long-term support of refugees is expensive, it pays off in the long run, even benefiting the children of refugees who might otherwise struggle with integration issues themselves.

Conclusions

We had two principal aims for this chapter. First, we wished to investigate how refugees are securitized and under what conditions such processes are more or less likely to occur. To that end, we paid particular attention to how refugees can come to be perceived as threats to a population's military, economic, political, societal, and environmental security. We hope this analysis and framework will help readers of this volume understand better why and how so many Syrian refugees have been securitized by governments as well as political and social groups in eastern Mediterranean countries during the last decade. Second, we sought in this chapter to focus on the policies that receiving states should enact and the actions they should undertake to integrate refugees effectively into their societies. We did so to provide readers with benchmark criteria by which to assess how successful the countries of the eastern Mediterranean have been, and are likely to be, in integrating Syrian refugees into their national societies.

References

Adamson, Fiona. 2006. Crossing Borders: International Migration and National Security. *International Security* 31(1), 165–199.

Bali, Sita. 1997. Migration and Refugees. In Brian White, Richard Little and Michael Smith (eds.), *Issues in World Politics*. New York: St. Martin's Press, 207–214.

Balzacq, Thomas. 2005. The three Phases of Securitization: Political Agency, Audience and context. *European Journal of International Relations* 11(2), 171–201.

Benedicto, Ruiz Ainhoa. 2019. Guarding the fortress. *Transnational Institute. 26 November.* https://www.tni.org/en/guarding-the-fortress

Berry, J. W. 1997. Immigration, acculturation and adaptation. *Applied Psychology: An International Review* 46, 5–61.

Barry Buzan et al. 1990. *The European Security Order Recast.* London: Pinter.

Buzan, Barry. 1991. *People, States and Fear. 2nd edition.* London: Harvester Wheatsheaf.

Buzan, Barry and Waever, Ole. 2003. *Regions and Powers: The Structure of International Security.* Cambridge: Cambridge University Press.

Buzan, Barry, Waever, Ole, and de Wilde, Jaap. 1998. *Security: A New Framework for Analysis.* Boulder: Lynne Rienner.

Deudney, Daniel. 1990. *The Case Against Linking Environmental Degradation and National Security. Millennium: Journal of International Studies 19(3), 461–476.*

Faist, Thomas. 2005. The Migration-Security Nexus: International Migration and Security. In: *Migration, Citizenship and Ethnos: Incorporation Regimes in Germany, Western Europe and North America*, edited by Y. Michal Bodemann and Gökce Yurdakul, pp. 103–120. New York: Palgrave Macmillan.

Gerard, Alison. 2014. *The Securitization of Migration and Refugee Women.* New York: Routledge.

Huysmans, Jef. 2006. *The Politics of Insecurity: Fear, Migration, and Asylum in the EU.* Routledge: London.

Schultz, Charles, L. 1977. The Economic Content of National Security Policy. *Foreign Affairs*, 51(3), 529–535.

Stivachtis, Yannis A. 1999. Kosovar Refugees and National Security, *Refuge*, Special Issue, August 1999, 41–46.

Taureck, Rita. 2006. Securitization theory and securitization studies. *Journal of International Relations and Development* 9(1), 53–61.

United Nations Department of Economic and Social Affairs (UNDESA). 2022. The Sustainable Development Goals Report. https://sdgs.un.org/goals/goal16

United Nations Department of Economic and Social Affairs (UNDESA). 2018. Refugees and Social Integration in Europe. https://www.un.org/development/desa/family/wp-content/uploads/sites/23/2018/05/Robila_EGM_2018.pdf

UNHCR. 2014. The Integration of Refugees: A Discussion Paper. https://www.unhcr.org/cy/wp-content/uploads/sites/41/2018/02/integration_discussion_paper_July_2014_EN.pdf

UNHCR. 2021. Promoting integration through social connections. https://www.unhcr.org/handbooks/ih/social-connections/promoting-integration-through-social-connections

Waever, Ole. 1993. Securitization and Desecuritization. In: *On Security*, edited by Ronnie. D. Lipschutz, pp. 46–86.

Waever, Ole, Buzan, Barry, Kelstrup, Morten, and Lemaitre, Pierre. 1993. *Identity, Migration and the New Security Agenda in Europe*. New York: St. Martin's Press.

Weiner, Myron. 1992. Security, Stability, and International Migration. *International Security* vol. 17(3), 91–126.

Widgren. Jonas. 1990. International Migration and Regional Stability. *International Affairs* vol. 66(4), 749–766.

Williams, Michael C. 2003. Words, images, enemies: Securitization and international politics. *International Studies Quarterly* 47(4), 511–531.

World Economic Forum (WEF). 2016. 10 ways countries can help refugees integrate. https://www.weforum.org/agenda/2016/05/10-ways-countries-can-help-refugees-integrate/

PART I

International Governmental and Non-Governmental Responses to the Syrian Refugee Crisis

2

UNHCR, National Policies and the Syrian Refugee Crisis in Lebanon and Jordan

NEDA MOAYERIAN AND MAX O. STEPHENSON JR.

According to the UNHCR, since the onset of Syrian political unrest and the civil war in 2011, more than 6.6 million residents of that nation have been displaced. Approximately 84 per cent of those fleeing the conflict have sought refuge in neighboring countries, namely Turkey, with 3.6 million registered Syrian refugees; Lebanon, with about 1 million; and Jordan, with 750,000 (UNHCR 2019a). These figures should be understood in the context of the overall populations of the receiving countries. In addition, many refugee families entered these nations with limited means to support their basic needs. Even for those who could at first rely on their savings or assistance from host families, life since their arrival has emerged as a daily struggle. Indeed, approximately 88 per cent of Syrian refugee families lived below the poverty line in Lebanon in 2020, while that figure for Jordan was 93 per cent (UNHCR 2020).   More generally, as the conflict has continued, with host countries confronting an overwhelming demand for services, even those with historically welcoming policies toward refugees reduced their support to decrease the costs that the relatively rapid influx had created for their infrastructures, economies and citizenries.

The 1951 Refugee Convention definition of a refugee, along with the provisions on non-refoulement, established the basic obligations of countries to individuals seeking protection. That agreement defined a refugee as, 'someone who is unable or unwilling to return to their country of origin owing to a well-founded fear of being persecuted for reasons of race, religion, nationality, membership of a particular social group, or political opinion' (UN General Assembly 1951, 3). The rights of individuals and the corresponding obligations of states differ depending on the legal status of asylum seekers, that is, those with confirmed protection status (refugee or other) or applicants whose sanctuary claim has been denied (Stern 2016). Importantly, neither Lebanon nor Jordan has ratified the 1951 convention relating to the status of refugees or its follow-up 1976 protocol. As Janmyr has contended, 'It is arguable that the reasons for non-accession to the Convention vary between States, and, although some explanations may be valid throughout the [Middle East] region, important nuances may be lost by viewing these States as a group' (2017, 439). Whatever their specific reasons for non-adoption, refugee rights and state obligations toward them are tightly intertwined with national regulations and political climates in non-signatory countries. This chapter reviews the political and historic context of refugee policy action during the recent Syrian Civil War in these two countries. Changes in regulations and policies in Lebanon and Jordan tell a story of increasing reticence toward hosting Syrian refugees where each nation can take that stance with relative impunity because the European Union (EU) is keen to prevent additional exodus to its member states, and because both countries are non-signatories to the Convention.

This chapter also explores the strategies the UNHCR has adopted to address changing national policies and regulations in these nations in order to ensure humanitarian support for Syrian refugees and families. Our review of UNHCR's effectiveness in protecting Syrian refugees' rights in Lebanon and Jordan during the recent civil war suggested that the international organization has found itself addressing the traditional tension in its role of serving as the creature of a state centered body (the UN) whose members are sovereign within their territories, while also trying to protect the rights of individuals whom it cannot itself directly – that is, alone – assist. We also found that UNHCR is dependent on host states that have inadequate social, political and economic capacity to respond to refugees' needs. That is, the organization cannot control, nor can it directly affect those states' residents without their governments' cooperation. In addition, we contend that UNHCR's acceptance (willingly or not) of the neoliberalization of the humanitarian space has exacerbated its structural challenge in multiple ways. We have sought to highlight those conditions in our analysis.

Lebanon's Response to the Syrian Refugee Crisis

Lebanon, a country with the highest per capita population of refugees in the world, today hosts approximately 1.5 million Syrians, 'including 918,874 [individuals] registered as refugees with UNHCR, along with 27,700 Palestinian refugees from Syria and a population of an estimated 180,000 Palestinian refugees from Lebanon living in 12 camps and 156 gatherings' (UNHCR 2020, 8). In addition to the fact that the country is not a partner to the international refugee convention, it also does not have any specific national legislation addressing the rights and living conditions to be accorded refugees. As was clear in the terminology section of the Lebanon Crisis Response Plan (LCRP) – developed among 112 partner organizations and published by UNHCR in 2017 to assist more than 2.8 million crisis-affected people living in Lebanon – this situation has led to an ongoing in-principle conflict between that country and the UN concerning the status of Syrian Civil War refugees:

> The UN characterizes the flight of civilians from Syria as a refugee movement and considers that these Syrians are seeking international protection and are likely to meet the refugee definition. The Government of Lebanon ... refers to individuals who fled from Syria into its territory after March 2011 as temporarily displaced individuals, and reserves its sovereign right to determine their status according to Lebanese laws and regulations (UNHCR 2020, 4).

Lebanon's declining economy, its growing public debt-to-GDP ratio, recent political unrest, the COVID-19 pandemic and a huge explosion at Beirut's port, which killed nearly 200 people and caused billions of dollars in damage in 2020, have all deepened Lebanon's financial and political challenges and contributed to a less generous stance towards refugees than the Convention outlines (UNHCR 2019a).

A variety of concerns have shaped the nation's non-compliance with the Convention and 1976 protocol, despite sustained international pressure to ratify them. Political researchers have attributed Lebanon's non-ratification of the Convention to a fear of endangering its fragile social and sectarian cohesion. After signing the Taif agreement, which reinstated the country's sectarian power-sharing system in 1989, Lebanon, home to 18 different religions, has striven to maintain a delicate demographic balance among these disparate groups, despite frequent struggles for political and social power among them (Nagle and Clancy 2019; Rizkallah 2017). As Janmyr has observed, 'Opposing accession may also serve the political purpose of appearing to 'defend' Lebanon from refugee naturalization, and thus be seen to preserve Lebanon's sectarian balance' (2017, 543). Several analysts have also investigated the importance of power-sharing negotiations and practices aimed at stabilizing the country during the Arab Spring (Fakhoury 2015; Hazbun 2016).

Moreover, continuing bitter feelings among many of its citizens concerning Palestinian refugees, whom they blame for the 1975–1990 Lebanon civil war (Hanafi and Long 2010; Janmyr 2017), have led the nation's politicians, almost unanimously, to decrease the number of Palestinian refugees in the country through systematic marginalization (e.g., restricting employment to all but the most menial of professions) and equally restrictive legislative changes related to residence, travel and freedom of movement, right to work and social security, as well as ownership and inheritance of property (Hanafi and Tiltnes 2008; Suleiman 2006).

Decree No. 478 of September 1995, 'Regulating Entry and Exit of Palestinians' into and out of Lebanon, for example, 'set a precedent in discouraging both Palestinian refugees to seek employment abroad, and the Gulf states to grant them visas'(Suleiman 2006, 15). As the policy was a violation of Article 9 of the Universal Declaration of Human Rights (UDHR) stating that no one shall be subjected to arbitrary arrest, detention or exile, the Salim Al-Hoss government revoked the Decree on 12 January 1999. Nevertheless, Palestinian refugees' right to employment and to social security continue to be regulated by Decree No. 17561 of 1964. That policy restricts the employment of Palestinians and requires that they obtain a work permit prior to employment. In addition, the order requires the Minister of Labor and Social Affairs to determine which professions will be reserved specifically to Lebanese citizens on an annual basis (Suleiman 2006, 15). Various ministerial-level decisions since, including No. 621/1 in 1995, have limited the number and variety of jobs available to foreign nationals residing in Lebanon. Finally, in April 2001, the Lebanese parliament passed a law (No. 296), which amended the first article of Decree No. 11617 of 1969 regarding non-Lebanese acquisition of property to read: 'It is prohibited to any person who is not a national of a recognized state, or anyone whose ownership of property is contrary to the provisions of the Constitution relating to 'Tawteen' to acquire real-estate property of any kind' (Suleiman 2006, 18).

The provisions of a Memorandum of Understanding (MoU) between Lebanon and the UNHCR in 2003 also play a role in governing refugees' status in the country (Saliba 2016). In the early stages of Syrians' mass exodus to escape their nation's civil war, Lebanon received considerable praise from UNHCR and human rights groups for opening its borders and adopting a non-encampment policy. The country initially offered refugees free entry and the right to work based on a 1991 Treaty of Brotherhood, Cooperation And Coordination Between The Syrian Arab Republic And The Lebanese Republic (Tsourapas 2019). Some critics, taking into account Lebanon's later policies toward Syria's refugees, have viewed this apparent early hospitality as the result of the government's mismanagement and lack of clear strategy rather than an intentionally beneficent approach (Yassin et al. 2015). In later years, clashing views among the nation's political parties regarding the conflict in Syria have led to continuing controversy concerning the establishment of refugee camps, which have been favored by one political group and vigorously opposed by another (Meier 2014). In the summer of 2012, Prime Minister Miqati's government established a dissociation policy regarding the events in Syria, claiming to be neutral in that nation's conflict. However, in practice, the Lebanese government's decision to use, 'force to close the border, [efforts] to expel Syrian civilians seeking refuge in Lebanon, and even [threats] to jail several people [while] deporting others' supported the links between major political elements ... and the Assad regime' (Meier 2014, 386).

The Lebanese government swung from its initial open policy to an urgent international call for assistance by the end of 2012, claiming that the country was coping with a massive influx of Syrian refugees. Following that shift, the Lebanese government has assumed a passive, when not openly hostile, stance toward those displaced by the Syrian Civil War. In an article based on 16 months of fieldwork in Lebanon undertaken between 2015 and 2017, including more than 40 interviews with key informants working in UN, non-governmental (NGO) and public agencies, Janmyr concluded that international and nongovernmental entities were the most significant and influential forces in supporting that population. She found that, 'between 2012 and 2014, host communities, civil society networks and UNHCR constituted primary providers for Syrian refugees with the Lebanese government more or less in the back seat' (Janmyr 2018, 396).

In response to the large numbers of Syrian refugees, Lebanon's Council of Ministers approved what it dubbed its 'October Policy' in October 2014, to tighten restraints on their entry and residency (Janmyr 2016; Tsourapas 2019). The imposition of expensive renewal fees for registered refugees and a new requirement that a Lebanese national sponsor individuals who had not already registered for UNHCR refugee status, left many Syrians in the nation illegally and hence vulnerable to exploitation (Janmyr 2016; Tsourapas 2019). In May 2015, with nearly 1.2 million Syrian refugees registered by UNHCR residing in the country, Lebanon's government asked the UN agency to suspend registration and even to de-register refugees who traveled to Syria, 'as they did not appear to fear returning to their home country, [and so] were not entitled to their UN-designated refugee status' (Janmyr 2018, 407). Accordingly, UNHCR registration of Syrian refugees in Lebanon formally ended in 2015. While the UN organization continues to update its information concerning the previously registered population, the organization has found itself in the position of advocating for the resumption of registration even as it seeks to prepare those it is assisting for a safe and dignified return to Syria when conditions are ripe.

The international nongovernmental organization, Human Rights Watch, has argued that General Security officials in Lebanon have applied residency policies incoherently by requiring refugees already legally registered with

UNHCR to obtain a Lebanese sponsor and by demanding that Syrians sign a pledge not to work, even after the government formally dropped that requirement in 2016. Human Rights Watch and many other organizations have documented for several years how the Lebanese government's kafala (sponsorship) system has provided employers unwarranted power and control over refugee workers' lives, 'leading to an array of abuses, including non-payment of wages, forced confinement, excessive working hours, and verbal, physical, and sexual abuse' (Human Rights Watch 2021b, 418).

For its part, UNHCR has contended that since 2017, host community fatigue in Lebanon has made it quite challenging to preserve 'a dignified protection space for refugees' (UNHCR 2017). Perceived competition for employment has been the main source of tension and conflict. Indeed, during 2017 several Lebanese municipalities imposed and subsequently increased restrictions on Syrian refugees through, 'curfews, confiscation of IDs, restrictions on residency and evictions justified with reference to pressures on local infrastructure, on economic, security, law and order, or on no particular grounds' (UNHCR 2017). The call on Syrian refugees to return to their country by local and national Lebanese officials continued in 2018 after the elections that May and surfaced again during the Brussels II Conference on 'Supporting the Future of Syria and the Region,' hosted by the EU and the UN in April 2018. The participants in that event concluded their work by agreeing to the following broad aim:

> The Government of Lebanon and its international partners reiterate that the main durable solution for Syrian refugees in Lebanon is their safe, dignified and non-coercive return to their country of origin, in accordance with international law and the principle of non-refoulement. ... The international partners expressed their support for UN-facilitated returns (Brussel II Conference 2018, 6).

In 2019, with continued negative public and political discourse concerning Syrian refugees as pernicious forces in Lebanon's economy, employment and society, the government again toughened its relevant laws and regulations. Those steps, 'led to instructions to dismantle unauthorized shelter structures, to consider deportation for Syrians who had entered Lebanon irregularly after 24 April 2019, and to enforce the permit requirements for foreign workers' (UNHCR 2019b). The 2019 Construction Law stipulated that only 'non-permanent' building materials, including wood, stone, and canvas, could be used for building on agricultural land. The law explicitly forbade concrete structures, including those with cement foundations. While the Construction Act had existed since 2004, it had gone largely unenforced until the 2019 statute.

Approximately 24,000 Syrian refugees (a 44 per cent increase compared to 2018) left Lebanon to return to Syria during 2019. The most frequently cited reasons for those decisions were to reunite with their families as a result of improved security in their sites of return and unfavorable socioeconomic conditions in Lebanon (UNHCR 2019b).

With the global COVID-19 pandemic in 2020–2021, Syrian refugees in Lebanon faced an obvious and potentially fatal risk and a growing need for basic assistance, including healthcare, shelter, water, sanitation and hygiene (UNHCR 2019a). The public health crisis heightened the dangers of the Lebanese government's increasingly draconian approach to Syrian refugees. As an example, Human Rights Watch has highlighted the fact that, 'Living conditions for the Syrian refugees living in Arsal [who had been] forced to dismantle their shelters in 2019 remain dire. … Their situation, compounded by COVID-19 movement restrictions, threatens their safety and their very lives' (Human Rights Watch 2021a).

Jordan's Response to the Refugee Crisis

As a major destination country for refugees in the Middle East, Jordan has hosted several million displaced people since the 1940s. The 1948 Palestinian exodus, the Six-Day War in 1967 and the 1987 Intifada led many Palestinians to seek refuge in Jordan. Today, Jordan hosts the largest number of Palestinian refugees (an estimated 1.9 million) of any nation in the world. The country also received thousands of Iraqi refugees following the U.S. invasion of that country in 2003. The Iraqi refugee population in Jordan exceeded 66,700 persons in February 2021 (UNHCR 2021a).

As noted above, Jordan, like Lebanon, has never signed the refugee convention and it now hosts approximately 665,000 Syrian refugees registered with UNHCR and 1.3 million when those not registered are considered (about 10 per cent of Jordan's population of 10.1 million in 2019). More than 83 per cent of the Syrian refugees now residing in Jordan live outside of Zaatari and al-Azraq, the two refugee camps created for them (UNHCR 2021b). Many analysts praised Jordan's hospitality toward refugees at the onset of Syria's civil war. Zetter and Ruaudel, for example, in their comparative study of international legal provisions for refugees' right to work, claimed that 'Signatory States do not necessarily offer "best" or "better" practice than nonsignatories' and commended 'the leadership shown by Jordan in providing a quota of work permits to Syrian refugees as part of the donor-supported [Jordan] Compact' (2018, 5). The EU and Jordan signed that agreement in February 2016. That pact obliged the Kingdom to improve Syrian refugees' access to education and lawful employment in return for grants and loans and preferential trade agreements with the Union and its member states.

Other scholars have viewed Jordan as a rent-seeking (or a semi-rentier) nation whose, 'various policy strategies [have been] adopted in an attempt to attract higher levels of funding [that] reveal them as important actors in aid negotiations, with greater agency than is commonly portrayed' (Kelberer 2017, 150; Tsourapas 2020; Morris 2019). A brief overview of Jordan's response to the Syrian refugee crisis during the past decade illuminates the factors that have led to these contrasting claims.

In the first years of the Syrian conflict, Jordan kept its borders open to Syrian refugees due partly to the existence of a pre-war bilateral non-visa regime that allowed Syrians free entry to the country (International Labor Organization 2015). However, beginning in 2013, the Jordanian government gradually applied stricter controls and border restrictions. Authorities formally denied entry to Palestinians residing in Syria beginning in April 2012 and officially declared a non-admittance policy to Palestinians in January 2013. From January to April 2013, only 300 Syrians were allowed to enter Jordan per day. By mid-2014, nearly 12,000 Syrians were stranded on the Syria-Jordan border, even as the Kingdom shifted to a closed-door policy that prevented Syrians from arriving via its international airport (Human Rights Watch 2014). Without regular entry possible since December 2013, all Syrian refugees must report to one of Jordan's two camps, which are jointly administered by the national government and UNHCR.

Tsourapas has argued that the encampment strategy 'enabled the Jordanian state to highlight that it was facing a clearly enumerated influx of Syrian refugees, and to strengthen its appeals for international aid' (2020, 9). Turner, when comparing Lebanon and Jordan's (non-)encampment strategies has similarly suggested that, while acknowledging the importance of both states' differing historical experiences hosting refugees, and the security and budgetary motivations for policies of (non-)encampment, one can consider camps as tools 'through which states spatially segregate refugees, of certain socio-economic classes, whom they deem surplus to labor market requirements' (2015, 386).

Stave and Hillesund (2015) have compared the Syrian refugees who fled to Lebanon to their counterparts in Jordan. On average, the latter group is less economically advantaged, more rural in origin and less well-educated than its host population. As a result, and as Turner has argued,

> The 'bailout' system [a process through which Syrians who have identified a Jordanian sponsor are able to leave the

camps and settle in urban areas] has an important class element as it has often enabled those Syrians with sufficient access to capital and connections to leave refugee camps and move into Jordanian host communities, but has simultaneously effectively consigned to camps the poorest Syrians, who might be expected to exert the strongest downward pressure on wages (Turner 2015, 395).

Jordan's government introduced the bailout system in July 2014 and suspended it in early 2015. With that action, there are now few legal ways for refugees residing in Jordan's camps to leave them to settle in host communities and those require approval by the government's Humanitarian Committee. That group may allow resettlement based on family reunification imperatives, medical requirements or for a small number of other extreme circumstances and conditions (Jordan INGO Forum 2018).

Registered with the UNHCR as refugees or not, all Syrians residing outside the camps in Jordan are required to enroll with the Ministry of the Interior (MoI) and receive a MoI Service Card. In 2015, the Ministry of Interior launched what it dubbed the Urban Verification Exercise (UVE) to re-register/verify all Syrian nationals living in the nation and to provide them with new biometric MoI cards. The identification entitles its holder to move freely throughout the Kingdom and to access public services, including health and education, within the district in which it is issued. Refugees must visit police stations to apply for and renew the card annually to maintain their legal status. Alternatively, they may do so with a valid work permit.

To obtain a MoI card, refugees 12 years or older must first obtain a health certificate from the Ministry and present it along with proof of address (e.g., certified lease agreement, non-certified lease agreement with the presence of the landlord or proof of place of residency issued by UNHCR). Common issues refugees have faced to obtain their MoIs have included long wait times at health centers and police stations, police asking for additional documentation beyond the official requirements (NRC 2016) and difficulties obtaining and providing lease contracts and/or proof of residence (Jordan INGO Forum 2018). The Norwegian Refugee Council (NRC) has studied Syrian refugees' documentation of legal status in Jordan and found,, 'Most refugees interviewed sought to obtain lease contracts (many were living in NRC shelter properties); few discussed bringing their landlord to the police station, and none discussed knowing about or using the UNHCR mechanism' (NRC 2016, 15). The NRC interviews revealed that, 'some landlords ha[d] been reluctant to certify leases because of potential tax consequences. ... In other cases, landlords were unwilling to provide copies of their identity documents or accompany refugees to the police station' (NRC 2016, 15).

Syrians found by Jordanian authorities not to possess a Ministry card are typically arrested and relocated to a refugee camp.

As we noted above, in an effort formally aimed at ameliorating Syrian refugee and vulnerable host communities' living conditions, the EU and Jordan signed the Jordan Compact in February 2016. The agreement obligated the Jordanian government to provide Syrian refugees access to the formal labor market by issuing up to 200,000 work permits for jobs in sectors with low native citizen participation and a high ratio of foreign workers, as well as sectors with a high degree of skills match. The Kingdom also agreed to allow Syrian refugees to register businesses more readily by revising its pertinent legal standards and regulations. For its part, to spur job creation in Jordan, the EU reduced trade barriers on products manufactured in 18 designated Special Economic Zones (SEZs), if at least 15 per cent of the factories' laborers were Syrian refugees (Agulhas 2020). The Compact also removed restrictions on Syrian refugees in camps that prevented those individuals from engaging in financial activities with people outside of them and it also permitted Syrians to become involved in municipal works projects through private sector contractual employment.

While this political commitment to integrate Syrian refugees into the formal Jordanian labor market has resulted in an increased number of work permits for that population, many commentators have expressed skepticism concerning whether the Jordan Compact is genuinely serving the needs of Syrian refugees. Prioritization of state-centric agendas (Arar 2017; Moayerian and Stephenson 2021) via uninformed/non-participatory decision making processes (Lenner and Turner 2018), the underwhelming (and decreasing) growth of new jobs since the adoption of the Jordan Compact (ICMC 2021), an increase in the number of Syrian refugees working in the informal sector since the Jordan Compact's adoption, linear thinking and an overemphasis on agreement-stipulated outputs rather than outcomes (e.g., number of work permits issued versus jobs secured) (Huang et al. 2018) and lack of human rights considerations are among the major critiques of Jordan Compact planning and implementation (Al-Mahaidi 2021).

Morris has argued that financial aid from the EU has discouraged Jordanian officials from negotiating and preparing a plan for a return project as 'government policy is partially as a result of this aid funding tied to refugee integration in Jordan' (2019, 33). On the other hand, ongoing uncertainty about the situation in Syria has sharply reduced the voluntary return rate among Syrian refugees. Chaotic conditions in Syria, frequent policy changes in that country and circulation of misinformation on social media have left refugees in limbo concerning when or whether to seek to return. Morris has claimed that UNHCR has neither the infrastructure in place, nor the arrangements with the Syrian and Jordanian governments to facilitate large-scale voluntary return of Syrians from Jordan.

The influx of Syrian refugees has necessarily resulted in increased demand for education and health services. Prior to the Syrian crisis, the Jordanian Government had committed to raising education standards and reducing the number of students attending double-shift schools (Francis 2015). With more than half of the Syrian refugee population in Jordan under the age of 18, however, the school system has been forced to accommodate a notably higher number of students. Consequently, the hours children spend in school in the country and the quality of education for many of those students due to larger class sizes have both declined. In 2014, the Jordanian Government announced a need to build an additional 72 schools to address the needs of Syrian and Jordanian students (Majali 2014). Meanwhile, El Arab and Sagabaken (2018, 1079) have reviewed the healthcare research addressing Syrian refugees in Jordan and found that, 'The healthcare needs of the refugee, as well as the host population in Jordan, cannot be adequately met without the international society acknowledging a collective responsibility, including a financial commitment'. Many scholars and observers have contended that a major structural barrier for Syrians' access to healthcare and educational services in Jordan is their frequent lack of formal documentation. As a result, several analysts have called for more flexibility in the provision of needed services and improvements in ensuring refugee access to adequate documentation (El Arab and Sagbakken 2018; Norwegian Refugee Council (NRC) 2016).

More generally, Francis (2015) has argued the Syrian refugees' arrival illuminated an existing governance crisis in Jordan. With the government's now more obvious lack of capacity to deliver essential services (e.g., healthcare, education and waste management) and deterioration of service quality in many municipalities, Jordanian citizens have increasingly blamed not only the influx of Syrian refugees, but also the government for those conditions. In this regard, a number of studies have suggested that, 'many of the barriers faced by refugees also exist for vulnerable nationals, and that supporting refugees can provide an opportunity to improve protection conditions for host communities' (Durable Solutions Platform and Migration Policy Institute 2021, 7).

Having surveyed the shifting reactions and policies of the Lebanese and Jordanian governments to the Syrian Civil War refugee crisis, the following sections review the specific roles the UNHCR has played in responding to that still unfolding challenge in Lebanon and Jordan with an eye to gauging its relative effectiveness in providing long-term protection and support to the Syrian Civil War refugee population.

UNHCR Response to Syrian Crisis in Lebanon and Jordan

The overall refugee response in Jordan and Lebanon has resulted from a close collaboration between the governments of the host countries, UN agencies and national and international nongovernmental organizations under the aegis of UNHCR as the lead UN agency for refugee support. UNHCR is responsible for formal assignment of refugee status, resettlement designation and management of formal camps for refugees. As outlined in 1998 (Jordan) and 2003 (Lebanon) separate memoranda of understanding (MOUs) with UNHCR, that institution is responsible for overseeing the refugee application and registration process for all asylum-seekers and providing those who qualify with official certification as persons of concern. Jordan and Lebanon have each pledged to respect the principle of nonrefoulement for those granted refugee status. The MOUs, however, did not provide a blueprint for long-term integration or naturalization of refugees. Lack of a comprehensive domestic legal framework covering refugees with dedicated implementation mechanisms in Lebanon and Jordan has limited UNHCR's capacity to address the protection concerns faced by Syrian refugees. The refugee agency has faced three major challenges as it has sought to address this enduring mismatch of need and capability. We treat those next.

Lack of Downward Accountability

While both MOUs and many scholars/practitioners have placed UNHCR at the center of the refugee regime complex (Betts, Loescher, and Milner 2013), others have rightfully 'conceive[d] of regime complexes as dependent ultimately on a nation state for their foundation' (Barry-Murphy and Stephenson 2018, 791).

In the current era, neoliberalism has provided the leading narrative governing such arrangements by prizing the market, profitability and efficiency. Lebanon's formal request that the UNHCR de-register Syrian refugees by arguing that many of them are not truly refugees, but merely economic migrants seeking jobs, highlights the dominance of this way of thinking in that nation's political decision-making during the crisis. Critics have suggested that UNHCR's willingness to comply with such demands, and its too casual attitude to delisting Syrian refugees at government request, are examples of its lack of downward accountability and failure to ensure humanitarian protections to those it ultimately is charged with protecting (Kagan 2014). As a UN agency ultimately responsible to the nations that comprise that body, UNHCR leaders have argued they were duty bound to comply with Lebanon's suspension order, especially when individuals had not yet fully completed the registration process (UNHCR 2015).

Those refugees who do not obtain registered status do not receive a UNHCR certificate, which as mentioned earlier, for many is essential for continued residency in Lebanon. Without access to full legal status, as a recent report by the Durable Solution Platform and Migration Policy Institute has stated, 'refugees are often unable to obtain basic identity documentation, which limits their access to vital services and makes them vulnerable to harassment, detention, and even deportation' (Durable Solutions Platform and Migration Policy Institute 2021, 7). The result is a classic example of author Joseph Heller's famous Catch 22, a situation from which there is no escape due to conflicting conditions. In this case, it has arisen because relevant responsible organizations have informally refused to accept ultimate accountability and thereby place the affected individuals (refugees) in extraordinary and often supremely difficult straits, whatever their formal rights and responsibilities (Heller, 1961). In this case, this ironic scenario has arisen due to these nations' difficult situations, their past refusal to accede to international humanitarian claims and the tensions implicit in UNHCR's dual mission of serving individual refugees via member states.

In both Lebanon and Jordan, UNHCR adopted biometrics technology in the registration process hoping to enhance downward accountability by enabling faster and fairer refugee assistance, while also improving upward accountability to UN member states through more accurate registration and population data. However, with its strong concern with upward accountability (avoiding fraud and duplication), UNHCR adopted a framing of its role that ultimately did little to improve overall conditions for Syria's refugees. In 2014, the Lebanese government requested access to UNHCR's biometric refugee data and, given the lack of an official UNHCR stance on the issue, many refugees reported concern about their personal information thereby indirectly reaching the Syrian government, with some refusing iris scans, even if it meant forfeiting food and cash aid from the UNHCR and other international agencies (Jacobsen 2016).

Overemphasis on Measurable Outcomes

Several critics of UNHCR have argued that its embrace of a more (economic) developmental approach (versus a humanitarian one) has corroded what should be its main focus: ensuring legal protection and a more vocal and political engagement with governments that fail to honor or that abrogate those obligations to refugees. Jacobsen and Sandvik, in their analysis of UNHCR's approach to increasing its accountability, have argued that the organization's Results-based Management (RBM), biometrics (iris recognition technology) and cash-based interventions (techno-bureaucratic technologies) have, 'yield[ed] an understanding of protection in which quantification, measurability and accuracy are assigned greater value than qualitative perspectives and contextual understanding' (2018, 9). Put differently, the organization's emphasis on measurable outcomes has led critics to question its contributions to humanitarian relief as, 'neither its reports nor its performance measurement systems [have] provided a clear and complete picture of how it was improving the circumstances and well-being of persons of concern' (MOPAN 2015, 64).

As briefly noted in our discussion of the Jordan Compact above, the initial idea framing that agreement was to turn a humanitarian crisis into a development opportunity, a schema that did not target refugees' well-being as its goal, but instead considered them a means to increase Jordan's economic prosperity and not coincidentally, to limit potential Syrian migrants to EU nations. Development-led responses to large-scale, protracted refugee crises, a frame that has gained remarkable traction in recent years, has been popularized as the humanitarian-development nexus (HDN). Zetter (2019) has argued that this approach to the refugee regime is a straightforward manifestation of the neoliberal framework,

> seeking to incorporate a small, but as-yet untapped, component of the global economy. Converting refugees from welfare recipients into market actors as consumers and producers through employment promotion and cash-based transfers (CBTs), and the increasing privatization of humanitarian space through entrepreneurial activity (Zetter 2019, 8).

With its cash-based intervention (CBI) approach in Lebanon and Jordan, UNHCR adopted a vulnerability-assessment framework (VAF) to map the needs of the Syrian non-camp population in both nations. Nominally, VAF provides a vulnerability score that UN agencies and international nongovernmental organizations (INGOs) can employ to identify household needs. Those who have investigated how this method has operated in practice have expressed concerns about a 'system that doesn't see people but data sets, not individuals but numbers, not families but scores,' in which families lose cash assistance because of being shifted among categories of vulnerability (2018, 8). In such terms, 'these families haven't turned down a magical road to a better life, but a data set, based on an annual registration process, has decided their fate for them' (Jacobsen and Sandvik 2018, 8).

Assistance Versus Agency Mobilization

In a neoliberal international system, 'refugees must petition for a citizenship relationship, most typically based on persecution or other hardship. … That is, to gain citizenship, refugees need first to be conceptualized as victims' (Barry-Murphy and Stephenson 2018, 793). Agier (2011) has contended that due to their exclusion from formative roles in the refugee regime and denial of their agency, refugees have no choice but passively to accept their status or pursue illegal solutions/channels to their plights. Examples of structures that have worked to limit refugees' possibilities for exercising agency are myriad in the Jordanian and Lebanese Syrian crises profiled here. Predefined living districts, rigid employment sectors and class-based bailout mechanisms are obvious illustrations of the neoliberal mindset that values a certain narrow stratum of refugees and views others as socio-economic burdens or threats on (inter)national resources. Criticizing UNHCR's use of its vulnerability framework in Lebanon, Janmyr (2018) has warned that such supposed efficient pragmatism has actively endangered humanitarian values.

Conclusions

Displaced Syrians' protection within the refugee regime complex during the present crisis has depended heavily on (and often been limited by) affected states' capacities and the norms they have been willing to accept. In the case of Jordan and Lebanon, the omnipresent neoliberal worldview has led these host countries to cultivate legal ambiguity and uncertainty along with complicated/expensive processes for documentation and/or self-employment for the Syrians they have hosted in the present crisis. Taken together, this stance has de facto constituted a strategy that has blamed and demonized refugees for their situations and, even more perversely, curtailed others' willingness to recognize their political rights and agency. To overcome this unsustainable and inhuman worldview, the dominant framing of refugees as passive and vulnerable and in need of state protection/reunification must change. However, as mentioned earlier, the challenging relationship between the UN agency and its sovereign members limits such potentials. Certainly, as we have argued, UNHCR has been unable or unwilling to press such claims.

In order for leaders of the refugee regime governance complex and refugees to view themselves as agents of their own future, it is essential 'to re-interpret the narrative of vulnerability prescribed for them by the regime's overseers and to rethink how they and those who play a role in protection decisions regarding them can revise their prescribed story' (Barry-Murphy and Stephenson 2018, 793). It appears essential not simply to regard refugees as passive actors in search of a market defined niche, but instead as human beings with complex needs and the full array of rights that accompany that standing.

References

Agier, Michel. 2011. *Managing the Undesirables: Refugee Camps and Humanitarian Government*. Translated by David Fernbach. Cambridge: Polity Press.

Agulhas. 2020. Independent Monitor's Assessment Report Jordan Compact and Brussels Meetings. 3. UK.

Al-Mahaidi, Ala. 2021. Securing Economic Livelihoods for Syrian Refugees: The Case for a Human Rights-Based Approach to the Jordan Compact. *The International Journal of Human Rights* 25 (2): 203–30. https://doi.org/10.1080/13642987.2020.1763314.

Arar, Rawan. 2017. The New Grand Compromise: How Syrian Refugees Changed the Stakes in the Global Refugee Assistance Regime. *Middle East Law and Governance* 9 (3): 298–312. https://doi.org/10.1163/18763375-00903007.

Barry-Murphy, Emily, and Max Stephenson. 2018. Democratizing the Refugee Regime Complex. *VOLUNTAS: International Journal of Voluntary and Nonprofit Organizations* 29 (4): 790–800. https://doi.org/10.1007/s11266-018-9967-0.

Betts, Alexander, Gil Loescher, and James Milner. 2013. *The UN High Commissioner for Refugees (UNHCR): The Politics and Practice of Refugee Protection*. Routledge.

Brussel II Conference. 2018. Supporting the Future of Syria and the Region: Lebanon Partnership Paper. https://www.consilium.europa.eu/media/34145/lebanon-partnership-paper.pdf

Durable Solutions Platform and Migration Policy Institute. 2021. A Bridge to Firmer Ground: Learning from International Experiences to Support Pathways to Solutions in the Syrian Refugee Context. Research Report. https://www.migrationpolicy.org/sites/default/files/publications/dsp-mpi_syria_refugees_fullreport.pdf

El Arab, R., and M. Sagbakken. 2018. Healthcare Services for Syrian Refugees in Jordan: A Systematic Review. *European Journal of Public Health* 28 (6): 1079–87. https://doi.org/10.1093/eurpub/cky103.

Fakhoury, Tamirace. 2015. Lebanon's Perilous Balancing Act. https://laur.lau.edu.lb:8443/xmlui/handle/10725/8286

Francis, Alexandra. 2015. Jordan's Refugee Crisis. *Carnegie Endowment for International Peace*. https://carnegieendowment.org/files/CP_247_Francis_Jordan_final.pdf

Hanafi, Sari, and T. Long. 2010. Governance, Governmentalities, and the State of Exception in the Palestinian Refugee Camps of Lebanon. *Journal of Refugee Studies* 23 (2): 134–59. https://doi.org/10.1093/jrs/feq014.

Hanafi, Sari, and Åge A Tiltnes. 2008. The Employability of Palestinian Professionals in Lebanon: Constraints and Transgression. *Knowledge, Work and Society* 5 (1): 1–15.

Hazbun, Waleed. 2016. Assembling Security in a 'Weak State:' The Contentious Politics of Plural Governance in Lebanon since 2005. *Third World Quarterly* 37 (6): 1053–70. https://doi.org/10.1080/01436597.2015.1110016.

Heller, Joseph. 1961. *Catch 22*. New York: Simon and Schuster.

Huang, Cindy, Nazanin Ash, Katelyn Gough, and Lauren Post. 2018. Designing Refugee Compacts: Lessons from Jordan. *Forced Migration Review*, no. 57 (February): 52–54.

Human Rights Watch, ed. 2014. *Not Welcome: Jordan's Treatment of Palestinians Escaping Syria*. New York, NY: Human Rights Watch.

———. 2021a. Lebanon: Dire Conditions for Syrian Refugees in Border Town. https://www.hrw.org/news/2021/01/19/lebanon-dire-conditions-syrian-refugees-border-town

———. 2021b. *World Report 2021: Events of 2020*. New York: SEVEN STORIES PRESS.

ICMC. 2021. Refugees and Host Communities Seeking Direction from the Margin of Jordan's Labour Market. Labour Market Assessment. https://data2.unhcr.org/en/documents/details/84614

International Labor Orgnization (ILO). 2015. Access to Work for Syrian Refugees in Jordan: A Discussion Paper on Labour and Refugee Laws and Policies. *Beirut: ILO*, 30.

Jacobsen, Katja Lindskov. 2016. UNHCR, Accountability and Refugee Biometrics. *UNHCR and the Struggle for Accountability: Technology, Law and Results-Based Management*, 184.

Jacobsen, Katja Lindskov, and Kristin Bergtora Sandvik. 2018. UNHCR and the Pursuit of International Protection: Accountability through Technology? *Third World Quarterly* 39 (8): 1508–24. https://doi.org/10.1080/01436597.201 8.1432346.

Janmyr, Maja. 2016. Precarity in Exile: The Legal Status of Syrian Refugees in Lebanon. *Refugee Survey Quarterly* 35 (4): 58–78.

———. 2017. No Country of Asylum: 'Legitimizing' Lebanon's Rejection of the 1951 Refugee Convention. *International Journal of Refugee Law* 29 (3): 438–65. https://doi.org/10.1093/ijrl/eex026.

———. 2018. UNHCR and the Syrian Refugee Response: Negotiating Status and Registration in Lebanon. *The International Journal of Human Rights* 22 (3): 393–419. https://doi.org/10.1080/13642987.2017.1371140.

Jordan INGO Forum. 2018. Syrian Refugees in Jordan: A Protection Overview.

Kagan, Michael. 2014. Refugee Status Removed After a Routine Interview? UNHCR, Please Explain. *RSD Watch*, 23 October 2014. https://rsdwatch. com/2014/10/23/refugee-status-removed-after-a-routine-interview-unhcr-please-explain/

Kelberer, Victoria. 2017. Negotiating Crisis: International Aid and Refugee Policy in Jordan. *Middle East Policy* 24 (4): 148–65. https://doi.org/10.1111/mepo.12313.

Lenner, Katharina, and Lewis Turner. 2018. Learning from the Jordan Compact. *Forced Migration Review* 57: 48–51.

Majali. 2014. Jordan Needs 72 New Schools to Accommodate Refugee Children. *Jordan Times*, 3 December 2014. http://www.jordantimes.com/news/local/jordan-needs-72-new-schools-accommodate-refugee-children-%E2%80%94-majali

Meier, Daniel. 2014. Lebanon: The Refugee Issue and the Threat of a Sectarian Confrontation. *Oriente Moderno* 94 (2): 382–401. https://doi.org/10.1163/22138617-12340063.

Moayerian, Neda, and Max Stephenson Jr. 2021. Human Rights, Economic Assumptions, the Jordan Compact, and the Syrian Refugee Crisis. *Academia Letters*, June. https://doi.org/10.20935/AL1429.

MOPAN. 2015. Synthesis Report UN High Commissioner for Refugees (UNHCR). Multilateral Organisation Performance Assessment Network.

Morris, Julia. 2019. The Politics of Return from Jordan to Syria, 4.

Nagle, John, and Mary-Alice Clancy. 2019. Power-Sharing after Civil War: Thirty Years since Lebanon's Taif Agreement. *Nationalism and Ethnic Politics* 25 (1): 1–8. https://doi.org/10.1080/13537113.2019.1565171.

Norwegian Refugee Council (NRC). 2016. Securing Status: Syrian Refugees and the Documentation of Legal Status, Identity, and Family Relationships in Jordan. https://data2.unhcr.org/en/documents/details/52314

Rizkallah, Amanda. 2017. The Paradox of Power-Sharing: Stability and Fragility in Postwar Lebanon. *Ethnic and Racial Studies* 40 (12): 2058–76. https://doi.org/10.1080/01419870.2017.1277031.

Saliba, Isaam. 2016. Refugee Law and Policy: Lebanon. Legal Reports. Library of Congress. https://www.loc.gov/collections/publications-of-the-law-library-of-congress/about-this-collection/#ftn5

Stave, Svein Erik, and Solveig Hillesund. 2015. Impact of Syrian Refugees on the Jordanian Labour Market. *International Labour Organization (ILO)*, 160.

Stern, Rebecca Thorburn. 2016. Responses to the 'Refugee Crisis': What Is the Role of Self-Image among EU Countries? *Swedish Institute for European Policy Studies*, 16. https://ssrn.com/abstract=2933381

Stevens, D. (2016). Rights, needs or assistance? The role of the UNHCR in refugee protection in the Middle East. *The International Journal of Human Rights*, *20*(2), 264–283. https://doi.org/10.1080/13642987.2015.1079026

Suleiman, Jaber. 2006. Marginalised Community: The Case of Palestinian Refugees in Lebanon. https://assets.publishing.service.gov.uk/media/57a08c4be5274a31e0001112/JaberEdited.pdf

Tsourapas, Gerasimos. 2019. The Syrian Refugee Crisis and Foreign Policy Decision-Making in Jordan, Lebanon, and Turkey. *Journal of Global Security Studies* 4 (4): 464–81. https://doi.org/10.1093/jogss/ogz016

———. 2020. The Jordan Compact. *Signature* 2: 3.

Turner, Lewis. 2015. Explaining the (Non-) Encampment of Syrian Refugees: Security, Class and the Labour Market in Lebanon and Jordan. *Mediterranean Politics* 20 (3): 386–404.

UN General Assembly. 1951. Convention Relating to the Status of Refugees. Vol. 189. UN Treaty Series. UN General Assembly. https://www.refworld.org/docid/3be01b964.html

UNHCR. 2015. MID-YEAR DASHBOARD. https://reliefweb.int/sites/reliefweb.int/files/resources/28072015_ProtectionSectoralDashboard.pdf

———. 2017. Lebanon. UNHCR Operations Worldwide. https://reporting.unhcr.org/node/2520?y=2017#year

———. 2019a. 2020 Planning Summary: Lebanon. https://reporting.unhcr.org/sites/default/files/pdfsummaries/GA2020-Lebanon-eng.pdf

———. 2019b. Lebanon. UNHCR Operations Worldwide. https://reporting.unhcr.org/node/2520?y=2019#year

———. 2020. Lebanon Crisis Response Plan 2017-2020. https://reliefweb.int/sites/reliefweb.int/files/resources/74641.pdf

———. 2021a. Jordan: Operational Update (February 2021). https://data2.unhcr.org/en/documents/details/85613

———. 2021b. Syria Regional Refugee Response: Jordan. https://data2.unhcr.org/en/situations/syria/location/36

Yassin, Nasser, Tarek osseiran, Rima Rassi, and Marwa Boustani. 2015. No Place to Stay? Reflections on the Syrian Refugee Shelter Policy in Lebanon. UN Habitat. https://www.aub.edu.lb/ifi/Documents/publications/ books/2015-2016/20150907_noplacetostay.pdf

Zetter, Roger. 2019. Theorizing the Refugee Humanitarian-Development Nexus: A Political-Economy Analysis. *Journal of Refugee Studies*, no. fez070 (August). https://doi.org/10.1093/jrs/fez070.

Zetter, Roger, and Héloïse Ruaudel. 2018. Refugees' Right to Work and Access to Labour Markets: Constraints, Challenges and Ways Forward. *Forced Migration Review*, no. 58 (June): 4–7.

3

The European Union's Response to the Syrian Refugee Crisis

EVANTHIA BALLA

The crisis began in Syria ten years ago, following a wave of popular unrest that swept the Arab world, also commonly known as the Arab Spring. In March 2011, pro-democracy protesters demanded an end to the authoritarian practices of Bashar al-Assad's regime, posing an unprecedented challenge to his authority. The Syrian government used police, military, as well as paramilitary forces to suppress demonstrations. Resistance militias began to form and, by 2012, the conflict had expanded into a full-fledged civil war, which drew in regional and extra-regional forces.

The Assad regime has received external support from Iran and Russia and indirect support from China. Russia and China's veto against western-sponsored proposals to the UN to take actions against Assad's regime also corroborate that support. Based on this backing, the regime managed to maintain control of crucial areas in terms of population, such as in Aleppo, Syria's largest city. On the other hand, the rebels, and later the coalition of Syrian Democratic Forces (SDF), obtained support from the United States of America (USA) and some European States, such as France (Kienle 2019; Phillips 2020). In addition, the country also experienced a fierce sectarian contest between the Shiite forces led by Iran and the Sunni camp backed by Saudi Arabia, Turkey, and Qatar. As far as the war against terror is concerned, an apparent aim of the USA to defeat terrorism, as well as a Global Coalition against Da'esh, all contribute to a further involvement of various players in the region. Nonetheless, peaceful attempts by institutional actors, such as efforts from the UN-led Geneva process based on UN Security Council Resolution 2254 or the ad hoc Astana process, which works to enforce the Resolution, comprising Russia, Iran and Turkey, have all so far failed to progress toward a political settlement to the conflict. What began with demonstrations against the Syrian regime is now a civil war with regional and international dimensions (Haass 2017; Baczko et al. 2018; Hinnebusch and Saouli 2020; Phillips 2020; Matar and Kadri 2019).

Considering the European Union's perspective, at the beginning of the crisis, the block presented a united front against Bashar al-Assad's repressive leadership, including severe sanctions against the regime. However, the EU failed to reach a genuinely Common Foreign and Security Policy (CFSP). As Cavatorta and Turcotte (2020) point out, the EU's involvement in Syria has swung between constructive engagement with the Syrian regime to marginalization of it. In addition, the refugee crisis that the Syrian Civil War provoked revealed the EU's internal malfunction and limits.

The massive refugee waves from Syria are exacerbating the economic and social conditions of Syria's neighbors and Europe itself. According to the Regional Strategic Overview 2021–2022 (3RP, co-led between UNHCR and UNDP), there are more than 5.5 million Syrian refugees across the region - whether fleeing the brutality of the Assad regime or Da'esh depravity, seeking safety in Lebanon, Turkey, Jordan and beyond. The UN Refugee Agency also reported around 6.2 million people displaced within Syria as of 2021 – the largest internally displaced population in the world. Furthermore, poverty rates for Syrian refugees exceed 60 per cent in some countries, while unemployment and uneven access to basic services, such as education, persist. Thousands of civilians have also suffered at the hands of brutal non-State armed groups, including Da'esh, as stated by the Regional Strategic Overview (3RP). The European Council has characterized the conflict in Syria as 'the world's largest humanitarian disaster, with no parallel in recent history' (European Council, no date).

The Impact of the Refugee Crisis on the EU

During the last two decades, the Middle East has experienced a dramatic forced migration. The war in Syria alone produced one of the greatest shares of the Middle East's refugees. Millions have also fled wars, especially in Libya, Iraq, Afghanistan, Somalia, Sudan, and Yemen. North African States and Turkey have emerged as key transit hubs for refugee flows into Europe.

In 2015, at the peak of the EU's refugee crisis, the main countries of origin of refugees and migrants arriving in Greece were Syria (57 per cent), followed by Afghanistan (22 per cent) and Iraq (5 per cent). Those who traveled as far as Italy were mainly from Eritrea (25 per cent), Nigeria (10 per cent) and Somalia (10 per cent), followed by Syria (7 per cent) and The Gambia (6 per cent).

According to Eurostat, 1.3 million migrants applied for asylum in the Member States of the EU, United Kingdom (an EU Member State at the time), Norway, and Switzerland in 2015. In the same year, refugees from Syria totaled 378,000, accounting for 29 per cent of all of Europe's asylum seekers – the highest share of any nation. Similarly, the largest group of beneficiaries of protection status in the EU in 2015 remained citizens from Syria (166,100 people, or 50 per cent of the total number of persons granted protection status in EU Member States). The applications for international protection have ever since been a lasting reality. In 2019, EU countries granted protection to 295,800 asylum seekers, from which almost one in three (27 per cent) came from Syria. Still in 2020, Syrians (84 per cent), Eritreans (80 per cent), and Yemenis (75 per cent) had the highest recognition rates.

It is also worth highlighting that in 2015 and 2016 alone, more than 2.3 million illegal crossings were detected. Although the total number of illegal crossings had dropped to 114,300 in 2020, the lowest level in the last six years, Afghanistan and Syria, along with Tunisia and Algeria, remain the main countries of origin of people detected making an irregular border crossing. Under this prism, the necessary balance between, on the one hand, respecting human rights, while, on the other hand, prevention and protection from potential threats such as terrorism, required a special statecraft by the European governments and by the block itself (Goździak et al. 2020).

Migration has been posing significant challenges to European societies so far and has raised serious concerns over its medium and long-term economic and fiscal impact. The current migrant and refugee crisis has also been a disintegration challenge for Europe. Tassinari (2016, 72) has claimed that,

> [t]ogether with common foreign and defense policies—another item on the European agenda that is becoming increasingly enmeshed with the refugee crisis—migration is the epitome of a highly sensitive issue that is threaded carefully at the domestic level by each European Union (EU) member state before it gets negotiated in the EU, almost always resulting in watered-down compromises.

Dinan, Nugent and Paterson (2017, 1) contend that apart from the 2009 financial crisis, 'the most recognizable feature of the EU in crisis has been the migration crisis'. Similarly, Buonanno (2017, 122) has suggested that the 'migration crisis is widely thought to threaten many of the foundations and bases on which European integration has been built'.

On the other hand, Webber (2019, 170) has argued that '[u]nlike the Eurozone Crisis, the Refugee Crisis did not produce a higher level of (horizontal, sectoral and vertical) political integration'. Instead, because of the restoration of border controls, the crisis resulted in limited political fragmentation. For Brack and Gürkan (2021, 13), 'during the Schengen crisis, cultural issues were central to debates in many Member states and attempts to depoliticize the issue through a delegation of power to a supranational structure failed'.

In the end, the EU responded to the Syrian Refugee Crisis using the power vested in it by its Member States. EU policy and its Member States' distinct national strategies have not always coincided. Consequently, unity was threatened, and the EU's credibility challenged.

The EU's Response to the Refugee Crisis: Policy and Politics

In times of crisis and in events of disintegration, the EU has been responding through institutional and operational adaptations (Niemann and Zaun 2018; Buonanno 2017; Schilde and Goodman 2021; Bosilca 2021). Within the Union's area of freedom, security and justice, measures have been taken in relation to asylum, immigration, borders, police and judicial cooperation. The EU has established a Common European Asylum System (CEAS) and a European Migration Network. On the external front, the EU has been functioning within the context of its CFSP, and its Neighborhood Policy, seeking to enhance prosperity and stability to neighboring countries. The Union has also used the framework of its Common Security and Defense Policy (CSDP), implementing humanitarian and rescue tasks.

However, it was on the European Agenda on Migration (European Commission 2015) that Europe would establish a comprehensive approach to improve the management of migration in all its aspects. The plan focused on three fronts: action at the border of the EU, by saving lives and securing the borders of the Union; action inside the EU, by developing a new policy on legal migration, and by relocating refugees to other Union Members and strengthening the common asylum policy; and last but not least, external action, by reducing the incentives for irregular migration, as well as assisting the refugees where they are and resettling them when possible.

How was this to be implemented in practice? A new European Border and Coast Guard (EBCGA–Frontex) was launched in October 2016 to ensure that Europe could protect its common external borders and face the new migration and security challenges in a united fashion. Its budget of 254 million euros in 2016 rose gradually, reaching 543 million euros in 2021. In addition, the EU has strengthened the role of Europol as well as of Eurojust. Other EU agencies have also been experiencing a similar transformation. The European Asylum Support Office (EASO) based in Malta, which facilitates the implementation and improves the functioning of the CEAS, became the EU Agency for Asylum (EUAA). The EUAA began its activities with a 172 million euros budget for 2022.

An altogether new concept, the Hotspot, was also inaugurated as part of the European Agenda on Migration, allowing EBCGA, Europol, and EUAA to work on the ground in affected EU Member States to identify, register and fingerprint arriving migrants and to assist in dismantling migrant smuggling networks (Niemann and Zaun 2018). Moreover, according to the Agenda, a series of other policies would be implemented, such as a return and resettlement policy, as well as emergency measures including the relocation of asylum-seekers from the frontline Member States to other Member States.

On 18 March 2016, the EU signed a controversial agreement with Turkey, aiming at stopping the flow of irregular migrants via Turkey to Europe. According to the deal, irregular migrants arriving on the Greek islands should be returned to Turkey, and, for every Syrian returned to Turkey, the EU would take in a Syrian from Turkey (European Council 2016). In exchange, the EU also agreed to reduce visa restrictions for Turkish citizens, to update the customs union, re-energize the accession process and to provide 6 billion euros in financial aid.

As far as the asylum claims are concerned, the Dublin Regulation establishes that the country where an asylum seeker enters EU territory is responsible for dealing with the asylum claim. During the height of the refugee and migrants' arrivals, this deal placed a particular burden on Greece and Italy, where most asylum seekers arrived. Under this prism, in 2016, the European Commission proposed a new corrective allocation mechanism. According to the document, although the point of entry would still determine which state was responsible, if, in turn, that government faced a disproportionate number of asylum seekers, the mechanism would trigger the transfer of cases to less-burdened states (European Commission 2016a).

In 2017, the European Parliament and the Council reached a broad political agreement on reviewing some of the CEAS legislative instruments. It agreed on establishing a full-fledged EU Asylum Agency, to reform Eurodac, review the Reception Conditions Directive, examine the Qualification Regulation and the EU Resettlement framework. However, the Council did not reach a common position on the reform of the Dublin system and the Asylum Procedure Regulation. In 2020, the Commission proposed a fresh start, a New Pact on Migration and Asylum, aiming at tackling the imbalances in member states' burdens related to migrant arrivals and simplifying the asylum process (European Commission 2020). Concerning EU funding for migration, asylum and integration policies in the EU's budget, 10 billion euros went to migration and asylum management in 2014–2020. This amount rose to 22.7 billion euros for the 2021–2027 period.

The EU has taken some important steps towards managing the crisis, strengthening its institutions and tools. However, the overall approach can be considered as an example of 'defensive integration,' inclining to finding solutions to deal with the refugee flows outside the EU borders, but not managing the challenge adequately within its own borders (Kriesi, et al. 2021). The New Pact on Migration and Asylum has also been criticized as mainly technical and that it has not seemed to have simplified the asylum process so far (Donatienne and Erol 2020). The hotspots have given a significant contribution in managing the refugee and migrant flows, but there has been a lack of a precise legal framework governing the whole strategy and guaranteeing refugees' human rights. (Niemann and Zaun 2018). In addition, there has reportedly been an inadequate response to the refugees' needs for medication, food supply and accommodation supplying (UNHCR, no date). Furthermore, the Dublin Regulation fell short of the urgent solution to such a humanitarian drama. Entry countries carrying a disproportionate weight of migrants and refugees often neglected their obligations and allowed asylum seekers to move on to Northern European States. As a result, Northern States chose to temporarily reinstall border controls within the Schengen area, jeopardizing one of the greatest achievements of internal integration by the Union, the free movement of people, goods, services and capital. In this context, the EU Member States' response resembled what Biermann et al (2019) have called 'a 'Rambo' game situation,' in which 'the States least affected by migratory pressure were satisfied with the institutional status quo and were thus able to leave the more affected states aggrieved'. European Funds are important instruments of support. However, there are a series of other issues, such as monitoring allocations, that still need to be addressed.

Regarding the relocation plan, it did not fulfil its purpose and was ultimately abandoned. Indeed, the 'corrective allocation mechanism' immediately became a divisive issue. Proponents of the relocation deal supported the view that managing the refugee crisis was a shared responsibility, while opponents responded that no country should be under obligation by EU decisions to accept third-country citizens on their territories. The United Kingdom did not opt into the solidarity relocation scheme. The Czech Republic, Hungary, and Poland openly refused to comply with the decision, based on their national political needs, triggering court cases (Niemann and Zaun 2018). The voluntary resettlement plan ended up being 'an enormous flop' (Buonanno 2017, 116).

The EU places 'building resilience' (European Commission 2016b) as a central objective of development and humanitarian assistance. Yet, as far as the CSDP is concerned, existing crisis management procedures and mechanisms remain limited and slow. Similarly, the EU-Turkey agreement has been criticized by EU Member States, as well as by other signatories to the 1951 Geneva Convention Relating to the Status of Refugees (and its 1967 Protocol), as to have avoided their international obligations to refugee protection (Rygiel et al. 2016; Niemann and Zaun, 2018; Abdat 2018; Ghosh 2018; Kaya 2020). Moreover, the EU, while considering Turkey a safe country of origin – this seems to contradict the Commissions' (2019) criticism to the country for discrimination against minorities and the politicization of the judiciary. The weaknesses in the EU's refugee management were further evident when Turkey, during the end of February 2020, suspended the deal, by opening its land border with Greece and leading to a deadlock situation. Both sides placed strategic interests above humanitarian principles (Kriesi et al. 2021).

Thus far, the EU-Turkey Statement has allowed the continuation of the resettlement process. It also significantly contributed to the reduction of irregular border crossings within the EU. However, it was the product of a 'German kind of solution format,' not a common approach to a common challenge. It appeared to be a way of protecting the Member States from supranational activism. As a result, the EU continued muddling through the crisis (Crawford 2021, 482).

Finally, the EU's lack of coherence and the subsequent weak responses to the crisis, were soon manipulated by the dangerous populist and extremist parties. In fact, the refugees arrived at a moment when Europe was just emerging from the worst economic crisis of the post- war period. As a result, a series of far-right parties seized the opportunity to exploit public distress and build a 'factless' discourse against the migrant challenge in order to gain more power. In January 2015, the neo-fascist Golden Dawn became the third-largest political party in the Hellenic Parliament. Likewise, in 2017, the Freedom Party (FPO) became a coalition partner in Austria's new government, and Germany's Alternative for Germany (AfD) entered Germany's Bundestag for the first time in 2017, becoming the country's third-largest political party. In Italy, two populist movements – the Five-star Movement and the League – made large gains in the March 2018 elections, while Hungary's re-elected prime minister, Viktor Orban, has grown increasingly far-right and authoritarian. The rise of these forces put further negative pressure on the EU's national governments, making it more difficult for the Union to act with unity.

The EU's struggle to manage the flow of refugees has allowed the highest boosting of xenophobic and nationalistic forces in Europe since World War II, and the Syrian drama was not able to trigger any breakthroughs to the sharing practices in the EU. Overall, there has been a lack of comprehensive solidarity rules and EU governments have employed mostly unilateral and security-driven responses aimed at limiting the number of refugees that would enter Europe (Karageorgiou 2016, 210; Kriesi et al. 2021). Regarding the European Union's involvement in Syria's civil war, there has been unity in humanitarian aid, yet also division in external policy making.

The EU's Particular Response to the Syrian Crisis

The EU's response to the refugee crisis concerning Syrian refugees has been based on the European Agenda on Migration and on the New Pact on Migration and Asylum, as previously discussed. Under this prism, steps have been made concerning humanitarian assistance to the Syrian people, as well as to neighboring hosting countries. The EU and its Member States have provided more than 17 billion euros in aid since the beginning of the conflict to help those who have fled the war, inside and outside Syria. The EU's regional trust fund, the Madad Fund, has reached almost 1.4 billion euros in combined funding from the EU and its Member States. The EU focused on helping Syria's neighboring states not only through the Madad Trust Fund, but also through the Regional Development and Protection Programme for refugees and host communities in Lebanon, Jordan, as well as Iraq (Rosanne and Sinatti 2020).

A series of Brussels Conferences on Supporting the future of Syria and the region, seeking to mobilize humanitarian aid to Syrians within the country and in the neighboring countries, have also been taking place since 2017. On 29 and 30 March 2021, the Brussels V Conference pledged 5.3 billion euros for 2021 and beyond for Syria and the neighboring countries hosting the largest Syrian refugee population, the largest amount of that support came from Europe. Nonetheless, as Barbulescu (2017) has contended, such measures increased financial aid to the region – rather than shared the need to provide protection to refugees.

As far as the Union's external policymaking in Syria is concerned, before the 2011 Syrian Uprising, it was based on a policy of constructive engagement, despite the absence of an Association Agreement (AA). Syria was a partner in the 1995 Barcelona Process, set to create an area of shared prosperity between the EU and the Mediterranean countries of the southern bank. After the dramatic foreign intervention in Iraq in 2003, Europeans became even more convinced that diplomatic engagement was far better than military involvement in the region; and that dialogue combined with economic development could gradually contribute to more democratic accountability by the Syrian government (Cavatorta and Turcotte 2020, 261). However, the Syrian Uprising against the Syrian government put an end to that constructive engagement. The EU reverted its position turning against Assad's regime and focused on a strategy to bring peace and security in the region, as outlined in the EU's regional strategy for Syria and Iraq (Council of the European Union 2015), as well as the ISIL/Da'esh threat and the EU strategy on Syria (Council of the European Union 2017).

Indeed, the terrorist threat of Da'esh and other terrorist groups in Syria implies a serious challenge not only to the internal stability of the nation, but also to its broader region and the international community. Hence, the regional strategy for Syria was set to support efforts by the Global Coalition to counter Da'esh; reduce the influx of foreign terrorist fighters, funds and weapons to Da'esh; prevent regional spillovers and improve border security; and provide humanitarian aid and international protection to those affected.

Since 2012, the EU and its Member States have also been implementing some restrictive measures, including sanctions. Overall, 270 individuals and 70 entities have been targeted by a travel ban and an asset freeze. EU sanctions also include an oil embargo and export restrictions on equipment and technology that might have been used for internal repression, among others. As part of its security response and the fight against terrorism, the EU has implemented UN Security Council sanctions freezing the funds of persons and entities associated with Osama bin Laden, the al Qaida network, the Taliban and Da'esh.

Nevertheless, the threat of Da'esh, in addition to the refugee crisis, has also triggered significant different policy positions by EU Member States, leaving the EU with a weak and divided voice in the face of one of the world's largest humanitarian disasters. Countries, such as Germany and Sweden were open to admitting refugees at the beginning of the crisis, while others, namely Denmark, Hungary, and Poland, refused entry from the very start. Europe's divisions were immediately apparent and also were revealed by attitudes toward the arms' embargo on the rebels. France and the UK pursued an end to the arms' embargo against the rebels in the spring of 2013, based on humanitarian arguments. In turn, several others, including the Czech Republic, the Netherlands, and Sweden, were more skeptical. The arms embargo was allowed to lapse, but all the other EU measures against Syria continued (Cavatorta and Turcotte 2020, 271).

In practice, as Saatçioğlu (2020) has pointed out, EU member states eventually united around the 'lowest common denominator solution' represented by the refugee deal, which illustrated Thin Europe (focused on a strategy aiming at resolving the 'crisis' on the ground – i.e., an EU-Turkey deal) at the expense of a more norm-based policy associated with Thick (a more EU integration approach) and Global Europe (focused on international cooperation and the EU's corresponding responsibilities to refugee protection). The current institutional architecture of the EU's foreign policy has resulted in a lack of determining influence on developments in the Syrian Civil War, be it from the EU collectively or from Member States individually.

Ultimately, the EU is what its members allow it to be. As Cavatorta and Turcotte (2020, 273) claim, 'the EU can only be a "player" in international affairs if its constituent parts allow it'.

Explaining the EU's Response to the Syrian Refugee Crisis through Theoretical Lenses

During the last years, there has been a vibrant theoretical discussion on European (dis)integration tendencies due to the successive crises of the last decades, including the refugee crisis, as well as on the applicability of grand theories to the study of crisis (Schimmelfennig 2018; Börzel and Risse 2018; Hooghe and Marks 2019; Smeets and Zaun 2021; Schilde and Goodman 2021; Biermann at al. 2019). For the purposes of this chapter, the theories, that were conceived with European integration in mind – neofunctionalism, liberal intergovernmentalism and post-functionalism – also provide important explanatory tools by which to gauge the strengths and weaknesses of the EU's response to the Syrian Refugee crisis.

As previously discussed, the refugee crisis has revealed a series of EU flaws, related to the incoherent European reaction that led to the Schengen crisis and to the related failure of the relocation scheme, the rise of extremism inside the EU, the externalization of the solution through the EU-Turkey agreement and finally the failure in speaking with one voice in the world scene and reaching its humanitarian objectives.

Liberal intergovernmentalism explains cooperation based on the European States' functional interests and asymmetrical interdependence. States will only delegate or pool the authority needed to comply with a deal (Moravcsik and Schimmelfennig 2009; Hooghe and Marks 2019). In this regard, weak interdependence and incompatible preferences led to a fragile intergovernmental bargaining during the refugee crisis, and particularly the Schengen crisis, as well as a mix of unilateral measures that produced temporary disintegration. The Dublin system, besides tackling border crossing issues in the Schengen Area, was not designed to deal with such a shock as the 2015–2016 peak of the refugee crisis. It was not intended to prevent uncoordinated and subsequently damaging actions by some Member States either. Greece and Italy were incapable of controlling the unprecedent refuge flows from crossing their borders and heading to the North. Germany's action also had a negative impact. At the beginning of the crisis, Germany suspended the Dublin Regulation for Syrian refugees to admit them directly. However, just weeks later, the country changed its strategy and temporarily restored border controls with Austria. Several other Schengen states followed the same strategy, such as Austria, Denmark, France, Slovenia, Norway and Sweden. Furthermore, Member States interpreted the Refugee Convention definition differently. As a result, 'the Schengen/Dublin regime has been up in the air since the summer of 2015' (Schimmelfennig 2021, 68).

At the same time, liberal intergovernmentalism points out that the EU failed to replace the provisions laid down in the Dublin Regulation with a system of shared responsibility or reallocation. The European Commission's proposal for a Regulation on a permanent crisis relocation mechanism, as previously discussed, was rejected not only by Eastern Member States but also by some Western Member States, refugee's entry doors, such as France and Spain, (Schimmelfennig 2018). In the end, Europeans agreed on a one-time reallocation of up to 160,000 refugees. Still, even this ad hoc measure had a mixed record of implementation, and it was legally challenged by several Eastern Member States. In practice, over the last years, only dedicated schemes and voluntary relocations coordinated by the Commission have taken place.

The EU has also focused on externalization tactics to overcome the Schengen crisis. Member States, instead of strengthening the capacity of the EU to deal with migrants, have enhanced intergovernmental cooperation with third countries to prevent migrants from reaching the EU's borders, as seen in the 2016 EU agreement with Turkey. However, supranational institutions are not accountable for that agreement, leaving the process unsupervised and thus highly unpredictable. Ultimately, the Schengen crisis led to a quantitative expansion rather than qualitative deepening of the activities of EU agencies (Schimmelfennig 2018; Smeets and Zaun 2021).

In intergovernmentalist theorizing, Member States determine the course of European integration, while institutional actors play a minor role. (Moravcsik 1993, 1998; 2018; Smeets and Zaun; Hooghe and Marks 2019). Indeed, there was not 'a profound effect on governance institutions' (Crawford 2021, 482). The EU's agencies have been reinforced in terms of budget and personnel but remain dependent on Member States' decisions. They do not have any acquired supranational competencies (Schimmelfennig 2018).

EASO/EUAA continues to be limited to supporting the implementation of a Common European Asylum System and coordinating national authorities in the implementation of EU asylum rules. It cannot impose uniform asylum decisions across the European Union.

As far as the EBCGA (Frontex) is concerned, the original Commission proposal had provided supranational competences to the Agency in case of urgent situations. However, supranational competences for the agency were not part of the legislation adopted by the Council and the Parliament. Instead, the new Regulations provided that in case of situations at the external borders requiring urgent action, the Council may make a decision (Article 42, Regulation (EU) 2019/1896; Article 19 and 80 Regulation (EU) 2016/1624). Similarly, they allow member states to reintroduce border controls at their internal borders if another government fails to cooperate with EBCGA (Frontex) or to protect its external Schengen borders effectively. This is renationalization rather than supranational enforcement (Schimmelfennig 2018, 16). Smeets and Zaun have argued that the EU level actors involved played a significant role in Eurozone asylum crisis outcomes (2021), such as the Commission and the European Central Bank.

Although the EU's difficulties in coherently responding to the refugee crisis can mostly be explained by intergovernmentalism, neofunctionalism captures other important aspects of the EU's actions. Neofunctionalism highlights supranational activism in proposing reforms to face the refugee threat. In May 2015, the European Commission proposed the European Agenda on Migration to equip the EU with the tools to better manage migration in the areas of irregular migration, borders, asylum and legal migration. Although the relocation scheme was rejected, supranational cooperation was upgraded concerning external border control, police and judicial cooperation inside the EU and registration of the incoming immigrants, as was the case of EBCGA and EUAA.

For neofunctionalists, European integration can address crises. Nonetheless, integration advances, but it does so while dependent on the effects of prior integration, transnational interdependence, and supranational institutional capacity (e.g., Niemann 2006; Niemann and Speyer 2018; Sandholtz and Sweet 1998, 2018; Lefkofridi and Schmitter 2020). In the case of the refugee crisis, Member States moved forward with the suspension, but not abandoning the Schengen *aquis*. That fact suggests that, at a time of economic recovery, the internal market benefits appeared more important than the costs of ending a key pillar of European integration – the free movement of people (Hooghe and Marks 2019; Niemann and Speyer 2018, 31). For Hooghe and Marks (2019, 1121), 'while intergovernmentalism is pertinent to headline bargaining on refugee quotas, neofunctionalism's wider lens helps to explain why, beyond the limelight, there has been an incremental, albeit haphazard, increase in supranational activity'.

Neofunctionalists also see common interest in cooperation and interdependence among Member States concerning the Schengen *acquis*. Indeed, disintegration would represent high costs of policy adjustment, and at a time when States were trying to recover from a long financial crisis. Furthermore, permanent reinstallation of borders would put an end to the most popular achievement of the European project, the free movement of people. This would have a negative impact on the internal policy of the Member States (Niemann and Speyer 2018, 31). As far as the supranational activism is concerned, it was the Commission's European Agenda on Migration that outlined immediate steps to tackle the crisis along with medium-term reform of the Dublin system. The Commission's plan for a permanent refugee relocation mechanism was rejected, but supranational cooperation was upgraded for managing flows and monitoring borders (Hooghe and Marks 2019). Similarly, even in the case of the EU-Turkey deal, an extensive involvement from the Commission on the main issues of funding, visa liberalization, and the re-energizing of accession was ultimately required (Meets and Beach 2020).

As far as the rise of the extremist parties in Europe is concerned, post-functionalism highlights identity politics (Börzel and Risse 2018; Hoogh and Marks 2019). Börzel and Risse (2017, 20) assert that '[t]he influx of migrants and refugees changed identity politics, since populist forces framed the Schengen crisis in terms of "us" vs "them" and propagated an exclusionary "fortress Europe"'. For Kuhn (2019, 1221), '[t]his conflict about European integration, and relatedly, immigration, increasingly structures European and domestic politics in general'. Thus, the rising support for xenophobic parties made it even more difficult for national governments to harbor culturally dissimilar people and transfer power to supranational institutions to work on common European solutions. Hence, helping millions of refugees from Syria or other conflict zones intensified social cleavage in European societies and challenged European solidarity. Nationalist challengers across Europe impelled governments in re-imposing border controls in Germany, Austria, Sweden, France and Denmark. Three other countries – Hungary, Poland, and the Czech Republic – even breached EU law by failing to take in their share of asylum seekers. Even today, they oppose the EU's new migration pact. As a result, the increase of Euroscepticism seems to have diminished the EU's margin of action to collectively respond to crises.

Conclusions

The Syrian drama and the exodus it provoked occurred at a time when the EU was already facing a set of massive challenges, financial instability, Brexit uncertainties, the rise of extremist populist parties within numerous EU Member States, along with regional conflicts, and a persistent threat from terrorism. All in all, the EU has taken some important steps towards managing the refugee and migration test, by strengthening its institutions and tools and by introducing some new concepts, such as the hotspot approach. However, supranational institutions have not gained autonomous decision-making powers, which could allow them to reduce intergovernmental conflict and transnational pressures. Instead, the EU focused on externalization to overcome the Schengen crisis, revealing once again the limits of its commitment to act as a political union capable of offering strong common solutions.

The EU has offered crucial humanitarian assistance to Syrians inside and outside the country, imposing restrictive measures, such as sanctions and undermining the Assad regime. However, this strategy has not proven to be sufficient, with the Union not having played a decisive role in resolving the conflict to date. The paradox is that the EU deals with a substantial part of the refugee crisis, having assumed most of the humanitarian costs, suffering from growing extremism, besides being threatened by terrorism and instability. Yet, it has not been able to resolve the conflict that creates these problems. In addition, the lack of a common stance towards the crisis by the Member States and the complexity of the EU policies themselves, all diminish the value of the EU as a trustworthy regional and global player.

Ultimately, all European responses, in terms of common policy and policies, touch on the very essence of the European integration debate. Should the EU advance in a more integrated way as a political union, or should it continue working as a platform of cooperation and integration *a la carte?* The EU needs to internally set up a genuinely integrated asylum system and better coordinate migration policy, while also externally coordinating a coherent and credible CFSP and a CSDP. For this to be achieved, deficits in solidarity among Member States must be addressed, and decisions over the future integration model of the EU should be made. If this does not happen, the EU will remain vulnerable to crisis.

Today's key security challenges such as demography, climate change, human rights and pandemics all have an impact on EU policy and policies. Member States should address those questions in a coordinated manner and not in isolation. In the same way, further integration and not disunity is the key to confronting the refugee crisis as well as the Syrian Civil War. It is basically a matter of security. After all, there is nothing new in that a correlation among crisis, security, and integration has been at the heart of the European project since its genesis.

References

Abdat, Ahmed. 2018. *The EU-Turkey Refugee Deal. First Lessons for the Mediterranean Neighborhood Strategy*. Grin Verlag.

Anholt, Rosanne and Sinatti, Giulia. 2020. Under the guise of resilience: The EU approach to migration and forced displacement in Jordan and Lebanon. *Contemporary Security Policy*. 41:2. 311–335. DOI: 10.1080/13523260.2019.1698182

Baczko, Adam, Dorronsoro, Gilles and Quesnay, Arthur. 2018. *Civil War in Syria: Mobilization and Competing Social Orders*. New York: Cambridge University Press.

Barbulescu, Roxana. 2017. "till a Beacon of Human Rights? Considerations on the EU Response to the Refugee Crisis in the Mediterranean. *Mediterranean Politics*. 22:2. 301–308. DOI: 10.1080/13629395.2016.1194546

Biermann Felix, Guérin Nina, Jagdhuber Stefan, Rittberger Berthold and Weiss Moritz. 2019. Political (non)reform in the euro crisis and the refugee crisis: a liberal intergovernmentalist explanation. *Journal of European Public Policy*. 26:2. 246–266. DOI: 10.1080/13501763.2017.1408670

Bordignon, Massimo and Moriconi, Simone. 2017. The case for a common European refugee policy. *Bruegel Policy Contribution*. Policy Paper Issue. n8. http://aei.pitt.edu/85410/

Börzel, Tanja A. and Risse, Thomas. 2018. From the euro to the Schengen crises: European integration theories, politicization, and identity politics. *Journal of European Public Policy*. 25:1, 83–108, DOI: 10.1080/13501763.2017.1310281

Bosilca, Laura-Ruxandra. 2021. The refugee crisis and the EU Border Security Policies. In Riddervold Marianne, Trondal Jarle and Newsome Akasemi (eds). *The Palgrave Handbook of EU Crises*. Palgrave Macmillan.

Brack, Nathalie and Gürkan, Seda. 2020. *Theorising the Crises of the European Union*. New York: Routledge.

Buonanno, Lauri 2017. The European Migration Crisis. In Dinan; Nugent; Paterson (eds) 2017. *The European Union in Crisis*. The European Union Series. Red Globe Press.

Cavatorta, Francesco and Turcotte, Pierre-Michel. The Disintegration of European Security: Lessons from the Refugee Crisis. In Hinnebusch Raymond and Saouli Adham (eds.) *The War for Syria*. Routledge/ St. Andrews Syrian Studies Series. Taylor and Francis. Kindle Edition.

Council of the European Union. 2015. Council conclusions. 7267/15. 16 March. https://www.consilium.europa.eu/media/21843/st07267en15.pdf

Council of the European Union. 2017. Outcome of the Council Meeting. 7922/17, 03 March. https://www.consilium.europa.eu/en/meetings/fac/2017/04/03/

Crawford, Beverly. 2021. Moral Leadership or Moral Hazard? Germany's Response to the Refugee Crisis and Its Impact on European Solidarity. In Riddervold Marianne, Trondal Jarle and Newsome Akasemi (eds). *The Palgrave Handbook of EU Crises*. Palgrave Macmillan.

Dinan, Desmond, Nugent, Neill and Paterson, William (eds). 2017. *The European Union in Crisis*. The European Union Series. Red Globe Press.

Donatienne, Ruy and Erol, Yayboke. 2020. Deciphering the European Union's New Pact on Migration and Asylum. Critical Questions. *Centre for Strategic and International Studies/CSIS*. 29.092020

European Commission. 2015. Communication from the Commission to the European Parliament, the Council, the European Economic and Social Committee and the Committee of the Regions. "A European Agenda on Migration." https://eur-lex.europa.eu/legal-content/EN/TXT/?uri=celex%3A52015DC0240

European Commission. 2016a. Proposal for a Regulation of the European Parliament and of the Council establishing the criteria and mechanisms for determining the Member State responsible for examining an application for international protection lodged in one of the Member States by a third-country national or a stateless person (recast). COM (2016) 270 final. 4 May. https://eur-lex.europa.eu/legal-content/EN/TXT/?uri=CELEX%3A52016PC0270

European Commission. 2016b. Building Resilience. The EU Approach. Fact Sheet. 2016. https://ec.europa.eu/echo/files/aid/countries/factsheets/thematic/EU_building_resilience_en.pdf

European Commission. 2019. Commission Staff Working Document: Turkey 2019 Report. Accompanying the document Communication from the Commission to the European Parliament, the Council, the European Economic and Social Committee and the Committee of the Regions 2019 Communication on EU Enlargement Policy. COM(2019) 260 final. 29 May. https://ec.europa.eu/neighbourhood-enlargement/sites/default/files/20190529-turkey-report.pdf

European Commission. 2020. Communication from the Commission on a New Pact on Migration and Asylum. COM (2020) 609 final. 23 September. https://eur-lex.europa.eu/legal-content/EN/TXT/?qid=1601287338054&uri=COM:2020:609:FIN

European Council. No date. Syria: EU response to the crisis. https://www.consilium.europa.eu/en/policies/syria/

European Council. 2016. EU-Turkey statement, 18 March. https://www.consilium.europa.eu/en/press/press-releases/2016/03/18/eu-turkey-statement/

Ghosh, Bimal. 2018. *Refugee and Mixed Migration Flows. Managing a Looming Humanitarian and Economic Crisis.* Palgrave Macmillan. 10.1007/978-3-319-75274-7

Goździak, Elżbieta M., Main, Izabella and Suter, Brigitte. 2020. *Europe and the Refugee Response. A Crisis of Values?* New York: Routledge.

Haass, Richard. 2017. *A World in Disarray. American Foreign Policy and the Crisis of the Old Order. Penguin* Press.

Hinnebusch, Raymond and Saouli, Adham (eds.) *The War for Syria.* Routledge/ St. Andrews Syrian Studies Series. Taylor and Francis. Kindle Edition.

Hooghe, Liesbet and Marks, Gary. 2019. Grand theories of European integration in the twenty-first century". *Journal of European Public Policy.* 26:8, 1113–1133, DOI: 10.1080/13501763.2019.1569711

Karageorgiou, Eleni. 2016. Solidarity and sharing in the Common European Asylum System: the case of Syrian refugees. *European Politics and Society.* 17:2. 196–214. DOI: 10.1080/23745118.2016.1121007

Kaya, Hülya. 2020. *The EU-Turkey Statement on Refugees: Assessing its Impact on Fundamental Rights.* Cheltenham: Edward Elgar. ISBN 978178990 9203. ISBN 978178990 9210

Kienle, Eberhard. 2019. Introduction: Syria in the Imperialist Cyclone. In: Matar Linda, Kadri Ali (eds) *Syria: From National Independence to Proxy War.* Palgrave Macmillan. Cham. https://doi.org/10.1007/978-3-319-98458-2_3

Kriesi, Hanspeter, Altiparmakis, Argyrios, Bojar, Abel and Oana, Ioana-Elena. 2021. Debordering and re-bordering in the refugee crisis: a case of 'defensive integration.' *Journal of European Public Policy.* 28:3. 331–349. DOI: 10.1080/13501763.2021.1882540

Kuhn, Theresa. 2019. Grand Theories of European Integration Revisited: Does Identity Politics Shape the Course of European Integration? *Journal of European Public Policy.* 26:8. 1213–1230. https://doi.org/10.1080/13501763.2 019.1622588

Lefkofridi, Zoe and Schmitter, Philippe C. 2020. Neofunctionalism in the Decade of Crises . In Brack Nathalie and Gürkan Seda. *Theorising the Crises of the European Union.* New York: Routledge.

Moravcsik, Andrew and Schimmelfennig, Frank. 2009. Liberal intergovernmentalism. In Wiener Antje and Diez Thomas (eds.). *European Integration Theory.* Oxford: OUP. 67–87: 71.

Moravcsik, Andrew. 1993. Preferences and Power in the European Community. A Liberal Intergovernmentalist Approach. *JCMS: Journal of Common Market.* 31:4. 473–524.

Moravcsik, Andrew. 1998. *The Choice for Europe. Social Purpose and State Power from Messina to Maastricht.* Ithaca: Cornell University Press.

Moravcsik, Andrew. 2018. Preferences, Power and Institutions in 21st Century Europe. Special Issue: Liberal Intergovernmentalism and its Critics. *JCMS: Journal of Common Market.* 56:7. https://doi.org/10.1111/jcms.12804

Niemann, Arne and Speyer, Johanna. 2018. A Neofunctionalist Perspective on the 'European Refugee Crisis': The Case of the European Border and Coast Guard. *JCMS Journal of Common Market.* Special Issue: EU Refugee Policies and Politics in Times of Crisis. 56:1. https://doi.org/10.1111/jcms.12653

Niemann, Arne and Zaun, Natascha. 2018. EU Refugee Policies and Politics in Times of Crisis: Theoretical and Empirical Perspectives. Special Issue: EU Refugee Policies and Politics in Times of Crisis. *JCMS: Journal of Common Market.* 56: 1. 3–22 https://doi.org/10.1111/jcms.12650_

Phillips, Christopher. 2020. *The Battle for Syria: International Rivalry in the New Middle East.* New Haven, CT: Yale University Press.

Riddervold, Marianne, Trondal, Jarle and Newsome, Akasemi (eds). 2021. *The Palgrave Handbook of EU Crises.* Palgrave Macmillan.

Rygiel, Kim, Baban, Feyzi and Ilcan, Suzan. 2016. The Syrian refugee crisis: The EU-Turkey 'deal' and temporary protection *Global Social Policy.* 16:3. 315–320 https://journals.sagepub.com/doi/full/10.1177/1468018116666153

Saatçioğlu, Beken. 2020. The EU's response to the Syrian refugee crisis: a battleground among many Europes. *European Politics and Society.* DOI: 10.1080/23745118.2020.1842693

Sandholtz, Wayne and Sweet, Stone. 1998. *European integration and supranational governance.* New York: Oxford University Press.

Schilde, Kaija and Goodman, Sara Wallace. 2021. The EU's response to the Migration crisis. Institutional Turbulence and Policy Disjuncture. In Riddervold Marianne, Trondal Jarle and Newsome Akasemi (eds). *The Palgrave Handbook of EU Crises.* Palgrave Macmillan.

Schimmelfennig, Frank. 2018. European integration (theory) in times of crisis. A comparison of the euro and Schengen crises. *Journal of European Public Policy.* 25:7. 969–989. DOI: 10.1080/13501763.2017.1421252

Slominski, Peter and Trauner, Florian. 2018. How do member states return unwanted migrants? The strategic (non)use of 'Europe' during the migration crisis. *JCMS.* 56:1. 101–118. https://doi.org/10.1111/jcms.12621

Smeets, Sandrino and Beach, Derek. 2020. When success is an orphan: informal institutional governance and the EU–Turkey dea". *West European Politics*. 43:1. 129–158. DOI: 10.1080/01402382.2019.1608495

Smeets, Sandrino and Zaun, Natascha. 2021. What is intergovernmental about the EU's '(new) intergovernmentalist' turn? Evidence from the Eurozone and asylum crises. *West European Politics*. 44:4. 852–872. DOI: 10.1080/01402382.2020.1792203

Tassinari, Fabrizio. 2016. The Disintegration of European Security: Lessons from the Refugee Crisis. *PRISM*. 6:2. https://cco.ndu.edu/Portals/96/Documents/prism/prism_6-2/Tassinari.pdf?ver=2016-07-05-104622-137

Taylor, Paul. 2008. *The End of European Integration Anti-Europeanism Examined*. Routledge/UACES Contemporary European Studies.

UNHCR. No date. Emergency Handbook. Commodity distribution (NFIs, food). https://emergency.unhcr.org/entry/43130/commodity-distribution-nfis-food

Webber, Douglas. 2019. Trends in European political (dis)integration. An analysis of post functionalist and other explanations. *Journal of European Public Policy*. 26:8. 1134–1152. DOI: 10.1080/13501763.2019.1576760

Webber, Douglas. 2019. *European Disintegration?: The Politics of Crisis in the European Union*. The European Union Series. London: Red Globe Press.

Wurzel, Rüdiger and Hayward, Jack. 2012. *European Disunion: Between Sovereignty and Solidarity*. Basingstoke: Palgrave Macmillan.

Zielonka, Jan. 2014. *Is the EU Doomed?* Cambridge: Polity Press.

4

Civil Society and the Syrian Refugee Crisis

GEORGETA V. POURCHOT

This chapter evaluates the rise of civil society in the context of the 2011 Syrian civil conflict and the resulting refugee crisis. The evolving nature of the conflict, from a grass-roots protest against the Assad regime to a full-scale revolution involving the entire country, followed by the involvement of foreign actors, both state (Russia, Iran, Turkey, the US) and non-state (Islamic State of Iraq and the Levant/ISIL, Hezbollah), left the country in ruins, without basic services and with large numbers of Syrians either displaced internally, or fleeing the country. As of this writing, there are 6.7 million Syrian refugees and asylum seekers hosted by 128 countries, and approximately 6.8 million internally displaced people (IDPs) in Syria. The total of 13.5 million Syrians represented in these two groups comprises more than half of the country's pre-war population (UNHCR 2021). Syrian civil society 'barely existed' prior to the 2011 revolution (Crawford, 1). Faith-based groups catered to the needs of specific ethnic groups. The Government Organized Non-Governmental Organizations (GONGOS) were patronized by the Syrian government and catered only to the needs of those who supported the government's policies (Alhousseiny and Atar, 101). The popular revolution put in motion scores of people working either to make the plight of Syrians visible to their own government and to the outside world, or to hold the government accountable for its actions against its own population, or to help those directly affected by the conflict such as refugees and internally displaced populations. The work of domestic groups engaged in such activism resembles what Western researchers call 'civil society'. Their work, and the work of International Non-Governmental Organizations (INGOs) is described and recognized in this chapter.

The chapter proceeds with a brief introduction into conceptual frameworks of analyzing civil society to put the activity of Syrian groups in perspective. It continues with two sections evaluating two types of civil group activities: advocacy, and humanitarian relief. A conclusion summarizes aspects of the activities of these groups that warrant their description as a rising civil society in Syria.

Civil Society and Non-Governmental Organizations: Conceptual Frameworks of Analysis

Western scholars employ a variety of concepts to designate organizations or institutions that form 'civil society.' Alexis de Tocqueville is considered the original political thinker to discuss 'voluntary associations' in America, which he considered a landmark of a democratic society (de Tocqueville 2000). Anthropologist Ernest Gellner defined civil society as the collection of institutions and associations that are separate from the government and which free people join at will. This collection of institutions and associations is a must-have ingredient if a society is to be free, democratic, and keep its government accountable (Gellner 1996). In 1995, Robert Putnam popularized the concept of 'social capital,' defined as 'the features of social organization such as networks, norms, and social trust that facilitate coordination and cooperation for mutual benefit' (Putnam 1995, 67). While Putnam, an influential Harvard professor, based his study primarily on Italian and American data and examples, he identified three variables that remain important for any discussion of civil society: political and civic engagement, informal social ties, and tolerance and trust. A society in which citizens can associate freely, in 'horizontal bonds of fellowship' whether via membership in a club, or a neighborhood group, produces a strong society, in which governments, constituted on 'vertical bonds of authority,' can be held accountable (Putnam et al. 1993, 175–6).

Arabic scholars caution that 'civil society' does not translate directly into the Arabic language, at least not in a 'Western' sense (Al-Om 2011). Concepts such as 'civil community,' 'brotherhood,' or 'kinship' have been proposed by various Arab scholars to denote a sphere of human activity that is separate from the state, but which does not exclude religion. An influential Arab thinker who defined civil society as a mix of group feeling, tribal ties, and a brotherhood based on kinship and religion was Ibn Khaldūn. His concept of *aṣabīya* as a powerful social cohesion force remains influential in Islamic studies (Esteban 2004, 27–37).

The analytical concepts described above indicate one main similarity between the two conceptual frameworks: that civil society happens outside government control. One main difference between Arabic and Western concepts of civil society is the inclusion of religion and tribal ties as vehicles for the creation and facilitation of what Putnam calls 'horizontal bonds of fellowship,' de Tocqueville calls 'voluntary associations,' and Gellner calls 'associations that free people join at will'. A second important difference appears to be the exclusion from the Arabic concept of 'government accountability' as a function to be performed by freely formed associations of people.

In the Syrian case, the terminology used to designate civil society groups is important particularly considering the position of the Syrian authorities regarding this sector of human activity. Art. 4.a of the Law of Emergency, imposed in 1963 prohibited freedom of assembly and movement, and Art. 4.b made provisions to 'monitor all types of letters, phone calls, newspapers, bulletins, books, drawings, publications, broadcasts, and all forms of written expression, propaganda, and advertisements prior to publication' (Syrian Human Rights Committee 2003), a clear mark of government censorship. As a result of the 2011 mass protests across Syria demanding reform, the Assad administration issued Legislative Decree no. 54, which permitted peaceful demonstrations and promised that 'duly licensed civil society organizations have the right to organize demonstrations in accordance with the principles of the (Syrian) Constitution' (Parliament of the Syrian Government 2011, Art. 3). A day after the decree was issued, fresh peaceful protests in the streets calling for the fall of the Assad regime were met with live ammunition by security forces.

The notion that civil society organizations should not operate outside a formal framework approved and monitored by the Syrian government – consequently cannot hold the government accountable in a Western sense – is also supported by the views of its president. In 2001, President Assad explained that civil society and non-governmental organizations are not and should not be independent of the work of the authorities. On the contrary, he viewed them as tools of the authorities in meeting certain governmental goals: 'T] hese institutions are not an alternative to government institutions as some suggest, and they should not precede them in the process of construction,' Assad stated. 'On the contrary, civil institutions are based on government institutions and support them and are not a replacement for them' (Al-Assad 2001). This view contrasts directly with Gellner's conceptual framework of civil society as a network of institutions and associations separate from the government, working to keep the government accountable, and Putnam's horizontal bonds of fellowship created outside a government frame of control. It also contrasts with both Western and Arabic concepts that civil society constitutes a sphere of human activity separate from the government.

It is therefore fitting to ask whether civil society groups could function at all in Syria, in conditions of martial law (imposed in 1963), severe censorship (under the Law of Emergency, 1963), and a civil war (since 2011). To do that, this author proposes to evaluate this question by drawing on both Western and Arabic concepts of civil society to identify which, if any, conceptual elements of civil society may apply to Syria in the context of the 2011 civil conflict and the resulting refugee crisis.

A Western framework of analysis would look for variables such as the organizational capacity of a civil society group or formal non-governmental organization (NGO), and its operational experience on the ground (Hurd 2017; Tavares 2010). While it would be useful to the researcher to know which groups and organizations have a strong operational capacity, illustrated in their charter, administrative staff, leadership and plan of work; and demonstrated operational capacity with results of the ground, the situation in Syria is that of a society in prolonged crisis, with decades of censorship. As such, the ability of groups of people to organize themselves and perform functions typically associated with the concept of civil society had to be modest, by Western standards.

Some authors describe early forms of civil society in Syria (pre-1963) as faith-based groups with charitable missions towards the poor, elderly, or the sick, a description consistent with the Arabic concept that civil society does not exclude religion. Between 1963 when the state of emergency was instituted and 2000, when Bashar al-Assad became president, the number of these groups declined from 596 to 513; and during the Damascus Spring (described in the next section), they were estimated to grow to 1,400 (Alhousseiny and Atar, 12). The question of whether civil society groups could function in Syria under such conditions is therefore a legitimate topic of research.

The next two sections offer an evaluation of two types of activities observed and documented by local groups and INGOs, that groups of Syrians performed in the context of the 2011 civil war: advocacy (with its associated functions of documentation, education and training), and humanitarian relief. This analysis seeks to identify whether these two types of activities were organized by voluntary groups of citizens, freely assembling whether to foster a community, a 'brotherhood,' or a (faith) community need, independent of a government mandate, and creating an *aṣabīya*, a powerful social cohesion force. These variables correspond broadly with the conceptual frameworks identified by de Tocqueville, Gellner, and Khaldūn. In addition, it sought to identify whether elements of Putnam's social capital framework are present, in how horizontal bonds of fellowship emerged, in order to hold the government accountable for its actions.

One caveat is in order: Western and Arabic practitioners and scholars use the concept of 'civil society' or 'civil society organizations' (CSOs), understood as the organizations that have close ties to the Syrian society, provide public goods that the government cannot or does not provide, and operate mainly or exclusively in Syria (Crawford, 3; Al-Om 2011). This chapter uses the terms CSOs, local groups, civic groups, NGOs, and INGOs interchangeably. This author also recognizes that listing, describing, and recognizing the work of every single CSO group in Syria is not feasible given space constraints and availability of reliable data. The activities and patterns described in the following two sections are representative of the work of many more organizations than can be highlighted in the space of a chapter.

The Syrian Conflict and the Rise of Civil Society: Advocacy and Government Accountability

Public anger against the Syrian government predated 2011. It can be traced to 1970, when Hafez al-Assad, the father of current president Bashar al-Assad, appointed himself as leader of Syria after a coup d'état that he engineered. To maintain his power, Hafez created a cult of personality around himself and his family, characterized by violent suppression of freedom and civil rights, and an imposition of a state of emergency under the Law of Emergency of 1963. Upon his father's death in 2000 and new to politics, Bashar al-Assad initially permitted freedom of expression and association, in what became known as the Damascus Spring. This short period of approximately one year was characterized by the formation of citizen-and intellectual-led groups, meeting in forums to discuss political reform in the country. This type of civic activity outside a government mandate was relatively new, and consistent with both Western and Arabic concepts of free people assembly outside government structures or mandates.

The result of this collective civic work was the publication of the 'Manifesto of the 99,' a pamphlet outlining political demands such as the abolition of the martial law, an end to the state of emergency, the release of political prisoners and securing the safe return of political exiles (Middle East Intelligence Bulletin 2000). At this point in the Damascus Spring, civil society groups were starting to display a distinct government accountability function.

The initial response of the regime was encouraging, with scores of political prisoners released. By 2001, however, the regime changed course and returned to the repressive policies of Hafez al-Assad, shutting down the citizen-led forums, arresting intellectuals, and reinstating martial law.

The conflict that started in February 2011 in Syria originated in Daraa, a town in the south-west of the country, when a group of 18 school-aged boys wrote graffiti on their school wall calling for the overturn of the Assad regime. The governor of Daraa, an Assad loyalist, launched raids on the homes of all 18 boys demanding that they be handed over. News of the raids and imprisonment of the boys spread, and residents flooded the streets, calling for the return of the boys to their families. In response, the governor of Daraa allegedly said to the boys' parents: 'My advice to you is that you forget you ever had these children. Go back home and sleep with your wives and bring other children into the world and if you cannot do that, then bring your wives to us and we will do the job for you' (Ridley, 2014).

Grass-roots demonstrations demanding the return of the boys continued and spread throughout the country. Large, peaceful protests started to be organized every Friday after prayers, underscoring the importance of faith-based civic activities in Syria. They were given names such as the Friday of Dignity, Good Friday, Friday of Steadfastness, Friday of Pride, and many more. The authorities responded with mass beatings, teargas, arrests and imprisonment of the protesters, and eventually resorted to using live ammunition. The 18 boys were eventually released, beaten and bruised, which further fanned public anger. The brutal response of the authorities ignited a mass movement that continues.

One of the constant features of the Syrian revolution has been the authorities' denial that first, it occurred at all, and second, that it was an uprising of Syrians against their government. In March 2011, Assad blamed the unrest in the country on a foreign conspiracy, terrorist and other foreign elements, and vowed to defeat it. In April 2013, he called it a 'fake revolution'. In 2019, he claimed that the revolution was not about the Syrian people's discontent with their government who, for the most part supported his administration, but about a 'third World War' for power and influence being fought on the territory of Syria by Western powers led by the United States against the legitimately elected authorities in Syria (Al-Assad 2013; 2019).

Activists on the ground made it clear on countless occasions that the uprising *was* against the Assad regime, for human rights and dignity for all Syrians, calling on the authorities to be accountable to 'the people'. 'The things we're asking for are basic human rights. No leader starves his population to death – there are nations that starve other nations – but no leader besieges his own people, and starves them to death, or forcibly expels them,' Mazen Kewara, an activist in a large civil society group coalition called *Save Our Syria* told *Al Jazeera* (Tahhan 2017). Groups such as *Save Our Syria* organized themselves outside government control and assumed functions of advocacy for 'the people,' for Syrians who were forced by oppressive government policies to leave their homes in search of safety. These incipient forms of civil society groups demanded justice and human rights from their government.

The Assad regime's response focused on violently suppressing mass protests, submitting cities or areas engulfed in the uprising to bombardment, curfews, and cutting off means of subsistence and basic services such as trash collection, food supplies, running water, and electricity (HRW June 2011). These government policies led to mass displacements of people. Civic groups stepped in to provide humanitarian relief to refugees and IDPs. I describe their activities below.

In the 10 years of this conflict, additional forces joined a fight that appears to have different meanings for different actors. Neighboring Turkey was concerned about the possible breakup of Syria and the emergence of a Kurdish state on its border. Iran and Russia supported the Assad regime for a variety of reasons, not all related or coordinated. Non-state actors such as ISIL and Hezbollah (both designated 'foreign terrorist organizations' by the US State Department since 2004 and 1997 respectively), plus a host of armed groups and militias supporting or opposing the regime also operated in Syrian territory, with loosely defined interests and sources of funding. The US and the EU initially supported regime change from within, encouraged by the work of domestic groups of citizens making political demands on their government. Both condemned the abuses of the regime against its people, reported by civil groups and INGOs as this section further discusses. Both imposed sanctions against the ruling government and companies that did business with it. US/EU air strikes were launched for a limited time against territory believed to be controlled by non-state actors such as ISIL. As a result, Syrians suffered from repercussions for their uprising from their own government, state and non-state actors, and US/EU forces. Many chose to flee the country in search of safety for their families. Some fled from unsafe to safer areas within Syria becoming IDPs. Some remained in their homes trying to wait out the crisis.

Regime forces used chemical weapons against the Syrian people between 2012 and 2015. The Assad regime claimed that opposition groups performed the attacks and demanded a UN investigation, but only agreed to an inquiry that confirmed the use of the weapons, not by which forces against whom. Subsequent UN resolutions and negotiations led to Syria joining the Chemical Weapons Convention and renouncing its chemical weapons program in 2013. The existing stockpiles were seemingly disposed of with US-Western-Russian backing and coordination. A 2016 report by the Organization for the Prohibition of Chemical Weapons (OPCW)-UN Joint Investigative Mechanism found that the Syrian government used chemical weapons again in 2014 and 2015 against its own people. It also found that ISIL used such weapons in 2015 in Northern Syria, in attempts to force the population to be sharia-law compliant. Additional chemical weapons attacks in 2017 prompted the US to bomb a Syrian government air base. Similar attacks and subsequent reports laying responsibility on the Syrian regime and ISIL led to a 2021 resolution by the parties of the Chemical Weapons Convention to suspend Syria's rights and privileges under the Chemical Weapons Convention.

The disproportionately punitive government response to the popular protests was a miscalculation. The regime counted on people getting hungry, tired, and hurting enough to prompt them to stop protesting. Instead, the opposite occurred. Syrian groups, both local and in diaspora raised awareness of the events inside the country. The day following the abolition of the Law of Emergency in 2011, which prohibited freedom of assembly and movement, a network of approximately 70 groups of media and grassroots activists connected to the revolt across the country began forming Local Coordination Committees (LCC). They advocated for the release of prisoners, the dismantling of the security forces, and their replacement with new security personnel that would apply the laws of the country without abusing their power. LCCs related events on the ground to international media outlets, highlighting abuses of power, including statistics on numbers of prisoners, casualties of war, and numbers of people missing since 1980. LCCs were also responsible for organizing anti-regime demonstrations and disseminating information about the popular revolution. Most of the people working under this umbrella group operated within Syria, with a smaller number of expatriate Syrians lending support. LCCs were creative in organizing themselves via social media and virtual coordination meetings, and they cooperated with Arab media outlets to keep the international community informed about developments in Syria. They also cooperated with other Syrian organizations such as the Center for Documentation of Violations in Syria, which focuses on reporting human rights abuses (Carnegie Middle East Center 2012).

Organizations such as the Violations Documentation Center (VDC) in Syria and the Syrian Revolution Martyrs Database collected information about martyrs and cross-referenced it with data from the Damascus Centre for Human Rights Studies (Damascus Center for Human Rights Studies n.d.). They also partnered with local groups to document, train, and educate Syrians about their human rights. All these activities were performed by groups of people organizing themselves outside government institutional frameworks to fulfill needs on the ground such as advocacy, education, training and government accountability functions. For instance, in 2013, VDC partnered with Sawa (Together), a youth coalition, to organize volunteers to support displaced groups and perform other civic duties in Qamishli in north-east Syria, on the Turkish border. Their joint 2013 campaign to 'document' numbers of martyrs, detained, missing or kidnapped people, the effects of the use of chemical weapons, and other violations by the regime against civilians led to the group's harassment and arrests by the authorities (VDC 2013).

VDC also called attention to and documented inhuman prison conditions in Adra, particularly in women's prisons where abuse and mistreatment was accompanied by a denial of a fair trial (The Creative Memory of the Syrian Revolution_2017).

Advocacy was performed throughout the decade of war by numerous organizations, large and small. In 2016, *The Syrian Observer* reported that 191 Syrian civil society organizations had been involved in documenting the war, raising the visibility of casualties and violations of basic human rights by the Assad government (al-Wasl 2016). The Syrian Human Rights Committee (SHRC) reported on the effects of the government's blockade on various urban and rural areas. Aside from high unemployment and a lack of medicine, food, and water in areas in which the Assad authorities prohibited humanitarian support, disease followed, leading to more people fleeing to safer areas. For many of those who chose to stay, severe trauma, disease or death followed. Environmentally, the lack of basic services such as trash collection led to an invasion of rodents and consequently, to more disease (SHRC 2013).

Pro Justice, The Day After, Syrians for Truth and Justice, Creative Memory, the Syrian Observatory for Human Rights, and the Syrian Center for Media and Freedom of Expression are just a few of the grass-roots organizations that worked to raise the visibility of the crimes committed by the Assad regime. They documented the plight of the population and the resulting large numbers of refugees and IDPs, pressured the international community to help Syrians seek justice and accountability for the actions that the regime committed against its people. These groups created networks of supporters bound by what Putnam calls 'horizontal ties' speaking truth to power, to the vertical bonds of authority of the Assad regime.

In addition to domestic and diaspora groups of Syrians organized for advocacy and government accountability, several INGOs had a prominent role in performing these civil society functions. Human Rights Watch (HRW), International Red Cross, and Mercy Corps are some of the INGOs that called attention to the crimes against the Syrian people at the hand of their government. In 2011, HRW reported that the crimes committed against civilians imprisoned because of their peaceful protests amounted to crimes against humanity. Prisoners were beaten and humiliated, electric shocks were administered, cases of rape against male and female detainees were reported. Extrajudicial executions of people in detention occurred. The first mass grave was discovered and reported in May 2011, in Daraa (HRW 2011a, 2011b, 2011c). HRW also reported that the authorities made 'enormous efforts to ensure such information did not get out'. Cell phone networks were disrupted by the government and security forces confiscated personal phones on which they could identify coverage of the events taking place in the streets. Journalists and independent observers were prohibited by the authorities in the areas of protests, and the only journalist who was able to report from Daraa was arrested on his return to Damascus (HRW 2011b).

Another INGO that reported human rights abuses as early as the revolution started is Amnesty International (AI). It documented examples of how the government tightened its grip on the population by instilling fear of reprisals. For instance, when a child was killed while watching a street protest in front of his house, the family had to sign a written statement to the police saying that he had been killed by 'armed gangs,' to avoid trouble with the authorities. 'They will punish us if we complain,' the sister of the killed boy said at the time (Rovera 2012). AI also reported abuses by ISIL against populations in the northern areas of the country that they controlled. For instance, in 2013, Syrians in the northern part of the country were subjected to cruel torture. Children as young as eight were not spared; they were beaten and abused in front of their parents. People suspected of not following ISIL's practice of sharia law were publicly executed and their bodies were left hanging in public view for days. Syrians in detention were subject to beatings with rubber cables, electric shocks, or forced to sit in painful positions for hours (AI 2013). Overall, the advocacy and raising awareness of the situation in Syria by domestic and diaspora groups and INGOs amounted to a public information campaign and exposure of the crimes of the Assad government against its own people. The advocacy of these groups had a strong government accountability function which further hardened the Assad regime against such groups and their activities. Local and international awareness of the plight of Syrian refugees, IDPs, and those who chose not to flee prompted humanitarian support and relief activities profiled briefly next.

The Syrian Conflict and the Rise of Civil Society: Humanitarian Relief and Support Operations

Local Syrian groups and INGOs had an important role to play in providing humanitarian relief to displaced populations and refugees resulting from the 2011 anti-Syrian government revolution. Syria Civil Defense (White Helmets), Syria Relief, and the Charity Commission are just some of the many groups and organizations that fit under this rubric.

Many local groups evolved in accordance with the needs on the ground and provided a mixture of services that spanned the continuum from advocacy to humanitarian relief. For instance, in Barza, northeast of Damascus, activists created an LCC to organize the revolutionary movement in the area. As a result of the armed response of the regime and the curfew imposed in the entire area, the Barza LCC expanded its mission to establish a medical center, a civil defense team, and a relief office to offer humanitarian relief to those wounded in, or displaced by, the bombardments. Activists also created an education office to keep area children in school (The Creative Memory of the Syrian Revolution 2017, 58–9). Similar grass-roots initiatives occurred in ar-Raqquah, an agrarian province on the northern bank of the Euphrates River in north-east Syria, which came under violent siege early in the war by Syrian authorities, and thereafter, by ISIL. Parts of the country in the north and east also came under bombardment by an international coalition led by the U.S. fighting against ISIL; and starting in 2015, by Russia, which lent support to Assad's armed forces. Activists organized to provide support to the population under siege. The Assembly of the Free Youth of ar-Raqqah launched several campaigns, including 'I will not leave my school,' during which as many as twenty schools were reported rehabilitated so that children could continue their education. The Stamps of the Syrian Revolution group issued a stamp showing the youth of ar-Raqqah after a street cleaning campaign organized by the Free Youth (The Creative Memory of the Syrian Revolution 2017, 289). In Adra, groups of citizens formed an LCC and created a medical center and a relief office. They also partnered with the United Relief Center based in eastern Ghouta to assist Syrians caught in the violence (The Creative Memory of the Syrian Revolution 2017, 17). Such local groups organized themselves along the horizontal bonds of fellowship described by Putnam, in order to provide a public good that the government did not offer – humanitarian relief.

In May 2012, observers on the ground described funeral processions turned into protests, or more traditional protests following Friday prayers, with demonstrators clapping their hands in the air, to show that they were not armed, and chanting 'silmiya,' meaning 'peaceful'. They were met with live ammunition by regime forces and associated militias. Wounded people would not go to a hospital to be treated out of fear of being arrested; they relied instead on sympathetic citizens who hosted them in their own homes, or they quietly sought the services of a doctor or nurse. These forms of healthcare support came to be known as field hospitals. The UN Office for the Coordination of Humanitarian Affairs (OCHA) defined field hospitals as informal self-settled sites, transit centers, collective centers, or planned camps across North-East and North-West Syria. Many of such last resort sites were created and inhabited by IDPs. The injured who could not be treated at these locations were evacuated by groups such as the White Helmets (described below) to a safe location while those who had more serious injuries were evacuated out of the city or the country, sometimes to Turkey. To avoid the official border crossing checkpoints, those involved in the transfer of the wounded used less trafficked agricultural roads to evade regime forces (Rovera 2012).

Some local groups were organized by women. For instance, Syria's Civil Defense is a women's volunteer search and rescue group also known as the White Helmets. The Helmets aided people affected by bombings. Rabia Kusairi, a 23-year-old and one of the 230 female volunteers who worked for the White Helmets, is the leader of the women's center in Shanam, where the group goes house-to-house or tent-to-tent administering first aid and providing essential medical referrals. She says being a woman in a Muslim community means having better access to women affected by war to treat them as 'it's not easy for a woman to be treated by a male volunteer. Despite doing this important work, I face a lot of attempts to silence me or to reduce my role' (Williams 2021).

The Mazaya Center is another example of an individual civic initiative that became a network of similar centers to empower women through training. In 2013, Ghalia Rahal, a 47-year-old woman, converted a beauty salon into a center for the vocational training and empowerment of women. Having experienced sexual harassment first-hand, Rahal has explained, 'as a conservative society, we are still afraid to talk about this publicly, because it's very hard for a woman to come forward and say I was abused, or I was assaulted in exchange for a food basket or in exchange for a job'. Rahal suggested that the main problem in Syria is that men are in charge of every aspect of life, from fighting the war, to civil society, and humanitarian organizations (Williams 2021). Groups of women thus assumed an important relief function by organizing themselves to support the wounded, be they refugees, IDPs, people on the run, or people staying in their homes. None of their activities were mandated by the authorities. Theirs was a civic initiative along horizontal bonds of caring for their fellow human beings in need.

INGOs have also had an important role to play in humanitarian relief and support functions. Mercy Corps, Oxfam, Save the Children, International Rescue Committee, the International Red Cross, Doctors without Borders, Physicians across Continents, World Vision International, International Humanitarian Relief, the Norwegian Refugee Council, Education without Borders, and many other organizations worked in Syria throughout the 10 years of war, and some of them before the 2011 revolution.

Mercy Corps worked in Syria before the 2011 crisis, providing emergency assistance. Between 2008 and 2021, the organization prioritized addressing the immediate needs of refugees and IDPs inside Syria and in neighboring countries. It provided potable water, desludging and garbage collection in camps and informal refugee settlements. It worked with displaced individuals to help them develop coping mechanisms. Relief teams worked to increase economic opportunities so people could adopt self-sustainable lifestyles in their new displacement locations and provided new skills training and cash grants to small businesses. Mercy Corps also tried to address the root causes and drivers of the conflict by providing training and assistance in mutual reconciliation and civic engagement (Mercy Corps Syria n.d.; Mercy Corps 2019; 2021).

Oxfam worked in Syria in cooperation with local groups to provide food, hygiene kits, and household essentials. The organization also worked in neighboring countries to which Syrians fled, such as Lebanon and Jordan, providing cash assistance for rent, distributing food vouchers, warm clothing and blankets for the winters, building latrines and showers in camps, including wheelchair-accessible facilities. Oxfam also conducted hygiene training and guided journalists on how to interview people in need (Oxfam 2013, 2). For the April 2018–March 2019 period, it reportedly spent 8.8 million euros on humanitarian relief in Syria (Oxfam 2018–2019, 47).

Official camps set up either by UNCHR or by neighboring countries were overwhelmed by the number of people fleeing violence, leading to the creation of last resort sites. The work of the UN Office for the Coordination of Humanitarian Affairs) is notable here. The Assad authorities placed restrictions on humanitarian aid missions by various INGOs, and closed border crossings in areas it did not control, restricting the process of registration of groups offering humanitarian aid, or denying them access altogether. OCHA advocated for better aid access and raised the visibility of those restrictions in its reports (OCHA 2014, 7; OCHA, UNCT 2014, 3).

OCHA and UNHCR reported that shelters were crowded, leading to unsanitary conditions, lack of privacy, and exposure to contagious diseases particularly during the pandemic. Some IDPs chose to stay out of shelters and live and sleep in the open air. That decision carries health risks, especially during adverse weather conditions (OCHA 2020, 7).

In addition to the tremendous work that relief agencies performed on the ground under difficult conditions, there are three aspects of relief assistance that merit attention.

First, providing humanitarian support directly to the affected populations was disrupted or prohibited by the Syrian government, who restricted aid access to areas in the country that it controlled. In some areas, the authorities closed border crossings altogether. In a remarkable conceptual shift, humanitarian aid became 'criminalized' by being linked to aiding 'terrorists,' when the relief aid was aimed at wounded ISIL members. The International Committee of the Red Cross and Doctors without Borders made this point during a conference in 2019:

In northern Syria, we've been working in a displaced peoples' camp in al-Hol, and there's a section in that camp where the ISIL families are. People there have been treated completely differently than the rest of the camp. There was no health screening. Water provision is terrible. The 12,000 children there have no access to any kind of mental health services, toys, or education. They can literally see – across the fence – that the other children have safe spaces and playgrounds. ... So, it's active discrimination against that population who have been tagged as terrorists or ISIL people (Elliott and Parker 2019).

Second, donors placed restrictions on how the aid should be used, with some funding clauses being restricted to specific areas and populations. This challenge applied primarily to areas of the country under the control of ISIL, which is considered a terrorist group by the US government, the EU and other countries (Alhousseiny and Atar 2021, 113).

Third, humanitarian relief funding from wealthy countries has been declining since 2014, which translates into fewer organizations being able to provide support. For instance, a Syria Emergency Response Fund (ERF) was set up by OCHA in 2012 to increase support for humanitarian projects in partnership with local and international NGOs. In 2014, the Syria ERF received more than $23 million from a variety of governmental and non-governmental donors. Seventy-five projects with a value of $32 million were reported under way, and 143 NGOs were active on the ground as a result (OCHA 2014, 1). As of 2020, decreased funding resulted in fewer organizations operating on the ground; 130 NGOs and 25 INGOs with a humanitarian mission remained in operation (OCHA 2020, 40).

The amounts pledged and delivered by the governments of the US and the UK have been declining since 2018. Germany has increased its donation since 2018 but not enough to offset the lower pledges of other big donors. At a time when the COVID-19 pandemic persists and the Syria crisis remains unresolved, lower funding affects the ability of INGOs and NGOs to deliver relief and support services, and leaves Syrians without basic means of subsistence. Ten NGOs working on the ground signed a public letter protesting the cuts and highlighting that they come as sixty per cent of the Syrian population are food insecure (Worley 2021). As of this writing, the funding situation has not improved.

Conclusion: Is There a Civil Society in Syria?

This chapter provides evidence that civil society groups have been rising in Syria since the civil war started in 2011. Local groups have been forming to fulfill civil society functions described by both Western and Arabic scholars: 1. Groups organized themselves outside government control – and despite the government's attempts to silence them. 2. They created networks of support for one another and the populations in need such as refugees and IDPs. 3. They held the government accountable with their actions and protests. Diaspora dissidents sometimes argue that while the Syrian revolution may be on the decline in terms of the ability of the population to resist the Assad regime, it amounted to a liberation of 'civil society' from the fear of that regime (Lababidi 2021).

Once the civil conflict erupted in 2011, local Syrian groups formed in support of two main public service functions: advocacy, and humanitarian relief. There is high connectivity between these two types of civil society groups. Advocacy and watchdog groups reported the repression and abuses of the regime against its own citizens, demonstrating a classic feature of the Western concept of 'keeping the government accountable'. The visibility of the repression via internet and social media led in turn to humanitarian relief groups being formed by local groups, INGOs, or both. In the words of a prominent Syrian civil rights activist and politician:

> [C]ivil society has been responding to Syrians' needs and raising awareness about the situation in Syria from the beginning of the revolution ... conveying to the world what was happening in Syria; took photos and published them to the entire world; helped refugees and those displaced; defended human rights; documented violations of human rights and crimes against humanity (USIP 2014).

In so doing, rising groups of people organized for action demonstrated a growing maturity akin to a nascent civil society. This society combined elements of both Western concepts of free and voluntary associations of people holding their government accountable for its actions, and Arabic concepts of bonds of kinship and religion exercised outside a government sphere of activity. If civil society was weak prior to 2011, the work of advocacy and humanitarian relief of the past decade can be said to resemble Putnam's 'social capital,' since it created political and civic engagement, informal social ties, and, to a certain extent, tolerance among some segments of the population. This development was possible because of all the efforts at local, regional, and national levels that organized individuals, whether through CSOs, NGOs, or INGOs, were able to make.

This review of reports, eyewitness accounts, and NGO and INGO fact sheets, and stories concerning the activities of civic groups indicates that the national government of Syria created the initial crisis with its repressive response to popular demands for reforms. The persistence of street protests eventually became a nation-wide revolution that attracted foreign actors. Civilians were caught in the crossfire, which resulted in a humanitarian crisis that continues more than ten years after the first protests began.

In estimating the contribution of the nascent Syrian civil society to mitigating the effects of the conflict, we should be mindful that the scale of the human crisis in Syria is such that any effort is better than nothing. The scale of the population displacement is massive, requiring a commensurate response at the highest levels of national and international governance, above and beyond what local groups, NGOs and INGOs can offer with their limited resources.

References

Al-Assad, Bashar. 2001. Interview with President Bashar Al-Assad. *Asharq al-Awsat*, 8 February 2001. https://al-bab.com/documents-section/interview-president-bashar-al-assad#CIVIL

Al-Assad, Bashar. 2013. President Bashar Al-Assad's Historic Speech: The West Has Brought Terrorists to Syria. *President Bashar al-Assad blog*, 6 January 2013. https://presidentbasharassad.blogspot.com/2014/12/president-bashar-al-assads-historic.html

Al-Assad, Bashar. 2019. Majority of Syrian People Support their Government. *The Syrian Observer*, 12 November 2019. https://syrianobserver.com/interviews/54185/president-assad-majority-of-syrian-people-support-their-government.html

Al-Om, Tamara. 2011. Empowering Syrian Civil Society. Paper presented at British Society for Middle Eastern Studies (BRISMES) conference. https://tamaraalom.wordpress.com/empowering-syrian-civil-society

Al-Wasl, Zaman. 2016. Syrian NGOs, Civil Activists Found New Civil Platform for Peace and Justice. *The Syrian Observer*, 13 December 2016. https://syrianobserver.com/features/24602/syrian_ngos_civil_activists_found_new_civil_platform_peace_justice.html

Alhousseiny, Mazen and E. Atar. 2021. The Evolution of the Syrian Humanitarian NGOs and External Challenges. *The Rest Journal of Politics and Development* 11, no.2: 101–120.

Amnesty International (AI). 2013. Syria: Harrowing Torture, Summary Killings in Secret ISIS Detention Centers. Amnesty International website, 19 December 2013. https://www.amnesty.org/en/latest/news/2013/12/syria-harrowing-torture-summary-killings-secret-isis-detention-centres

Armscontrol.org. Timeline of Syrian Chemical Weapons Activity, 2012-2021. Last modified May 2021. https://www.armscontrol.org/factsheets/Timeline-of-Syrian-Chemical-Weapons-Activity

Carnegie Middle East Center. 2012. Local Coordination Committees of Syria. Malcolm H. Kerr Middle East Center, 12 December 2012. https://carnegie-mec.org/diwan/50426?lang=en

Crawford, Nicholas. 2015. *Engaging with Syrian CSOs. How Can the International Community Engage Better with Syrian Civil Society Organizations During the Civil War?* ALNAP on-line. https://www.alnap.org/help-library/engaging-with-syrian-csos

Damascus Centre for Human Rights Studies. N.d. http://dchrs.org

De Tocqueville, Alexis. 2000 (first published 1835). *Democracy in America*. With an Introduction by Joseph Epstein. Translated by Henry Reeve. Complete and unabridged vol. I and II. New York: Bantam Classics.

Elliott, Vittoria; Ben Parker. 2019. Balancing Act: Anti-Terror Efforts and Humanitarian Principles. *The New Humanitarian*, 26 November 2019. https://www.thenewhumanitarian.org/feature/2019/11/26/balancing-act-anti-terror-efforts-and-humanitarian-principles

Esteban, Damian. 2004. Religion and the State in Ibn Khaldūn's *Muqaddimah*. Master's degree thesis, Institute of Islamic Studies, McGill University, Montreal, Canada.

Gellner, Ernest. 1996. *Conditions of Liberty: Civil Society and Its Rivals*. London: Penguin Books.

Human Rights Watch (HRW). 2011a. Syria: Rein in Security Services. Allow Peaceful Protests to Proceed this Friday. HRW 21 April 2011. https://www.hrw.org/news/2011/04/21/syria-rein-security-services

HRW. 2011b. We've Never Seen Such Horror. Crimes Against Humanity by Syrian Security Forces. HRW 1 June 2011. https://www.hrw.org/report/2011/06/01/weve-never-seen-such-horror/crimes-against-humanity-syrian-security-forces

HRW. 2011c. Syria: Defectors Describe Orders to Shoot Unarmed Protesters. HRW 9 July 2011. https://www.hrw.org/news/2011/07/09/syria-defectors-describe-orders-shoot-unarmed-protesters

Hurd, Ian. 2017. *International Organizations: Politics, Law, Practice*, 5th edition. Cambridge: Cambridge University Press.

Lababidi, Zaki. 2021. Syrian American Council Figure to the Syrian Observer: The Revolution Has Achieved Goal, Liberating Syrians from Fear. *The Syrian Observer,* 30 July 2021. https://syrianobserver.com/interviews/68400/syrian-american-council-figure-to-the-syrian-observer-the-revolution-liberated-the-syrians-from-fear.html

Mercy Corps Syria. N.d. Website. https://www.mercycorps.org/where-we-work/syria#meeting-needs

Mercy Corps. 2019. 44 Syrian and International NGOs Call for Immediate End to Attacks on Civilians and Hospitals in Idlib, Syria. Mercy Corps website, 24May 2019. https://www.mercycorps.org/press-room/releases/44-syrian-and-international-ngos-call-immediate-end-attacks-civilians-and

Mercy Corps. 2021. NGOs Warn: Reduced Humanitarian Access Impedes Response to Rising Cases of Covid-19 and the Harsh Effects of Winter in Northern Syria Amid Shortages of Humanitarian Aid. Mercy Corps website, 28 January 2021. https://www.mercycorps.org/press-room/releases/ngos-warn-humanitarian-access-COVID-winter-northern-Syria

Middle East Intelligence Bulletin. 2000. Statement by 99 Syrian Intellectuals. 5 October 2000, vol. 2, no. 9. https://www.meforum.org/meib/articles/0010_sdoc0927.htm

Office for the Coordination of Humanitarian Affairs (OCHA). 2014. Syria Emergency Response Fund. Annual Report. https://www.unocha.org/sites/unocha/files/dms/Documents/Syria%20ERF_Annual%20Report%202014.pdf

OCHA. 2020. Humanitarian Needs Overview. The Syrian Arab Republic." https://reliefweb.int/sites/reliefweb.int/files/resources/syria_2020_humanitarian_needs_overview.pdf

OCHA, UNCT. 2014. 2015 Strategic Response Plan: Syrian Arab Republic. UN Country Team. https://reliefweb.int/sites/reliefweb.int/files/ resources/2015_SRP_Syria_EN_AdvanceCopy_171214.pdf

Oxfam. 2013. Syria Crisis Fact Sheet. Oxfam website, 11September 2013. https://s3.amazonaws.com/oxfam-us/www/static/media/files/syria-fact-sheet-may-2013.pdf

Oxfam. 2018–2019. *Fighting Inequality to Beat Poverty*. https://oi-files-d8-prod.s3.eu-west-2.amazonaws.com/s3fs-public/2019-12/191219_Oxfam_ Annual_Report_2018-19.pdf

Parliament of the Syrian Government. 2011. Legislative Decree no. 54 of 2011 regulating the right to peaceful demonstrations by citizens. http://www. parliament.gov.sy/arabic/index.php?node=201&nid=4442&ref=tree&

Putnam, Robert D., Robert Leonardi, Raffaella Y. Nanetti. 1993. *Making Democracy Work: Civil Traditions in Modern Italy*. Princeton, NJ: Princeton University Press.

Putnam, R.D. 1995. Bowling Alone: America's Declining Social Capital. *The Journal of Democracy* 6, no.1: 65–78.

Ridley, Yvonne. 2014. How the Graffiti Boys Ignited the Syrian Revolution. *Al-Jazeerah CCUN*, 4 March 2013.   http://www.aljazeerah.info/Opinion%20 Editorials/2013/March/4%20o/How%20the%2018%20Graffiti%20Boys%20 of%20Dara%27a%20Ignited%20the%20Syrian%20Revolution%20By%20 Yvonne%20Ridley.htm

Rovera, Donatella. 2012. Dispatch from Aleppo: Victims of Syria's Brutal Crackdown. *Amnesty International*, 31 May 2012. https://www.amnesty.org/ en/latest/campaigns/2012/05/despatch-from-aleppo-victims-of-syrias-brutal-crackdown/

Syrian Human Rights Committee. 2003. Oppressive Laws in Syria: Law of Emergency, issued upon the Legislative Act no. 15 on 22/12/1962 by the Councils of Ministers of Syria. https://www.shrc.org/en/?p=19812

Syrian Human Rights Committee (SHRC). 2013. Genocide: The Politics of Blockade. Syrian Human Rights Committee website 16 November 2013. https://www.shrc.org/en/?p=23018

Tahhan, Zena. 2017. The Voices Missing from Syria's Peace Talks. *Al-Jazeerah*, 23 March 2017. https://www.aljazeera.com/features/2017/3/23/the-voices-missing-from-syrias-peace-talks

Tavares, Rodrigo. 2010. *Regional Security.* London: Routledge.

The Creative Memory of the Syrian Revolution. 2017. *The Story of a Place, the Story of a People. The Beginnings of the Syrian Revolution 2011–2015.* https://creativememory.org/en/archives/16189/

United Nations High Commissioner for Refugees (UNHCR). 2021. "Syria Refugee Crisis Explained." 5 February 2021. https://www.unrefugees.org/news/syria-refugee-crisis-explained

United Nations Security Council (UNSC). 2015. Resolution 2254 Adopted by the Security Council at its 7,588th Meeting. 18 December 2015. http://unscr.com/en/resolutions/doc/2254

U.S. Institute of Peace (USIP) blog. 2014. Syria's Civil Society: Wael Sawah on The Push for Influence. https://www.usip.org/blog/2014/02/syrias-civil-society-wael-sawah-push-influence

Violations Documentation Center in Syria (VDC). 2013. Campaign in the City of Qamishli. VDC website, August 2013. https://www.vdc-sy.info/index.php/ar/reports/1379617604#.Y_KDgLTP3m9

Williams, Jessie. 2021. How Syrian Women Are Fighting a War—and Patriarchy. *Al-Jazeerah*, 12 April 2021. https://www.aljazeera.com/news/2021/4/12/how-syrian-women-are-fighting-a-war-and-patriarchy

Worley, William. 2021. UK, US Announce Steep Cuts in Funding to Syria. *Devex*, 30 March 2021. https://www.devex.com/news/uk-us-announce-steep-cuts-in-funding-to-syria-99539

PART II

National Responses to the Syrian Refugee Crisis

5

The Jordanian Response to the Syrian Refugee Crisis from a Resilience Perspective

ZEYNEP S. MENCUTEK AND AYAT J. NASHWAN

The conflict in Syria has been both complex and protracted since it began in March 2011. It caused a severe humanitarian crisis in which many Syrian civilians were killed, disappeared, persecuted, or lost fundamental rights and livelihoods. At the same time, more than 5.6 million Syrians have fled their country, and 6.6 million are internally displaced (OCHR 2020). The initial reasons for their displacement – insecurity, instability, and lack of safety – continue. As the United Nations (UN) has reported, 'there [have been]regular spikes in violence and continuous violations of human rights across the Syrian Arab Republic' (UN 2020, 1). The deadly confrontation between pro-government forces and opposition armed groups continues in some locations (Council of EU 2020). Besides security problems, access to livelihoods is limited, the service infrastructure in health, education, sanitation, and housing has not been yet rebuilt (UN 2020, 4). Syria meets neither the safe country standard nor the UNHCR protection threshold (UN 2018, 1).

The Syrian crisis has severely affected neighboring countries, including Jordan, Lebanon, Turkey, Iraq, and Egypt, because more than five million displaced Syrians sought refuge there. More than 662,700 Syrian refugees are officially registered in Jordan by the UNHCR (JRP 2020–22, 5). According to the Jordanian government, Syrians' total numbers with unregistered ones are around 1.3 million (King Abdullah II 2018a). Approximately 10 per cent of them live inside refugee camps, while the rest are distributed principally across the urban areas, mainly in Amman, Mafraq, Irbid and Zarqa Governorates (JRP 2020–22, 5).

Jordan has a long-term reputation for hosting refugees with the historical experience of Palestinian and Iraqi refugees. More than two million registered Palestine refugees have lived in Jordan for decades, with the support of United Nations Relief and Works Agency for Palestine Refugees (UNRWA) (UNRWA 2020, 1). Jordan also hosts thousands of refugees from other countries, including Yemen, Sudan, and Somalia (UNHCR 2019, 1). Despite the country's substantial experience in refugee-hosting, the Kingdom has not signed the 1951 Refugee Convention, hence it has is no legal obligation to provide long term protection to any refugee group, including Syrians. It has closely cooperated with UNRWA, UN High Commissioner for Refugees (UNHCR), and donor countries to maintain humanitarian assistance and protection services in protracted refugee situations such as those of the Iraqis and Syrians (Achilli 2015; Schimmel 2015).

In the last five years, Jordan has increasingly used the concept of resilience in framing its refugee response and its cooperation with external actors. This interest in resilience also reflects the regional and global paradigm shift in the humanitarian assistance and international development sector and has mainly been tested in the Syrian displacement situation. The organized efforts to coordinate a regional response to Syrian displacement were renamed as the '3RP' – the Regional Refugee and Resilience Plans in 2015. We argue that the concept of resilience increasingly shapes the Jordanian government's perceptions of refugee governance and turns into a frame of action. Resilience is widely used and attributed to several positive but ambiguous meanings. It simultaneously refers to a pillar of governance along with a humanitarian approach. It is used to emphasize that not only the needs of refugees but also the needs of host communities and the service infrastructure of Jordan. Resilience is presented as a key characteristic of the refugee support system. Also, resilience is individualized because it is approached as the desired trait of refugees and host communities. It replaced the concept of the development needs of the country. Policy designers aim to invest in and cultivate resilience at macro (e.g., Jordan as a whole), meso (e.g., sectors), and micro levels (e.g., individuals). Resilience is strategically favored because of its potential benefits. First, it enables to claim national ownership in the refugee governance and addresses needs of impacted host communities. Second, through overemphasizing resilience, policymakers appropriate regional and global humanitarian policy shifts towards a long-term self-reliance agenda. Third, the vocabulary further helps to legitimize development support demands by providing evidence. Plans also address donors' other favorable vocabulary, such as transparency, crisis prevention, and vulnerability assessment. In these ways, resilience discourse allows to avoid refugee flows' securitization, shows moderate diplomatic tone and cooperation desire of Jordan, unlike blackmailing. Nevertheless, this terminology still suffers from several layers of ambiguity as has also been observed in other contexts (Joseph 2013). Its wide usage raises the question of the resilience for whom and how. It does not settle the balance between the humanitarian needs of refugees and the development needs of host states.

Methodologically, we adopt the qualitative approach to understand both policies and politics from the lenses of resilience. We conduct textual analysis of Jordan's Response Plans (cited in the reference list as JRP 2016–18; JRP 2017–19; JRP 2018–20; JRP 2020–22).

Additionally, we draw from national laws, compiled reports, press releases. We also rely on interviews conducted with multiple stakeholders during the several rounds of field work carried out by both authors since 2015 as well as participatory observations in policy-oriented workshops. To systematically analyze data, we used Critical Discourse Analysis (CDA) (Fairclough 2005, 2003) as a method and N-Vivo software as a tool to delve into resilience's discursive dimension.

The chapter proceeds as follows. Drawing from policymaking and governance literature, it first focuses on resilience as a concept and theoretical framework in addressing refugee situations. Thereafter we present Jordan's case by discussing the main characteristics of its response to the Syrian refugee flow. That section highlights the government's policy changes over time. Thereafter, we examine the diverse adoption of the resilience concept in the JRPs and conclude by summarizing our findings.

Literature on Resilience, Policymaking and Governing Refugees

Resilience has been a common concept in policymaking in recent decades, particularly in addressing national and global security challenges, such as climate change (Gaillard 2010), health crises (Elbe 2008), financial and infrastructure collapses (de Goede 2007) and security risks (Longstaff 2005). Analysts have developed the concept of resilience on the assumption that modern systems' complexity and global interconnectivity make actors such as governments, populations, and systems vulnerable to 'extreme events' and unpredictable environments, hence they must develop capacities for qualified swift responses, improvisation, coordination, flexibility, and endurance via resilience building (Comfort et al. 2010; Longstaff 2005). Scholars have considered resilience to be a desired trait, alongside adaptability and transformability in such efforts (Cork 2010).

The term was first used in engineering in 1802 and revived in environmental management science in the 1970s, and then employed in the psychology literature in the 1980s (Holling 1973). After that, social scientist Louise Comfort et al. (2010) adopted the term. International relations and security studies have also welcomed it (Brassett and Vaughan-Williams 2015, 33; Lundborg and Vaughan-Williams 2011). The concept of resilience made its way into policy studies, particularly those addressing urban, environmental, and financial security issues (Brassett and Vaughan-Williams 2015; Walker and Cooper 2011). It is widely used in the psychology field, too, because resilience along with coping strategies are treated as a protective factor for displaced people and refugees' psychological well-being and mental health. Such analyses often focus on individual resilience in which refugees are accorded the principal role in addressing trauma, stress, or mental problems (Arnetz et al. 2013; Montgomery 2010; Schweitzer et al. 2007). Besides individual resilience, community resilience is also used to describe interconnected system networks at grassroots levels (Doron 2005). It is argued that 'while the resilience of individuals, families or specific organizations are key components of community resilience as a whole, a resilient community is greater than the sum of its parts' (Fitzpatrich 2016).

International governmental and non-governmental organizations, states, businesses, and some scholars see resilience as an 'unquestionably "good" value to be striven for, invested in, and cultivated throughout society at whatever cost' (Brassett and Vaughan-Williams 2015, 46). It is believed to enable 'to anticipate and tolerate disturbances ... without collapse, withstand shocks, and rebuild as necessary' (Lentzos and Rose 2009, 34). It implies both narrow and broad meanings. For instance, resilience is treated as a system characteristic and an 'umbrella concept for a range of system attributes deemed desirable in climate change (Klein et al. 2003, 35). It is also used as a metaphor, theory, set of capacities, and strategy, such as being observed in disaster management (Norris et al. 2008).

One of the policy fields that extensively embrace the resilience concept is the humanitarian assistance field (Scott-Smith 2018). This field also mainstreamed resilience at practice level, as the term is appreciated in the discourses and action plans of the United Nations (UN) agencies, donors, governments, and (international) non-governmental organizations (I/NGOs). As part of humanitarian assistance, the term gained attraction in responding to displacement situations, mainly offering a paradigmatic shift to the humanitarian aid sector from responding to needs to empowering those affected by crises (Scott-Smith 2018, 662).

Despite positive value attached to resilience in the humanitarian sector, it is widely criticized by scholars on the basis that the term lacks conceptual clarity (Bourbeau 2013; Kaufmann 2013) and serves as a buzzword or empty signifier (Manyena 2006; Weichselgartner and Kelman 2014). As Brassett and

Vaughan-Williams point out, 'while in many respects highly seductive, the concept of resilience remains somewhat abstract – both in theory and practice' (2015; 46).

The usage of the term has consequences for practices at global and national levels. As Ulrike Krause and Hannah Schmidt (2020, 22) pointed out, 'global policies designed to promote the self-reliance and resilience of refugees strive to increase their abilities to deal with hardships; in doing so, they rhetorically shift refugees from the category of 'vulnerable" to that of capable actors'. For example, climate change-induced migration, the prior emphasis on risk management emphasis was shifted to resilience. This implied that the responsibility shifts from Western emitters seeking to 'save' climate refugees toward the affected populations who are now expected to prepare for the effects of climate change and makes those affected by it responsible for their survival' (Methmann 2014; Methmann and Oels 2015). Thus, the rise of resilience in the humanitarian sector goes along with depoliticizing the issues causing displacement, such as global warming (Methmann 2014, 416). It is also a way of 'responsibilizing refugees through humanitarian governance,' identified as 'resilience humanitarianism' (Ilcan and Rygiel 2015, 333). For example, as Anholt and Wagner (2020, 1) noted,

> the EU no longer suggests that protracted crises will be overcome *tout court*. Instead, the EU can only help to cope with them. ... Rather than promoting a one-size-fits-all blueprint, resilience suggests an appreciation for local actors and practices.

This shift potentially benefits international actors because,

> foregrounding local institutions and their capacities allow[s] international actors to make their local partners responsible for the success of the refugee response, while potentially reducing the focus on their roles in crisis management, and the roles of donor countries in creating those crises (Lenner and Turner 2021, 2).

Against this background, it is worth examining how resilience is adopted at the national levels in responding the mass displacement situations. We look to advance the existing policy and theoretical debate on resilience by offering a rich empirical case study of Jordan's policy response to Syrian refugees. Through an interpretive analysis, we seek to describe how the long-term policy plans present resilience and the rationalities behind this. We aim to contribute a theory-driven critique of resilience in policy plans concerning the Syrian refugee crisis.

Resilience in the Governance of Syrian Displacement

Resilience concept has been in circulation at the Jordanian policy field since 2013 when the United Nations Development Programme (UNDP) and under the framework of the Regional United Nations Development Group (R-UNDG), a Sub-regional Response Facility was established in Jordan. The aim was to develop a joint response and coordination structure that covered several countries (Turkey, Lebanon, Jordan, Iraq, Egypt). The R-UNDG worked closely with humanitarian and development stakeholders and governments to adopt a plan, called Resilience-Based Development Response to the Syria Crisis. The system's originality was to offer 1) 'a new programming and organizational framework for integrating humanitarian and development interventions'; 2) expansion of scope of intervention to host communities along with refugees; 3) bringing new partners into the programs such as around the table (private sector, international financial institutions, development funders); and 4) enhancing the role for the governments of hosting refugees, to facilitate national ownership of plans (Gonzalez 2016, 27). Along with these goals, in 2015, the UNHCR expanded the Syrian Regional Response Plan (RRP 2014) to the Regional Refugee and Resilience Plan, named the 3RP. It is co-led by UNDP and UNHCR. It is participated in by governments of five countries, their line ministries, agencies, and some hundreds of partners, including relevant UN agencies and national and international NGOs (RRRP 2015).

While previous response plans of the UNHCR focused on the humanitarian needs of a Syrian refugee in the neighboring countries, 3RP's aimed at a more comprehensive approach targeting both refugees and crises affecting host countries. The 3RP's defined as a strategic, coordination, planning, advocacy, fundraising, and programming platform for humanitarian and development partners to respond to the Syria crisis. It comprises one regional plan, with five country chapters. It has two prominent components: refugees and resilience. The refugee component focuses on the 'protection and humanitarian assistance needs of refugees while the resilience component emphasizes the resilience, stabilization and development needs of impacted individuals, communities and institutions, aiming to strengthen the capacities of national actors' (3RP 2020, 1). To this end, 3RPs brought together humanitarian actors and development actors by grouping coordination under sectors and sub-sectors (shelters, WASH, protection, etc.). UN programme, 3RP 'turned into one of the UN's biggest humanitarian operations ever realized' (Diogini 2016, 27). Developmental objectives of host countries are strongly reflected in the 3RPs and their translations into the more specific national Response Plans (3RP 2020). The London Conference–Supporting Syria and the Region in February 2016 gave further momentum to the mainstreaming resilience approach. Besides its mobilization of financial resources, 'for the first time, a Syria pledging conference was structured around the resilience-building themes of livelihoods and education, with protection as the third one' (Gonzalez 2016, 27).

It should be noted that the paradigmatic shift in the regional response to Syrian displacement is also a reflection of the governing actors' positionings and power. The UNDP, which had been active in the region for decades took a decisive role in refugee governance by advocating for 'integrating short-term emergency measures into a nationally owned and led "fast-track development response"' (Lenner and Turner 2021, 3). When countries encountered the Syrian mass flow, UNDP strengthened its collaboration with national actors like ministries, municipalities, and trade chambers to support infrastructures under stress in urban spaces including clean water, sewage, shelters, and refugees' employability by providing vocational education (Mencutek 2018). The UNDP is a well-respected actor in the national countries due to its close cooperation and extensive funding to the national infrastructures. In 3RP, a humanitarian response is coordinated by the UNHCR, whereas the resilience pillar is carried out by the development response led by the UNDP (Anholt 2020, 297).

Despite its popularity in different fields and adoption in policy papers like the regional 3RP Syria crisis and national response plans, resilience still lacks conceptual clarity in the humanitarian action targeting Syrian refugees. In a recent comparative study, Rosanne Anholt (2020, 294) addresses how resilience is differently interpreted and translated by the humanitarian and development practitioners in Turkey, Jordan, and Lebanon. She finds that 'resilience is translated as the economic self-reliance of refugees, and the capacity for crisis management of refugee-hosting states, enacted through "localization" and strengthening the "humanitarian-development nexus."' While Jordan's response plans strongly emphasize development and the system's resilience, Lebanon's plan highlighted social resilience and 'stabilization' and resilience (Anholt and Sinatti 2020; Diogini 2016).

Among Syrian hosting countries, Jordan has been the most eager to adopt resilience terminology. It produced the National Resilience Plan 2014–16 and participated in the Regional Response Plans. Jordanian response plan 2015 (JRP 2015) concretized a one-year comprehensive humanitarian and resilience-based response to the Syria crisis. It drafted eight refugee and 11 resilience sector assessments outlining the vulnerabilities, needs and gaps in assistance. For Jordan, 'resilience-oriented programming has become strongly equated with refugee self-reliance after the 2016 Jordan Compact that permits Syrian refugees formally to work in some selected sectors' (Lenner and Turner 2021, 5). Also, in 2015, the Jordanian Government, in collaboration with the United Nations, formed the Jordan Resilience Fund to 'ensure coherence, aid effectiveness and coordinated assistance' (UNDP

2015, 1). To understand these policy plans, it is necessary first to zoom in on the policy context in Jordan.

Jordan's Refugee Response: From ad-hoc to Restrictive Policies

When Jordan first encountered the Syrian refugee flow in April 2012, the Jordanian government pursued a hybrid settlement system where camps and self-settlement were allowed (Mencutek 2018, 197). Jordan first limited, and then eventually closed, its borders to arrivals. The restrictions were legitimized by demographic and security concerns in May 2013 because Syrians' number reached a half million in Jordan and the rise of Islamic State of Iraq and Syria (ISIS) in 2014 threatened Jordan. It was suspected that Syrian Salafists could cross Jordan's border and mix with civil refugees to get support to the rebellion (Mencutek 2018, 218). Jordan also toughened procedures to access services and rights. In 2015, the Jordanian Ministry of Interior, cooperating with the UNHCR, re-registered all Syrians residing outside the camps to issue service/identity residence cards. Without obtaining a verified card, refugees did not have a right to live outside of refugee camps, travel freely, and get a work permit (Ibid., 199). Also, a 'bailout' process that allowed refugees to leave camps if they found sponsors, called *kafils*, was suspended in 2015 (Ibid.). Syrian refugees in Jordan still have an option to leave the camps, but they need a Jordanian guarantor and intense paperwork (Chatty 2016, 35).

Accessing refugees to sustainable livelihoods and their labor market participation has been one of the most critical challenges for Syrians, the host government, and host communities (Sahin-Mencutek and Nashwan 2020a, 2020b), which worsened with the COVID–19 pandemics. Although Syrian refugees in Jordan are only allowed to work if they have a working permit, getting a permit has difficulties due to the bureaucratic hurdles and vast informal sector. Many refugees face risk if they have worked without a permit, locking them into precarity, vulnerability (Ibid.). From 1 January 2016 to 31 January 2020, only 179,445 permits were issued to Syrians in Jordan (Ministry of Labour 2020, 1). Approximately five per cent of them are given to Syrian women (Ibid.,2). There are several restrictions and barriers to finding a job legally. Alternatively, many Syrians work in the informal labor market, which is the place where the highest level of discrimination and exploitation is experienced (Sahin-Mencutek and Nashwan 2020a, b). As in other refugee host contexts, de-qualification refers to the fact that migrants often find jobs that do not match their skills are observable among Syrians in Jordan. The financial problems, mainly not working and limited access to sustainable livelihoods, inevitably create severe poverty among Syrian refugees (Sert 2016). Refugees have been more impoverished than Jordanians before and after the COVID–19 pandemic (World Bank 2020).

For Syrians, the financial problems intersect with the challenges in access to health, residence (scarcity of housing, high rents), and difficulties in access to primary education and dropouts (Doocy, Lyles, Akhu-Zaheya, Burton, and Burnham 2016; Chinnery 2019). As Syrians' flow into Jordan created an immense burden on the Jordanian health system (Alameddine 2019), initial free access of Syrians to the public health system ceased after a while. Before late 2014, registered Syrians in Jordan could receive full free primary, secondary and some tertiary health care at public facilities, but now they must make co-payments like those required of uninsured Jordanians.

It appears that Jordanians held quite positive attitudes toward Syrian refugees at the societal level at the onset of the Syrian migration. Jordanian society responded to refugees' needs with generosity, predicated on their religious and cultural affinity (Alrababa'h et al. 2020). Over time, the support for Syrians has waned, and there has been a widespread perception that Syrians' presence negatively affects Jordanian communities, particularly the already strained labour market and public services (health, water, education) (Kvittingen et al. 2019). Nevertheless, few studies provide empirical evidence that 'neither personal-nor community-level exposure to the refugee crisis' economic impact is associated with anti-migrant sentiments among natives' (Alrababa'h, et al. 2020).

Jordanian formal response to the Syrian refugee flow has inevitably been linked to the complex web of domestic and regional political dynamics concerning Jordanian elites and hosting communities at a policy level. More specifically, the perceptions and realities about security challenges, demographic balance and national economic development reflect on Jordanian restrictive policy choices over time (Mencutek 2020). Nevertheless, the policies are very receptive to the international dynamics and donor's frameworks, since Jordan used to be refugee rentier state (Tsourapas 2019).

Development and Resilience Focus in Jordan's Refugee Governance

From the start of the Syrian crisis, the Government of Jordan has consistently highlighted the mounting cost of hosting refugees as well as the Syrian crisis' adverse impact on the Jordanian economy (Nasser and Symansky 2014). The Government proposes that hosting Syrian refugees constitutes a global public good and it has therefore been willing to shoulder the responsibility of doing so. Nonetheless, it follows as King Abdullah II reiterated in a speech to the General Assembly of the UN in 2018:

> As many of you know, Jordan has carried a massive, disproportionate burden as a refugee host. Our people have opened their homes, schools, public services, hospitals. We

have shared our country's scarce resources, our food and energy, our precious water. The crisis has held back economic growth and job creation, jobs urgently needed by our young people, more than 60 per cent of our population. Jordanians have borne this refugee burden in full accord with our country's long humanitarian traditions, but we know, and the world knows, that this crisis is a global responsibility. The sacrifices we and other host countries make every day can only continue if donor nations hold up their side of the partnership. That means continued, multi-track efforts *in development support and humanitarian assistance*; efforts which not only prepare refugees to return home and rebuild their countries, but also give hope to the people of host countries, who have sacrificed so much (King Abdullah II 2018b).

Several academics have also argued that 'the latest wave of refugees from Syria put extra pressure on the Jordanian population' along with the fact that 'Jordan is a small country situated in a turbulent region' (Alshoubaki 2020). The strained infrastructure and public services are perceived as a significant risk that might hamper Jordan's development trajectory and 'relatively stable economic and social landscape' (JRP 2020–22, 1). Thus, Jordan calls not only for humanitarian assistance but also for development aid, requiring the support of strained infrastructure and vulnerable host communities. King Abdullah II's speech was illustrative in this regard:

Our economy has faced significant challenges over the past decade. In doing the right thing for desperate refugees, Jordan's own people have paid an enormous price, and we are working closely with international partners to increase help for refugees and host communities alike. (King Abdullah II 2019)

These high-level official speeches mainly target international partners, both European and Arab countries, to garner financial support for Jordan's response through burden-sharing. The Government of Jordan has built durable and robust communication with the international community in shaping its refugee response. Donors particularly favor Jordan due to its overall stability compared to other countries in the region and its positive relationships with regional and international stakeholders (Tahrir Institute for ME Policy 2020). After 2015 Jordan's rhetoric has gradually linked to the EU crisis rhetoric, as illustrated London Donor conference in 2016. Jordan used crisis language to highlight that it shoulders a heavy burden and need support, which was reflected in the design of the Jordan Compact (EC 2016).

Besides garnering development support, Jordanian government looked to claim national ownership in the refugee governance. Since the start of the crisis, the Jordanian government was involved in decision-making, planning, and coordination. It appointed the Ministry of Planning and International Cooperation (MoPIC) as the lead agency and established a secretariat and information management system (Anholt 2020, 300).

The first Jordanian response plan (2015) was launched on 1 September 2014, by the MoPIC's initiative, Jordan Response Platform for the Syria Crisis (JRSPSC). The Platform served to facilitate and support the partnership between the Jordanian government, donors, Jordanian ministries (e.g., Ministry of Education (Chinnery 2019), Ministry of Health and national and international humanitarian partners such as UN agencies and NGOs. Policy plans are prepared in collaboration with around 150 national and international partners, including government ministries, donors, UN agencies, national and international NGOs (JRP 2020–22, 1). The Government also developed an innovative method to approve externally funded projects that requires that such aid be divided between Syrian and Jordanian beneficiaries.

The concept of resilience legitimizes such a conditionality in a very sensible way in negotiating refugee hosting. In pursuing well-elaborated migration diplomacy, Jordan practised various techniques, including sophisticated planning for refugee response (JRP 2015, 2016–18; 2018–2020; 2020–2022). Jordan develops JRPs to align with current global processes such as the Global Compact on Refugees and the UN 2030 Agenda for Sustainable Development and the Sustainable Development Goals (SDGs). Analysis of plans demonstrated that they have at least three objectives: 1) claiming the ownership of Jordan in regulating Syrian refugee affairs and presenting them as a 'nationally-led response,' 2) integrating refugee and development responses in one comprehensive plan, and 3) to show the budgetary needs of Jordan empirically. The Plans advocated for emergency measures to meet the immediate needs of refugees and to invest in capacity building related to service provision and infrastructure (Al Makhamreh and Hutchinson 2018). A closer look at JRPs through the lens of resilience provides insights into key components of Jordan's refugee governance strategy.

Critical Discourse Analysis on 'Resilience' in the JRPs

Examination of word frequency in four JRP shows that the crisis concept is used 587 times, at the top list after generic concepts such as Syrian, refugee, Jordan, service, and sector. The crisis term was followed by health (n=525), access (n=448), vulnerable (n=429), and water (n=422). Other key terms include education (n=379), food (n=313) development (n=299), capacity (n=289), protection (n=250), energy (232), areas (n=192), and security (n=185). Resilience appeared among the most used concepts, used 172 times. Its usage was 84 times in 2016 JRP, 46 times in the JRP 2018–20, and 42 times at the JRP 2020–22.

Text mining illustrates that JRPs use the concept of resilience in both broad and narrow sense. The meanings can be grouped into at least four categories. 1) resilience as a framework/perspective/lens that shapes all interventions in refugee response, 2) resilience as a synonymy of development or justification of development aid demands, 3) resilience as the desired feature of the entire system, its components, and sectors, and 4) resilience as need and 'desired trait' of refugee individuals and hosting communities.

The first broad meaning attributed to resilience is treating it as framework, perspective, and a lens. JRPs consistently note that response has two pillars: Refugee/Humanitarian and Resilience pillars. For example, JRPs make calls to stakeholders to address the Syria crisis's impact from humanitarian and resilience perspectives. JRPs suggest 'assessing all interventions using a resilience lens' (JRP 2020–22, 14).

Resilience is often used as a synonym for development objectives. The resilience-based comprehensive framework seems helpful in bridging 'the divide between short-term refugee response and long-term development goals because humanitarian response cannot be dealt apart from resilience response' (JRP 2020–22, 3). Starting resilience with humanitarian and development programming under a common nationally-led and resilience-based framework is important for 'safeguarding human development and fostering resilience to future shocks' (JRP 2016–18, 3). Moreover, resilience terminology seems to legitimize why Jordan needs more development support. Adopting the terminology of resilience, demands for budget support are asked sensibly. In this way, Jordan commits to harmonizing short-term refugee and longer-term developmental responses within a 'resilience-based comprehensive framework'. In other words, it creates 'a nationally led resilience framework that integrates humanitarian and development support'. In one way, resilience is used to replace development and reflect a desire to continue development objectives in the case of a protracted refugee situation. In another way, by adopting resilience, Jordan also commits to meeting international standards by noting that a resilience approach would 'enhance transparency' and make the system 'cost-effective and transparent' (JRP 2020–22, 15).

Resilience is also set as a goal to penetrate the system as a whole and its various components. JRPs seek to ensure the resilience of Jordan, host communities and national institutions by highlighting 'Jordan's resilience' and the 'resilience of [its] national systems and institutions'. It aims to develop resilience and strengthen systems in Jordan. Regarding the system components, JRPs underlined that each sector – health, education, and sanitary – is crucial for the resilience of national systems and institutions. JRPs advocate that the resilience pillar should be consistently incorporated across all sectors as a medium- to long-term approach. Notably, there is a need to foster the resilience of infrastructure and effectiveness of Jordan's service delivery in the areas where many refugees and vulnerable host Jordanian communities live.

Resilience is adopted to single out the needs of each sector. JRP 2018–2020 informed that "twelve-combined refugee and resilience sector response plans" are prepared to support their resilience refugees and vulnerable Jordanians and contribute to Jordan's broader economic development strategies. Among sectors, health is found the most critical sector that needs resilience. It is underlined that there is an 'urgent need for humanitarian partners and donors to support the resilience of the Ministry of Health through the construction new infrastructure and the maintenance'. (JRP 2020–22, 32). The second highlighted sector is water infrastructure and its overall water governance system. For the resilience of the education sector, the emphasis is on 'ensure the adaptability and quality of its education system' (JRP 2020–22, 25). Besides sectors, governance levels such as local are put under the resilience umbrella. There are frequent references to enhancing 'resilience capacities for several municipalities' or 'resilience of local governance systems' to cope with the Syria crisis. In general, the response aims at strengthening the resilience of fragile ecosystems and communities (JRP 2016–18, 28; JRP 2018–2020, 63; JRP 2020–22, 26)

Resilience is also seen as a need and 'desired trait' of refugee individuals and hosting communities. The plans aim to meet 'the humanitarian and resilience needs of Syrian refugees and vulnerable Jordanians impacted by Syria crisis' (JRP 2020–22, 12). They set the goal of fostering "the resilience of Syrian refugees and host communities." (JRP 2020–22, 1). Ideally, a coordinated approach meeting both the resilience and humanitarian needs of those in need would 'decrease resorting to negative coping strategies' (JRP 2016–18, 84). Resilience is not only aimed at meeting today's needs, but to cope with 'future shocks' (JRP 2016–18, 3). In this regard, resilience is potentially valuable for enhancing social cohesion and community engagement. It is pointed out that there is a need to 'support efforts to strengthen refugee and host community resilience, social cohesion and peaceful coexistence and focus on the needs' (JRP 2020–22, 52).

Resilience ideally balances a claim on national ownership on refugee plans and aligns with the international humanitarian sector's expectations and standards that fund interventions in Jordan. Frequently, Jordan underlines that it 'serves as a leading model in responding to the crisis through its unwavering support and generosity by hosting 1.36 million Syrian refugees and meeting their humanitarian and resilience needs' (JRP 2020–22, 1). JRP is presented as 'a genuine model of a strong, longstanding partnership between the host country and the international community' (Ibid.). Although the national government acknowledges that there has been generous support of the humanitarian and resilience pillars of the JRP in the recent years, this is because Jordan carries out 'a global public good, in addition to pioneering resilience-based approaches with the development of the Jordan Response Plan' (JRP 2020–22, 7).

Conclusion

There is no doubt that systems' complexity and global interconnectivity made actors vulnerable to 'extreme events such as mass migration flows and protracted refugee situations' as the Syrian case has demonstrated since 2011. International, regional and national refugee governance systems need to develop ways to swiftly respond to such events by maximizing their capacity, coordination and endurance. The ability of resilience seems critical to do this. Besides being a system trait, resilience is a highly favorable concept for humanitarianism's scholarly and practical world, including interventions addressing refugee situations. Resilience terminology is adopted in different regional and national responses. It emerges as a multivalent conceptual tool for both development and empowerment at a macro system level on the one hand, local, community and individual level on the other.

This chapter has shown that Jordan has also adopted resilience terminology in response to Syrians' mass refugee migration at multiple scales (macro, meso, micro). Resilience as a tool is used as tool at macro scale, as exemplified in the Jordanian long-term refugee policy plans have adopted the vocabulary on resilience. The programs take resilience as a pillar of refugee governance with humanitarian assistance, substituting development objectives. At the meso level, reliance has been unduly emphasized for strengthening the capacity of several sectors such as health, education, and municipality services at local levels. Resilience is also associated with the needs of refugees and host communities. Advocates propose the cultivation of this desired trait at the micro level to ensure refugee self-reliance in the long run. The resilience approach seeks to balance the needs of vulnerable Jordanians, Jordanian host communities and infrastructure. Overall, resilience is approached as an intended characteristic of several system components: Jordanian national authorities, local organizations and individuals.

Jordan's approach to resilience is not only discursive, but also a frame of action. It has multiple objectives: to enhance refugees and host communities' self-reliance, strengthen Jordanian local authorities' capacity to serve them, and negotiate better with international donors by adopting their favorable vocabulary. First, by overemphasizing resilience, Jordanian authorities can claim more national ownership in the refugee governance. This ownership claim has not contradicted the regional and global humanitarian policies, but instead reflects their discursive shift towards long-term self-reliance and resilience agenda is appropriate. As a rentier refugee state, Jordan has employed resilience terminology to legitimize further its aid demands targeting donors and implementers, mainly EU and UN agencies. It has used this rhetoric and pursued this agenda with great sophistication by presenting statistically supported evidence concerning the costs of hosting refugees. It has employed donors' own rhetoric, centered on a resilience approach, including transparency, cost-effectiveness, crisis prevention, and vulnerability assessment in its presentation. In these ways, the resilience discourse has allowed Jordan to employ a moderate, diplomatic, and global humanitarianism vocabulary in negotiating refugee hosting.

On the one hand, this course has shifted responsibility to international donors by asking those actors to support refugee resilience. On the other hand, this approach begs the question of refugee capacity to cope and prove self-reliant as the conception assumes. There is, therefore, still a need for more research to understand more fully how Jordanian policymakers are implementing this policy.

References

3RP 2020. Regional Refugee and Resilience Plan. http://www.3rpsyriacrisis. org/

Achilli, Luigi. 2015. Syrian Refugees in Jordan: A Reality Check, Migration Policy Centre, Policy Briefs, no. 2. https://cadmus.eui.eu/handle/1814/34904

Alameddine, Mohamad, Fouad M. Fouad, Karin Diaconu, Zeina Jamal, Graham Lough, Sophie Witter, and Alastair Ager. 2019. Resilience Capacities of Health Systems, *Social Science & Medicine*, 220: 22–30.

AlMakhamreh Sahar Suleiman, and Aisha Jane Hutchinson. 2018. Unaccompanied and Separated Syrian Refugee Children. *Refugee Survey Quarterly* 37, no. 3: 353–377, https://doi.org/10.1093/rsq/hdy0009.

Alrababa'h, Ala', Andrea Dillon, Scott Williamson, Jens Hainmueller, Dominik Hangartner, and Jeremy Weinstein. 2021. Attitudes toward migrants in a highly impacted economy: evidence from the Syrian refugee crisis in Jordan. *Comparative Political Studies*, 54, no. 1: 33–76.

Alshoubaki Wa'ed. 2020. The Dynamics of Population Pressure in Jordan In Juline Beaujouan, and Amjed Rasheed (eds.), *Syrian Crisis, Syrian Refugees: Voices from Syria and Lebanon.* Mobility & Politics series, Palgrave Pivot Cham. https://doi.org/10.1007/978-3-030-35016-1_3.

Anholt, Rosanne. 2020. Resilience in Practice: Responding to the Refugee Crisis in Turkey, Jordan, and Lebanon. *Politics and Governance* 8, no. 4 (2020): 294–305.

Anholt, Rosanne and Giulia Sinatti. 2020. Under the Guise of Resilience: The EU Approach to Migration and Forced Displacement in Jordan and Lebanon. *Contemporary Security Policy* 41, no. 2 (2020): 320–321.

Anholt, Rosanne and Wolfgang Wagner. 2020. Resilience in the European Union External Action. In Cusumano Eugenio and Stefan Hofmaier, *Projecting Resilience Across the Mediterranean,* Cham: Palgrave Macmillan. https://doi.org/10.1007/978-3-030-23641-0_2

Arnetz, Judith, Yoasif Rofa, Bengt Arnetz, Matthew Ventimiglia, and Hikmet Jamil. 2013. Resilience as a protective factor against the development of psychopathology among refugees. *The Journal of Nervous and Mental Disease* 201, no. 3:167–172.

Bourbeau, Philippe. 2013. Resiliencism: Premises and promises in securitization research. *Resilience* 1, no. 1 (2013): 3–17.

Brassett, James, and Nick Vaughan-Williams. 2015. Security and the Performative Politics of Resilience. *Security Dialogue* 46, no. 1: 32–50.

Chatty, Dawn. 2016. The Syrian Humanitarian Disaster. *IDS Bulletin*, 47, no. 3: 19–35.

Chinnery, Julie. 2019. Jordan: Education Policy in Transition. *Forced Migration Review,* 60 (2019): 19–21.

Comfort, Louise K., Arjen Boin and Chris C. Demchak. 2010. *Designing Resilience: Preparing for Extreme Events.* Pittsburgh: University of Pittsburgh Press.

Cork, Steven (ed). 2010. *Resilience and transformation: preparing Australia for uncertain futures.* Csiro Publishing.

Council of European Union. 2020 Brussels IV 2020. Brussels IV Conference on 'Supporting the future of Syria and the region': co-chairs' declaration. https://www.consilium.europa.eu/en/press/press-releases/2020/06/30/brussels-iv-conference-on-supporting-the-future-of-syria-and-the-region-co-chairs-declaration/#

de Goede, Marieke. 2007. Underground money. *Cultural Critique* 65, no. 1: 140–163.

Diogini, Filippo. 2016. The Syrian Refugee Crisis in Lebanon State Fragility and Social Resilience, *LSE Middle East Centre Paper Series,* no. 15.

Doocy, Shannon, Emily Lyles, Laila Akhu-Zaheya, Ann Burton, and Gilbert Burnham. 2016. Health service access and utilization among Syrian refugees in Jordan. International Journal for Equity in Health 15, no. 1: 1–15. https://doi.org/10.1186/s12939-016-0399-4.

Doron, Esther. Working with Lebanese refugees in a community resilience model. 2005. *Community Development Journal* 40, no. 2: 182–191. https://doi.org/10.1093/cdj/bsi026

Elbe, Stefan 2008. Risking lives: AIDS, security and three concepts of risk. *Security Dialogue* 39, no. 2–3: 177–198.

European Commission (EC). 2016. *EU – Jordan Partnership the Compact.* https://ec.europa.eu/neighbourhood-enlargement/sites/near/files/jordan-compact.pdf

Fairclough, Norman. 2003. *Analyzing Discourse: Textual Analysis for Social Research.* London: Routledge.

Fairclough, Norman. 2005. Discourse Analysis in Organization Studies, *Organization Studies 26,* no. 6: 915–939. https://doi.org/10.1177/0170840605054610

Fitzpatrick, Tal. 2016. Community Disaster Resilience. In Bruce Clements and Julie Casani, *Disasters and Public Health (Second Edition),* 57–85. Butterworth-Heinemann.

Gaillard, Jean Christophe. 2010. Vulnerability, capacity and resilience: Perspectives for climate and development policy. *Journal of International Development* 22, no. 2: 218–232.

Gonzalez, Gustavo. 2016. New aid architecture and resilience building around the Syria crisis. *Forced Migration Review,* 52: 26–28.

Holling, Crawford S. 1973. Resilience and stability of ecological systems. *Annual Review of Ecology and Systematics* 4: 1–23.

Ilcan, Suzan and Kim Rygiel. 2015. Resiliency Humanitarianism, *International Political Sociology,* 9: 333–351

JRP 2015. *Jordan Response Plan 2015.* https://reliefweb.int/report/jordan/jordan-response-plan-2015-syria-crisis-march-2015-enar

JRP 2016–18. 2015. *Ministry of Planning and International Cooperation.* Jordan Response Plan for the Syria Crisis 2016–2018. https://static1.squarespace.com/static/522c2552e4b0d3c39ccd1e00/t/56b9abe107eaa0afdcb35f02/1455008783181/JRP%2B2016-2018%2BFull%2B160209.pdf

JRP 2017–19. 2016. *Jordan Response Plan for the Syria Crisis 2017–2019.* Ministry of Planning and International Cooperation. https://static1.squarespace.com/static/522c2552e4b0d3c39ccd1e00/t/5956897e78d1714f5b61f5c2/1498843547605/JRP+2017-2019+-+Full+-+%28June+30%29.pdf

JRP 2018–20. 2017. *Jordan Response Plan for the Syria Crisis 2018–2020,* Ministry of Planning and International Cooperation.

JRP 2020–22, *Jordan Response Plan for the Syria Crisis 2020–2022* https://reliefweb.int/report/jordan/jordan-response-plan-syria-crisis-2020-2022

Joseph, Jonathan. 2013. Resilience in UK and French Security Strategy *Politics* 33, no. 4: 253–264. https://doi.org/10.1111/1467-9256.12010

Kaufmann, Mareile. 2013. Emergent self-organization in emergencies: Resilience rationales in interconnected societies. *Resilience* 1, no. 1: 53–68. https://doi.org/10.1080/21693293.2013.765742

Kelberer, Victoria. 2017. Negotiating crisis: International aid and refugee policy in Jordan. *Middle East Policy* 24, 4: 148–165. https://doi.org/10.1111/mepo.12313

King Abdullah II. 2018a. Remarks by His Majesty King Abdullah II, During the government lunch hosted by the Dutch Prime Minister, The Netherlands, The Hague, 21 March 2018.

https://kingabdullah.jo/en/speeches/during-government-lunch-hosted-dutch-prime-minister

King Abdullah. II. 2018b, Plenary Session 73rd 'Remarks' 15 September 15 2018, https://kingabdullah.jo/en/speeches/plenary-session-73rd-general-assembly-united-nations

King Abdullah. 2019. Remarks by His Majesty King Abdullah II, Opening the World Economic Forum on the Middle East and North Africa, Jordan Dead Sea, 6 April 2019. https://kingabdullah.jo/en/speeches/opening-world-economic-forum-middle-east-and-north-africa-0

Klein, Richard J. T., Robert J. Nicholls, and Frank Thomalla. 2003. Resilience to natural hazards: How useful is this concept? *Global Environmental Change Part B: Environmental Hazards* 5, no. 1: 35–45, DOI: 10.1016/j.hazards.2004.02.001

Krause, Ulrike and Hannah Schmidt. 2020. Refugees as Actors? Critical Reflections on Global Refugee Policies on Self-reliance and Resilience, *Journal of Refugee Studies* 33, no. 1: 22–41.

Kvittingen, Anna, Marko Valenta, Hanan Tabbara, Dina Baslan, and Berit Berg. 2019. The conditions and migratory aspirations of Syrian and Iraqi refugees in Jordan. *Journal of Refugee Studies*, 32, no.1: 106–124.

Nasser, Razan and Steven Symansky. 2014. *The Fiscal Impact of the Refugee Crisis on Jordan*. Washington, DC: The United States Agency for International Development. https://jordankmportal.com/resources/the-fiscal-impact-of-the-syrian-refugee-crisis-on-jordan-2014

Lenner, Katherina, and Lewis Turner. 2021. Governing Displacement in the Middle East: From Vulnerability to Resilience? *Resilience and Inclusive Politics in the MENA Region* On-Line Commentary No. 3, March.

Lentzos, Filippa and Nikolas Rose. 2009. Governing insecurity: Contingency planning, protection, resilience. *Economy and Society, 38, no.* 2: 230–254. https://doi.org/10.1080/03085140902786611

Longstaff, Patricia, H.2005. *Security, Resilience, and Communication in Unpredictable Environments*. Center for Information Policy Research, Harvard University.

Lundborg, Tom and Nick Vaughan-Williams. 2011. Resilience, Critical Infrastructure, and Molecular Security: The Excess of 'Life' in Biopolitics. *International Political Sociology*, 5, no. 4 (2011): 367–383. https://doi.org/10.1111/j.1749-5687.2011.00140.x

Manyena, Siambabala Bernard. 2006. The Concept of Resilience Revisited. *Disasters* 30, no. 4: 434–450. https://doi.org/10.1111/j.0361-396 3666.2006.00331.x

Mencutek, Zeynep Sahin. 2018. *Refugee Governance, State and Politics in the Middle East*. New York, London. Routledge.

Methmann, Chris. 2014. Visualizing Climate-Refugees: Race, Vulnerability, and Resilience in Global Liberal Politics. *International Political Sociology* 8, no. 4: 416–435. https://doi.org/10.1111/ips.12071

Methmann, Chris, and Angela Oels. 2015. From 'Fearing' to 'empowering' Climate Refugees. *Security Dialogue* 46, no. 1: 51–68.

Ministry of Labor. 2020. Ministry of Labor Syrian Refugee Unit -Monthly Progress Report, 2020. https://reliefweb.int/sites/reliefweb.int/files/resources/73881.pdf

Montgomery, Edith. 2010. Trauma and resilience in young refugees: A 9-year follow-up study. *Development and Psychopathology* 22, no. 2: 477–489.

Norris, Fran H., Susan P. Stevens, Betty Pfefferbaum, Karen F. Wyche, and Rose L. Pfefferbaum. 2008. Community resilience as a metaphor, theory, set of capacities, and strategy for disaster readiness. *American Journal of Community Psychology* 41, no. 1–2: 127–150.

OCHR. 2020. Independent International Commission of Inquiry on the Syrian Arab Republic, February, 2020 https://www.ohchr.org/EN/HRBodies/HRC/IICISyria/Pages/AboutCoI.aspx.

RRP 2014. 2014 Syria Regional Response Plan, UNHCR. Available at http://www.unhcr.org/syriarrp6

RRRP 2015. *Regional refugee & resilience plan 2015–2016 in response to the Syria crisis: Regional strategic overview. Geneva and New York, NY: UNHCR and UNDP.* https://reliefweb.int/sites/reliefweb. int/files/resources/3RP-Report-Overview.pdf

Sahin-Mencutek, Zeynep, and Ayat J.J. Nashwan. 2020a. Employment of Syrian refugees in Jordan. *Journal of Ethnic & Cultural Diversity in Social Work*, 1-23.

Sahin-Mencutek, Zeynep, and Ayat J.J. Nashwan. 2020b. Perceptions About the Labor Market Integration of Refugees. *Journal of International Migration & Integration 1-19*.

Schimmel, V. 2015. UNHCR cash programming in emergencies–implementation and coordination experience during the Syrian refugee response in Jordan. *Field Exchange 48*, 76.

Schweitzer, Robert, Jaimi Greenslade, and Ashraf Kagee. 2007. Coping and resilience in refugees from the Sudan. *Australian & New Zealand Journal of Psychiatry*, *41*, no. 3 (2007): 282–288.

Scott-Smith, Tom. 2018. Paradoxes of resilience: A review of the World Disasters Report 2016. *Development and Change*, 49, no. 2.

Sert, Deniz Ş. 2016. From Skill Translation to Devaluation: The De-qualification of Migrants in Turkey. *New Perspectives on Turkey* 54: 97–117.

Tahrir Instutite for Middle East Policy. 2020. https://timep.org/explainers/part-1-syrians-in-neighboring-host-countries/

Tsourapas, Gerasimos. 2019. The Syrian refugee crisis and foreign policy decision-making in Jordan, Lebanon, and Turkey. *Journal of Global Security Studies* 4, no. 1: 464–481. https://doi.org/10.1093/jogss/ogz016

UN (United Nations). 2018 *The Comprehensive Protection and Solutions Strategy: Protection Thresholds and Parameters for Refugee Return to Syria*. https://data2.unhcr.org/en/documents/download/63223

UN. 2020. *Report of the Independent International Commission of Inquiry on the Syrian Arab Republic. Human Rights Council Forty-fifth session 14 September–2 October 2020.* Accessed 8 February 2021 https://undocs.org/A/HRC/45/31

UNDP 2015. Launch of the Jordan Resilience Fund, 28 March. https://reliefweb.int/report/jordan/launch-jordan-resilience-fund

UNHCR 2019. Jordan Fact Sheet, June 2019. https://reliefweb.int/report/jordan/unhcr-jordan-factsheet-june-2019.

UNRWA 2020. Where we work. https://www.unrwa.org/where-we-work/jordan

Walker, Jeremy, and Melinda Cooper. 2011. Genealogies of resilience: From systems ecology to the political economy of crisis adaptation. *Security Dialogue* 42, no. 2: 143–160.

Weichselgartner, Juergen, and Ilan Kelman. 2014. "Geographies of resilience: Challenges and opportunities of a descriptive 418 concept." *Progress in Human Geography,* 39, no. 3: 249–267. https://doi.org/10.1177/0309132513518834

World Bank. 2020. *Compounding Misfortunes. Changes in Poverty since the onset of Covid-19 on Syrian Refugees and Host Communities in Jordan, the Kurdistan Region of Iraq and Lebanon.* http://documents1.worldbank.org/curated/en/878321608148278305/pdf/Compounding-Misfortunes-Changes-in-Poverty-Since-the-Onset-of-COVID-19.pdf

6

The Syrian Refugee Crisis and the Lebanese Response

SUKAINA ALZYOUD, FATIMA ALZYOUD AND DANIA SHAHIN

Roughly 865,531 (194,331 households) Syrian refugees registered by the UN High Commissioner for Refugees (UNHCR) reside in Lebanon (UNHCR 2021). However, the Lebanese Government states that the country has the largest per capita population of Syrian refugees in the world estimating the number to be 1.5 million Syrian refugees. They are located in the north, center, and south regions of the country (UNHCR 2021). The refugees live in informal tent settlements or camps, deserted buildings, or cramped spaces either in community housing or the country's decades-old Palestinian camps (American Near East Refugee Aid 2021). This situation with the addition of the COVID-19 pandemic has put more burden on the country's already struggling economy, infrastructure and social systems (Abdallah 2020; American Near East Refugee Aid 2021).

According to the latest statistics Lebanon hosts 15.5 per cent of the total registered Syrian refugees in the MENA region (UNCHR 2021). This situation has created a need for Lebanon in all its components, 'governmental and non-governmental entities', to address and respond to the large influx of people and safety seekers. The official governmental response during the early stages of influx could be described as a response of no response. On the opposite side, several nongovernmental Organizations (NGOs) and international institutions took the lead in helping the Syrian refugees to fulfil their basic needs. As the situation developed and the conflict continued, forcing more people to flee, the responses of the Lebanese government and NGOs also changed. This chapter discusses the Lebanese response to the Syrian refugees' crisis from both governmental and non-governmental perspectives.

Lebanese Government Response

Lebanon has not signed the 1951Geneva convention and also does not have precise asylum laws (Lenner and Susanne 2016). Collaboration with the UNHCR has been based on a memorandum of understanding (MOU) (Lenner and Susanne 2016). There is a lack of an updated MOU regarding Syrian refugees in Lebanon, which means that the Lebanese government does not recognize UNHCR registration as a type of legal status (Janmyr 2016). Consequently, most Syrian refugees are unprotected legally and vulnerable to arrest as unauthorized immigrants (Janmyr 2016). In 2015, the Lebanese government directed UNHCR to temporarily suspend registration for both new guests and those already inside the country (Frangieh 2015). This led refugees to leave Lebanon (Lenner and Susanne 2016).

The Lebanese government was non-functional with weak state establishments; therefore, UNHCR has led the crisis response (Janmyr 2016). In 2014 the Lebanese administration issued new visa and residence regulations to replace its open-door policy and reassert itself (Frangieh 2015). The new laws made entry into Lebanon and the renewal of residence permissions extremely difficult (Frangieh 2015). Consequently, about half or more of the displaced Syrians in Lebanon are now considered to be without valid status documents (Frangieh 2015). This precarity greatly raises the vulnerability of refugees in Lebanon and blocks access to healthcare, education, and other services and limits mobility inside the country (Lenner and Susanne 2016).

Lebanon does not have official camps for Syrian refugees; nonetheless, new laws have strongly curtailed mobility in the country over the years (Lenner and Susanne 2016). The Lebanese government mostly gave the humanitarian response to various local and international organizations (Janmyr 2016). Due to security concerns, the government maintained a firm stance against building formal refugee camps for Syrians (Atallah and Mahdi 2017). The non-camp policy is also connected to demands for a readily available Syrian workforce (Lenner and Susanne 2016).

This disorganized management has led Syrians to mobilize their long-standing social relationships and work connections inside Lebanon (Lenner and Susanne 2016). Syrians live across the nation, mainly in the Bekaa Valley, the west/central region, and north Lebanon (Reliefweb 2017). Living conditions vary broadly, while some refugees live in informal tented settlements, others live in ruins, building shells and garages, and more than half rent an apartment or house. This flexibility of settlement and movement has become more limited. In 2014, a few cities imposed curfews, and during

2015–2016, numerous individuals lost their legal status documents and mobility (Frangieh 2015; Lenner and Susanne 2016); As a result, many now stay inside their living area, fearing being stopped at a checkpoint (Lenner and Susanne 2016).

The Lebanese healthcare system is largely private, and that fact has had a great impact on the Syrian refugee crisis (Parkinson and Behrouzan 2015). Private facilities as the American University Hospital provide excellent care; nevertheless, those facilities are accessible only with good insurance or extensive financial means (Parkinson and Behrouzan 2015). The Lebanese government has played a minimal role in building and managing healthcare (Batniji et al. 2014). Diverse providers control the health system, most of them connected to political parties who usually favor their supporters in health and social assistance (Batniji et al. 2014; Parkinson and Behrouzan 2015).

The Ministry of Public Health (MoPH), with the support of the World Health Organization (WHO) and the UNHCR, made a partnership with international and national NGOs to increase the accessibility of basic primary health care services (Blanchet, Fouad, and Pherali 2016; Truppa et al. 2019). Syrians registered with the UNHCR are given healthcare insurance; insurance covers 75 per cent of costs, and Syrians pay 25 per cent. Payment for the unsubsidized portion of care has imposed an additional burden on Syrians. While some poor refugees received financial aid from Islamic associations, others have gone into debt (Atallah and Mahdi 2013). Those who cannot pay have had their legal papers confiscated by hospitals, exposing them to detainment and deportation by Lebanese authorities (Parkinson & Behrouzan, 2015; Truppa et al. 2019). Syrian refugees have entered a fragmented, complex, and uncoordinated healthcare system that was already strained in Lebanon and has been put under additional pressure because of the abrupt influx of Syrian refugees (Blanchet et al. 2016). The system is informally discriminatory against non-citizens and many Lebanese citizens with limited financial resources (Blanchet et al. 2016; Parkinson & Behrouzan 2015). Therefore, Syrian refugees living in the North, the Bekaa Valley, Mount Lebanon, Beirut, and the South reportedly had trouble accessing healthcare (International Rescue Committee and Norwegian Refugee Council 2015).

In Lebanon, Syrian refugees encounter obstacles in accessing formal work opportunities and education (Lenner and Susanne 2016). The pledge for UNHCR-registered refugees work prohibition has led to full reliance on aid assistance. Limited access to formal work opportunities puts refugees at risk of being blocked from obtaining jobs or pushed towards informal and exploitative labor (Janmyr 2016). The Norwegian Refugee Council (NRC) field assessment (2014) proved that restricted legal status for Syrian refugees doubles the risk of abuse and exploitation, also diminishes their ability to seek redress and access justice (NRC 2014). Syrian nationals are exposed to the same risks in the sponsorship system, which builds upon Lebanon's sponsorship system for other migrants (Janmyr 2016). Under sponsorship, Syrian refugees can be subjected to state-sanctioned exploitation (Janmyr 2016). The sponsorship system was created to provide a legal relationship between employer and employee; however, this system has not improved legal or social security for Syrian employees (Lenner and Susanne 2016; Janmyr 2016). The sponsorship system has increased reliance on the employer, creating harsh work conditions due to fear of expulsion and deportation (Janmyr 2016; Lenner and Susanne 2016).

The Lebanese Ministry of Education and Higher Education (MEHE) is the only entity in charge of managing education in Lebanon and prohibits any handling or opening of schools by other entities, even NGOs. The MEHE facilitated the access of Syrian refugees into the schools by mandating Syrian students to be enrolled irrespective of their legal status. Moreover, it mandated the waiving of school fees (Reliefweb 2013). The Ministry also introduced second shift classes to public schools for refugee students (Charles and Denman 2013). However, access to formal education came with many challenges for these refugees, including transport costs, bullying, verbal and physical abuse, and adapting to the language of instruction (Charles and Denman 2013; Mahfouz et al. 2020). These challenges, caused many of the Syrian refugees' students to drop out of school (El-Ghali, Ghalayini, and Ismail 2016; Mahfouz et al. 2020). With all its efforts the MEHE schools and the education system was not able to accommodate the large numbers of refugees due to cost burden and lack of capacity (Reliefweb 2013; Mahfouz et al. 2020).

Nongovernmental Organizations' Response

As the Syrian refugee crisis gained momentum in Lebanon over the years, several NGOs and international institutions took the lead in helping Syrian refugees to address their basic needs. This section presents how NGOs and international entities responded to this crisis.

The complexity of the donors and sources of funding makes it hard to get a clear picture of the actual number of donors and total donations that has come to Lebanon related to the Syrian refugees' crisis. In the early phases of the Syrian refugee crisis, the Lebanese government authorized the UNHCR to take charge of the response (Anholt 2020).

One of the areas that donors worked on is to reduce the tension between the Syrian refugees and the host communities in Lebanon and assist local communities. For example, the UN-Development Program (UNDP) implemented a project called 'Support to Integrated Service Provision at the Local Level' (known as 4M) with the help of the European Decentralized Cooperation, to address issues in the health, social, and educational sectors. The project also supported the development of regional health services and plans with the aim of improving vulnerable local communities' access to excellent primary health care (Ministry of Public Health 2015). O'Driscoll (2018) reported on donors' response to the refugee crisis. According to that report the UNHCR has introduced a variety of community support initiatives in regions with high poverty and refugee populations, including new wells, community centers with water, sewage, and waste management systems, and enhanced medical facilities. Another form of the response funded by the EU is supporting a number of initiatives, attempting to enhance waste collection, water distribution, public health delivery, and community services, which have helped to reduce tensions between host and refugee populations to some extent. In addition, the Department for International Development funds were used by humanitarian organizations to support both refugees and Lebanese by implementing initiatives that include vaccination and food for livestock, work schemes for Lebanese and refugees, water and sewage infrastructure, repair, and school upgrades (O'Driscoll 2018).

The NGO response covered multiple areas including health care, education, food security, housing, and employment. The response for health care took many shapes and activities. The majority were to sport local communities and addition to the refugees. HelpAge International (HAI); AMEL Association International, Medical Teams International, and the Center for Public Health Practice at the American University of Beirut (AUB) implemented a program to improve primary healthcare services that are introduced for both Syrian refugees and Lebanese local host communities. This program targeted patients with Diabetes Miletus (DM) and Hypertension (HTN) for individuals older than 40 years. The interventions were carried out at six of AMEL's healthcare facilities: three Primary Health Centers and three Mobile Medical Units – situated in deprived areas in Lebanon: North Bekaa, West Bekaa, and Beirut suburbs. The interventions were divided into three components: 1) logistics and technical support Centers, which included supplying the facilities with essential technologies and tools such as blood pressure devices, glucometers, stethoscopes, weight/height scales, blood glucose test strips for managing and screening HTN and DM; 2) human resource development and the promotion of good practice through training the medical and pharmaceutical staff on HTN and DM management; and 3) improving patient knowledge by on-site patient educational and awareness-raising events.

In 2013, a Médecins Sans Frontières clinic was established as a nongovernmental primary healthcare center at *Shatila* Refugee Camp, south of the capital Beirut. It provided care for refugee patients and vulnerable host communities who suffer from non-communicable diseases such as DM, HTN and other cardiovascular diseases. Although this center allowed both host community and refugee patients to benefit from its program, this descriptive cohort study showed that from 3,500 patients who visited the center at the end of 2017, 76 per cent of them were Syrian refugees and they were not only from the catchment area of Shatila, but they came also from other different areas (Kayali et al. 2019). The other major organization contributing to the health care response was the UNHCR. The agency primarily covered the costs of entering primary health care centers in Lebanon for registered Syrian refugees. However, the UNHCR has criteria of eligibility for health care coverage with a payment scale of $1,500 (Akik et al. 2019).

The NGOs response to other areas was provided in the form of cash assistance which covered education, food security, housing, and employment. The cash assistance program consisted of providing Syrian refugees with financial aid in the form of monthly multi-purpose cash assistance with unconditional cash transfers. This package provided each refugee with $27 per person to cover food needs and $173.50 per household to meet other basic needs, for an average of $332 per household per month (Bastagli et al. 2021).

The NGO sector considered a main source of support for the Lebanese government and public to handle the Syrian refugee crisis impact on the Lebanese Education System. The involvement of the NGOs in education assistance included offering alternative classes to school aged students within the public schools, fast-tracked learning curricula to facilitate refugee students' integration in the Lebanese system, and basic literacy and proficiency for children who have never been to school (El-Ghali, Ghalayini, and Ismail 2016). Another method NGOs followed to aid is opening schools for the Syrian refugees, but those often had to risk operating without accreditation and certification by the Ministry of Education and Higher Education which prohibited such activities as it is the only authority in charge of managing education in Lebanon (El-Ghali, Ghalayini, and Ismail 2016). Moreover, help to cover their fees and transportation costs was provided by the UNHCR and other NGOs (UNHCR 2013).

Food security is another sector in which NGOs have aided and responded to refugees' needs. This aid and response came in the shape of providing a monthly food card or multipurpose cash card by the World Food Bank and other international agencies (Medina 2020; Bastagli et al. 2021), food items and care-packages by individuals and private donors (Medina 2020). Over the years of the refugee crisis and the COVID-19 pandemic burden hit them hard and high percentage of them survive on less than $2.90 per day (Medina

2020). According to the Country Director of the UN World Food Program (WFP) the hardship of the pandemic that was added to the collapsed Lebanese economy has pushed many refugees to adopt coping strategies like reducing health expenses, borrowing money from acquaintances and relatives living abroad, or withdrawing children from school. In the words of the WFT Director, 'If they had been eating meat twice per month, now they would not eat meat even once and they skip meals'. The WFP also reported plans to deliver in-kind food parcels to the families of school students who were included in the WFP school snack program (Medina 2020).

In terms of the NGOs' response to the refugee employment, at the early stages of Syrians residing in Lebanon they were allowed to work until early 2015 based on the 1993 Lebanese-Syrian bilateral agreement for Economic and Social Cooperation (Errighi and Griesse 2016). Starting in 2015, the Lebanese authorities suspended all Syrians' work rights under mounting social unrest and problems with public services provision. Since these changes Syrians who were displaced to Lebanon were required to sign a pledge not to work in the country (UNHCR 2015). This resulted in them only sustaining their livelihoods through humanitarian assistance provided by the Lebanese government and NGOs (UNHCR 2015). However, in some cases Syrian refugees were able to obtain sponsorship and a work permit, but their legal status was changed to 'migrant workers'. Nevertheless, they were employed without permit with less pay, facing harmful working conditions, and exploitation (Rescue 2016). Also, it was reported that they were able to work in three restricted sectors, construction, agriculture, and cleaning services, because of Lebanese nationals' labor shortage in these sectors as these occupations do not match the income expectations and skills of the Lebanese labor force (Rescue 2016). In a report by the International Labor Organization (ILO) (ILO 2020), the COVID-19 crisis has resulted in a high number of permanent and temporary job lay-offs in Lebanon, particularly among informal workers, which Syrian refugees made the majority. Additionally, 60 per cent of the Syrian refugees were permanently laid-off and 31 per cent were temporarily laid-off (ILO 2020).

In conclusion, the Lebanese response can be described as complex, strategic at times, unresponsive at other times, with total reliance on international agencies and donors. The response covered multiple sectors including health care, education, food security, housing, and employment. The economy and health care system were hard hit by the crisis. Moreover, the response appeared not to be strategically planned. It was also evident that the response appears to have been based on perceived short-term political imperatives, and the availability of donor funds.

References

Abdallah, I. 2020, 2/12/2020. Lebanese crisis deepens Syrian refugee misery. *Reuters*. Retrieved from https://www.reuters.com/article/us-lebanon-crisis-syrian-refugees-idUSKBN28D1SJ

American Near East Refugee Aid. 2021. Lebanon. Retrieved from https://www.anera.org/where-we-work/lebanon/

UN High Commissioner for Refugees, U. 2021. Situation Syria Regional Refugee Response. Retrieved from https://data2.unhcr.org/en/situations/syria/location/71. Retrieved 19/3/2021, from UNCHR https://data2.unhcr.org/en/situations/syria/location/71

Akik, Chaza, Hala Ghattas, Sandra Mesmar, Miriam Rabkin, Wafaa M. El-Sadr, and Fouad M. Fouad. 2019. Host country responses to non-communicable diseases amongst Syrian refugees: a review. *Conflict and Health* 13 (1): 8. https://doi.org/10.1186/s13031-019-0192-2. https://doi.org/10.1186/s13031-019-0192-2.

Anholt, Rosanne. 2020. Resilience in Practice: Responding to the Refugee Crisis in Turkey, Jordan, and Lebanon. *2020* 8 (4): 12. https://doi.org/10.17645/pag.v8i4.3090. https://www.cogitatiopress.com/politicsandgovernance/article/view/3090

Atallah, Sami, and Dima Mahdi. 2013. *Law and Politics of 'Safe Zones' and Forced Return to Syria: Refugee Politics in Lebanon.* Lebanese Center for Studies and Research. https://www.lcps-lebanon.org/publications/1515749841-lcps_report_-_online.pdf

Bastagli, Francesca, Fiona Samuels, Maria Stavropoulou, Nur Tukmani, Hiba Abbani, and Georgia Plank. 2021. *World Food Programme Multi-purpose Cash Assistance in Lebanon: Protection outcomes for Syrian refugees.* (reliefweb). https://reliefweb.int/report/lebanon/world-food-programme-multi-purpose-cash-assistance-lebanon-protection-outcomes-syrian

Batniji, Rajaie, Lina Khatib, Melani Cammett, Jeffrey Sweet, Sanjay Basu, Amaney Jamal, Paul Wise, and Rita Giacaman. 2014. Governance and health in the Arab world. *The Lancet* 383 (9914): 343–355. https://doi.org/https://doi.org/10.1016/S0140-6736(13)62185-6. https://www.sciencedirect.com/science/article/pii/S0140673613621856

Blanchet, K., F. M. Fouad, and T. Pherali. 2016. Syrian refugees in Lebanon: the search for universal health coverage. *Confl Health* 10: 12. https://doi.org/10.1186/s13031-016-0079-4.

Charles, Lorraine, and Kate Denman. 2013. Syrian and Palestinian Syrian Refugees in Lebanon: the Plight of Women and Children. *Journal of International Women's Studies* 14 (5): 96–111. https://vc.bridgew.edu/cgi/viewcontent.cgi?article=1729&context=jiws

El-Ghali, Hana A., Nadine Ghalayini, and Ghida Ismail. 2016. *Responding to crisis: Syrian refugee education in Lebanon* AUB Public Institute. https://www.aub.edu.lb/ifi/Documents/publications/policy_briefs/2015-2016/20160406_responding_to_crisis.pdf

Errighi, Lorenza, and Jörn Griesse. 2016. *The Syrian Refugee Crisis: Labour Market Implications in Jordan and Lebanon.* European Commission. https://ec.europa.eu/info/sites/info/files/dp029_en.pdf

Frangieh, Ghida. 2015. Lebanon Places Discriminatory Entry Restrictions on Syrians. *The Legal Agenda.* 22. http://english.legal-agenda.com/article.php?id=679&lang=en

ILO, International Labour Organization. 2020. *Impact of COVID-19 on Syrian refugees and host communities in Jordan and Lebanon.* https://www.ilo.org/wcmsp5/groups/public/---arabstates/---ro-beirut/documents/briefingnote/wcms_749356.pdf

International Rescue Committee and Norwegian Refugee Council, Rescue & NRCR. 2015. *Legal Status of Refugees from Syria: Challenges and Consequences of Maintaining Legal Stay in Beirut and Mount Lebanon.* http://www.nrc.no/arch/_img/9202281.pdf

Janmyr, Maja. 2016. Precarity in Exile: The Legal Status of Syrian Refugees in Lebanon. *Refugee Survey Quarterly* 35 (4): 58–78. https://doi.org/10.1093/rsq/hdw016. https://doi.org/10.1093/rsq/hdw016

Kayali, M., K. Moussally, C. Lakis, M. A. Abrash, C. Sawan, A. Reid, and J. Edwards. 2019. Treating Syrian refugees with diabetes and hypertension in Shatila refugee camp, Lebanon: Médecins Sans Frontières model of care and treatment outcomes. *Confl Health* 13: 12. https://doi.org/10.1186/s13031-019-0191-3.

Lenner, Katharina, and Schmelter Susanne. 2016. Syrian Refugees in Jordan and Lebanon: between refuge and ongoing deprivation? *EMed Mediterranean Yearbook 2016*: 122–126. http://www.iemed.org/observatori/arees-danalisi/arxius-adjunts/anuari/med.2016/IEMed_MedYearBook2016_Refugges%20Jordan%20Lebanon_Lenner_Schmelter.pdf

Mahfouz, Julia, Nizar El-Mehtar, Enja Osman, and Stephen Kotok. 2020. Challenges and agency: principals responding to the Syrian refugee crisis in Lebanese public schools. *International Journal of Leadership in Education* 23 (1): 24–40. https://doi.org/10.1080/13603124.2019.1613570.

Medina, Alicia. 2020. Syrian refugees strive to avoid the nightmare of food insecurity in Lebanon.

Ministry of Public Health. 2015. Support to Integrated Service Provision at the Local Level in Coordination with UNDP. Accessed 4 April. https://www.moph.gov.lb/en/Pages/6/783/support-to-integrated-service-provision-at-the-local-level-in-coordination-with-undp

NRC, Norwegian Refugee Council. 2014. *The Consequences of Limited Legal Status for Syrian Refugees in Lebanon.* https://www.nrc.no/resources/reports/the-consequences-of-limited-legal-status-for-syrian-refugees-inlebanon/

O'Driscoll, Dylan. 2018. *Donor response to refugee tensions in Lebanon.* University of Manchester. http://gsdrc.org/wp-content/uploads/2018/03/Donor_response_to_refugee_tensions_in_Lebanon.pdf

Parkinson, Sarah E., and Orkideh Behrouzan. 2015. Negotiating health and life: Syrian refugees and the politics of access in Lebanon. *Social Science & Medicine* 146: 324–331. https://doi.org/https://doi.org/10.1016/j.socscimed.2015.10.008. https://www.sciencedirect.com/science/article/pii/S0277953615301520

Reliefweb. 2013. Lebanon: RRP5 Update—August 2013 Education. https://reliefweb.int/report/lebanon/lebanon-rrp5-update-august-2013-education

Reliefweb. 2017. Lebanon: Inter-Agency Coordination January 2017 Statistical Dashboard. https://reliefweb.int/report/lebanon/lebanon-inter-agency-coordination-january-2017-statistical-dashboard

Rescue, International Rescue Committee. 2016. *Overview of Right to Work for Refugees Syria Crisis Response: Lebanon & Jordan.* rescue.org. https:// www.rescue.org/sites/default/files/document/987/policybrief2righttoworkforref ugees-syriacrisisresponsejanuary25.pdf

Truppa, Claudia, Enrica Leresche, Arlan F. Fuller, Ariana S. Marnicio, Josyann Abisaab, Nicole El Hayek, Carla Zmeter, Warda S. Toma, Hilda Harb, Randa S. Hamadeh, and Jennifer Leaning. 2019. Utilization of primary health care services among Syrian refugee and Lebanese women targeted by the ICRC program in Lebanon: a cross-sectional study. *Conflict and Health* 13 (1): 7. https://doi.org/10.1186/s13031-019-0190-4.

UNHCR. 2015. *Refugee Response in Lebanon: Briefing Documents.* https:// www.europarl.europa.eu/meetdocs/2014_2019/documents/droi/dv/95_ finalbriefingkit_/95_finalbriefingkit_en.pdf

UNHCR. 2021. *Syria Regional Refugee Response.* https://data2.unhcr.org/en/ situations/syria/location/71

UNHCR, United Nations High Commissioner for Refugees. 2013. *The future of Syria: Refugee children in crisis.* https://www.refworld.org/pdfid/529c3b4d4. pdf

7

Investigating Refugee Agency Amidst Widespread Popular, Political and Economic Discrimination and Alienation

MUDDATHER JAMEEL ABU. KARAKI, RENAD ABBADI
AND MAX O. STEPHENSON, JR.

Refugees of the now 11-year-long Syrian Civil War who fled to Jordan to escape that conflict today face a tortuously difficult dilemma: many Jordanian citizens increasingly perceive members of these groups as unwelcome interlopers who compete for limited resources and employment, rather than as innocents placed in peril by a conflict they did not create. Reflecting its population's growing concern, the government of Jordan has proved more unyielding in its policy stance that refugees must be prevented from competing with native citizens for positions and resources, leaving those individuals in a parlous economic state, with most of them unable officially to work. As it happens, that policy does not apply to migrant farmworkers, employment that many in Jordan do not otherwise wish to pursue. Accordingly, the Kingdom has been relatively open to allowing fleeing Syrians to work in such roles in agriculture. This fact was important to our study as we wished to interact with deeply vulnerable refugees, and our chosen population, migrant farmworkers, certainly met that criterion.

Meanwhile, and more broadly, many of the world's democratic nations, including the United States, Australia, France, Germany, and Great Britain, remain mired in a divisive nativist and nationalist politics of alterity that has exploited the fears and ignorance of a share those countries' populations for electoral gain, with those states now less likely vigorously to support international agreements concerning the human rights and protected status of refugees. This fact has produced a difficult political environment for those calling on those governments to respect the moral standing and human rights of those displaced by the Syrian conflict.

This scenario raised at least two abiding concerns for us, and we treat each briefly in this chapter. First, how do especially vulnerable Syrian refugees view their capacity to exercise their political agency in this circumstance, and secondly, what specific elements of the political and social environment now confronting them must change and how to allow either their repatriation or their permanent resettlement in Jordan or other nations? We explore these twin concerns by means of an analysis of personal semi-structured interviews with a sample of poor migrant laborer refugees in Jordan. We situate and interpret our interviews within Benhabib's and Arendt's conception of agency and analysis of how nationalism and 'othering' may limit the scope for its exercise. Overall, we were interested in exploring and describing the understanding of self-perceived political agency possessed by a group of particularly vulnerable Syrian Civil War refugees now residing in Jordan.

Situating Refugee Agency and this Study

The literature on refugees has burgeoned in recent years, as social turmoil and civil or international conflict has engulfed several nations, including Syria, Yemen, Myanmar, and the countries of the so-called Northern Triangle – Guatemala, Honduras, and El Salvador – in Central America. The brutal reality of social conflict has caused mass exodus from those countries and placed enormous stress on the United Nations (UN) and state institutions to respond. A backlash to this tide of humanity seeking refuge has arisen in many affected European nations, in Australia and in the United States, and a share of those countries' leaders have sought to stigmatize, scapegoat, and discriminate against members of these groups.

Jordan saw little of this sort of response until 2019–2020, when otherwise broadly sympathetic attitudes among some key government officials and many in the general public began to harden (The New Arab 2021). However, the Kingdom has accepted approximately 1.3 million Syrian refugees in recent years, a number that has deeply challenged the country's already thin social and economic capacity to respond and that is more than double the official total of those formally registered with the United Nations High Commissioner for Refugees (UNHCR). Roughly 80 per cent of this population lives in accommodations outside of UNHCR operated refugee camps and many agricultural workers, including those with whom we spoke, have received government-issued work permits allowing them to pursue employment. In this context, we thought it timely to examine how a particularly vulnerable subset of an already fragile population is now imagining its lived circumstances and prospects for moving forward in the harsh circumstances they confront.

Several authors have taken up this concern in refugee studies, although few more thoughtfully than Benhabib, who has searchingly developed ideas pressed by Arendt and others (Arendt 1979; Benhabib 2011, 2018). As political agency, our focus, is elemental to all democratic social change and certainly to that possibility in refugee lives, we employed Benhabib's conception of that construct to probe how our sample of individuals imagined their life prospects in such terms.

We interviewed a relatively small group of individuals (16, comprised of eight men and eight women) during a time in which their rights and agency were very much under threat to determine how they viewed their circumstances in such terms. We reckoned that those perceptions would be critical to their capacity to pursue and/or to cooperate with efforts to secure change in the status quo. We hoped our empirical inquiry would deepen our understanding of this critical valence in refugee studies and policy and politics in a mass migration scenario that has severely tested not only individual nations, but also the existing international refugee regime.

Benhabib has defined political agency as an expression of the communicative freedom of human beings (Benhabib 2018, 108). She has grounded her conception in Arendt's contention that individuals possess 'a right to have rights' because of the dignity that inheres in their humanity (Arendt 1979, 296–297). That norm and condition exceeds any specific national claim of rights, but also recognizes the paradox that such a possibility may yield unexpected results that constrain freedom, even as it may also enlarge the frame for the expression of such possibilities. In this sense, Arendt cautioned against the reality of freedom as an 'abyss under our feet' mediated by human will (Benhabib 2018, 107). As Benhabib has argued, the politics of human community in these terms may yield 'unexpected and contingent dimensions of the political' (Benhabib 2018, 107). One may not assume a simple linear causality that since innately humans possess rights and agency, it follows that when they exercise those perquisites the result will always protect or enlarge that freedom and agency. As Benhabib has noted in an analysis of Gündogu (2015) and Balibar's (2014) conception of Arendt's view on the premises of rights:

> Arendt, following Montesquieu, understands principle as animating spirit. What then is the principle that animates the call for a right to have rights?

> ... The context transcendent norms presupposed by speech acts raise validity claims [in which] the equality of speech partners and their equal freedom to say 'yes' or 'nay'—is counterfactually presupposed. Insofar as political authority is rationally justifiable and is not just based on force, coercion, violence, and deceit, we enact *equaliberty* counterfactually every time we address one another and seek to give reciprocal acceptable justifications (Benhabib 2018, 108).

This argument suggests in turn that:

> The principle of *equaliberty* animating the right to have rights [to possess and exercise agency] draws its force precisely from the fact that philosophy cannot deny *the other* the right to seek grounds as to why he or she is excluded from being recognized as a rights-bearing person. There are no such good reasons that would deny any human being the right to be an addressee of a validity claim that must eventually be addressed with reasons (Benhabib 2018, 109, emphasis in the original).

Importantly, this conception both provides the terrain, or metaphoric space, for human agency while also recognizing the difficulty of assuring the possibility for its exercise within the realities and vagaries of human disposition, nation-state sovereignty, and territoriality. In this sense, refugees face the ever-present possibility of witnessing an enervation of their right to have rights, 'of becoming *worldless*' and thereby seeing a share of their agency evanesce precisely because, as Benhabib has contended, following Arendt, 'they have no demonstrable, institutional, and interactional framework within which what they say and do can be recognized and responded to by others' (Benhabib 2018, 110). The refugees confronting this scenario do not lose their capacity for thought and opinion, but they may de facto exercise those faculties less and less meaningfully in the circumstances they confront.

Nonetheless, it is likewise clear that the right to have rights in this conception is contingent on all those engaged in dialogic interaction possessing that possibility, as its denial by one actor innately denies its possession to another. There is an in-principle paradox here, to be sure: Actions aimed at enervating the agency of others simultaneously degrade the rights of their purveyors, whether that fact is recognized by those discriminating against others or not. It is still the case, however, that such actions, especially when undertaken by a nominal majority, may damage or even hobble the capacities of those targeted and thereby limit their scope to imagine life's possibilities or to grasp the potential reach of their right to have rights. We were interested in exploring this dynamic among the refugees with whom we spoke.

Research Design and Methods

The lead author for this study has long maintained ties with a nongovernmental organization in Ma'an, Jordan, the Ma'an Orphanage Charitable Society, which has, in recent years, sought to provide support and succor to the various populations of refugees resident in its service area. For the past decade or so, that group has included migrant agricultural workers (farmers) who fled Syria to avoid persecution or death as that nation's civil war unfolded. Karaki worked with the Director of the Ma'an Orphanage Charitable Society to identify possible interviewees for this inquiry and to inform those individuals of the study team's interest in speaking with them to discuss their experiences as itinerant workers. Working together, the pair successfully approached a grower in the region who employs a substantial refugee workforce and gained his cooperation to allow the researchers to contact those in his employ to determine their willingness to participate in the study. Our sample arose from that contact.

We obtained Institutional Review Board approval for our study from Virginia Tech and Al-Hussein Bin Talal University and provided a recruitment flyer to Orphanage staff and the grower to share with potential interviewees. The study team also provided all individuals indicating possible interest in participation a consent form in Arabic. We imagined that each would sign the form and so it happened, but half of our interviewees did so only with an 'X' because they were illiterate, a fact that we had not previously predicted. Those individuals signed the form suggesting that they understood the character and risks and benefits of our effort after those were described to them orally before their interviews. We assured each participant that we would work to protect the confidentiality of their responses by assigning each a pseudonym and we have done so here by identifying individuals only with a number.

Karaki and Abbadi, of our study team, conducted the interviews in Arabic at the farm at which our interlocutors were working on 1 and 2 October 2019. This occurred at the request of the landowner/grower who, while willing to allow each individual time to participate in an interview, was unwilling also to have them take that time away from crop harvesting to travel to Ma'an for the purpose and return. Doing so would have likely meant each would miss a half-day of work and that was unacceptable to the farmer. Our team's Jordanian scholars served in this interviewing role, too, because of the fluency of each in the local language and the onset of travel difficulties from the United States linked to the COVID-19 pandemic, for Stephenson. The team also believed that the interviews might go more smoothly, and our interviewees prove more willing to share their views and perceptions, in the absence of an obvious foreigner (Stephenson). While not initially planned, we are persuaded that was indeed the case in retrospect.

We devised 11 semi-structured questions with which to approach our 16 interviewees (please see Appendix 1) and estimated that each conversation would take perhaps 60 minutes. As it happened, however, our respondents had little knowledge to share concerning many of our concerns and communicated that fact openly and concisely. Our interviewees offered by far their most detailed and complex responses to our initial question concerning how they came to take refuge in Jordan and to become employed in their current migratory/itinerant farmer role. Most of our interviews lasted approximately 30 minutes with the shortest completed in 22 minutes. We say more about this below.

The team had hoped to record our interview sessions and transcribe them verbatim, but as Karaki conferred with Orphanage Society officials and the grower, it became clear that our potential respondents were uncomfortable with that approach. For each, it was, and reasonably in our view, a matter of trust. Our interviewees were living in a foreign nation under difficult conditions, and they were concerned not to say something that might redound to harm themselves or their families, despite our aim to protect their confidentiality. Most also had good reason not to trust authority, given their experience under the autocratic and abusive Assad regime in their home nation. Accordingly, we shifted course and Karaki conducted each interview, with Abbadi taking as close to literal notes of each response as feasible. Abbadi is a professional linguist and she recorded contemporaneous notes for each response and interview in Arabic. Once assembled, she translated each completed conversation into English so that all members of the team could consider and code individuals' responses and review the interviews as a group as well.

We did not expect, nor conclude, that the findings from this study would be generalizable in a statistical sense, but we are and were hopeful that our arguments, rooted in thoughtful theorization, may help illuminate the character of the continuing challenges confronting refugees in an international context organized on the principle of state sovereignty and animated by the relentless capacity for othering exhibited by human populations across the globe. In this sense, we hope our findings may be analytically generalizable.

Team members independently coded – conducted a content/thematic analysis – the interview transcripts as our principal source of data and we thereafter discussed our conclusions amongst ourselves. We outline the principal themes/findings, on which we agreed, without debate, coincidentally, below. Table 1 provides an overview of some of the most salient characteristics of our interviewees. In brief, as a group they were relatively young, averaging 39 years of age, were supporting relatively large families comprised of an average of seven members, were as likely to be illiterate as literate (50/50 chance, assuming that those not reporting on the matter explicitly were, in fact, literate) and knew almost nothing about their nominal human rights as refugees. Five respondents suggested they knew 'a little' about their rights, principally the requirements to obtain a permit to work as an agricultural laborer in the Kingdom. While most of our interviewees were supporting nuclear families, a share, one-third or six, reported that they were residing with/helping to support, extended family members as well.

Themes Across the Interviews

As noted, the research team each parsed the interviews to identify central themes that crossed them. Together, the group agreed on the following key findings:

- Every interviewee provided a narrative of trauma in which conflict and murderous strife had forced them to flee their homes in Syria. All had to leave their communities and small farm holdings behind and many reported that they had lost siblings and relatives in the war and/or were themselves being pursued by militias when they fled.
- Our interviewees were uniformly poor, and they had also been poor in their home nation as well. In that respect, their material condition had not changed markedly, although their relative physical security had surely improved.
- Our respondents suggested that their poverty had dictated their choice to seek refuge in Jordan. The Kingdom was geographically close to their homes in Syria and its population was like their own culturally and linguistically as well. What is more, our interviewees argued that they saw Jordanians as generally welcoming and open to their presence, even as compared to life in UNHCR refugee camps, in which several of our interviewees had resided for a time following their exodus from Syria.
- A super majority, or three-fourths (12), of our interviewees indicated they would like to return to Syria when the situation permits and assuming they could again inhabit their original land and homes safely. Those conditions have not become broadly available to date.
- All our respondents indicated that they interacted little with Jordanians, other than their employers, due to the isolating conditions of their positions as migrant laborers. A quarter of our interviewees (4) noted that they obtained such information as they received on the security, political, and economic situation in the Kingdom and in Syria via radio and other itinerant harvesters.

- All but two of our respondents stated directly that they knew nothing about their human rights as refugees or about UNHCR efforts to track and assist them. Indeed, in so far as we could determine, none were receiving United Nations support of any kind, in part apparently, because they are not registered with the refugee agency. In any case, it would be difficult for that UN entity to track them since they spend roughly five months in Ma'an and seven months in Ghor harvesting crops each year and their interaction with groups and individuals beyond the farms on which they work is severely limited.
- Our interviewees lived in open-air tents on the farm on which they were working. Those living and laboring in these conditions were exposed to whatever weather occurred and utterly dependent on the good will of the grower employing them to supply them with sufficient potable water and wages to survive, which were far less than auspicious, especially for young children and older adults.

A Note on Literacy Levels in our Sample

We were especially struck that so many of our respondents volunteered that they were illiterate, as we did not include a question on the topic. As we noted above, we assume, but do not know with certainty, that those who did not indicate they were illiterate were in fact able to read and write. As a nation, Syria's overall adult literacy rate according to UNESCO in 2021 was 80.84 per cent, with 87.6 per cent of males and 73.63 per cent of females able to read and write (Countryeconomy.com 2022). Meanwhile, the similar statistic for Jordan in 2018 was 98.2 per cent overall, with males and females nearly equally likely to be literate (Statista 2022). Therefore, even acknowledging Syria's literacy rates and, assuming those who did not indicate their literacy status in our sample were literate, our interviewee group must be considered especially vulnerable in such terms.

While in Benhabib and Arendt's conception, agency does not depend on capacity to obtain and process information, it does seem likely nonetheless to be important in individuals' ability to understand their rights and position and this would appear to be especially significant for refugees working as itinerants in another nation. We suspect that those we interviewed know so little about their rights and context because so many of them are illiterate and all of them are also so isolated. These factors, while not per se impairing their capacity for agential action, make it difficult for them as individuals and as a group to exercise it. Or, if they do, illiteracy makes it materially more difficult for them to do so in anything like a probative way. While their living conditions are surely innately precarious, we believe this fact alone, illiteracy, significantly heightens this group's vulnerability to social predation and frailty.

Implications of our Findings

Perhaps the most striking finding of this modest empirical study is how little the affected refugees (our interviewees) knew about their rights, despite the precarity of their positions. Indeed, paradoxically, that very fragility may have contributed to their lack of knowledge concerning their situations. That is, their long working hours, marked social and geographic isolation, and itinerancy doubtless contributed to their ignorance of their rights.

Moreover, as we noted above, the high level of illiteracy in the group only aggravated these tendencies and made them still more difficult to address, let alone, to overcome. Indeed, an inability to mobilize and process information clearly exacerbated the isolation of the group and thereby deepened its innate vulnerability to the claims and actions of actors over whom they possessed no control and yet on whom they implicitly utterly depended. These included Jordanian government officials on whom their employment and resident status depended; citizens of the Kingdom whose decision to welcome or scapegoat them was critical to their capacity to survive; international actors with an interest in the Syrian crisis, especially the European Union and its member states whose aid to Jordan has been material to its capacity to respond to the influx due to the war in Syria; the United Nations, especially UNHCR, which nominally protects refugee rights under international law, but which has not been materially important to this group; and finally, the landowners for whom these individuals worked, on whose good will and honest behavior their daily lives literally depended.

Indeed, in Benhabib and Arendt's terms, what is noticeable about the situation these refugees confront each day is the precariousness of their claims on others for right action. Fully half were illiterate, all were extremely poor, all are living isolated lives permitted, at least in legal terms, only so long as the state in which they reside allows them to ply their tenuous work. More, they are largely invisible to the United Nations and the nongovernmental organization advocating on their behalf can only do so within the frame permitted by the nation and prevailing public attitudes.

This analysis suggests that these individuals run the very real risk of being deprived, in Benhabib's terms, of the space that affords them a 'demonstrable, institutional, and interactional framework within which what they say and do can be recognized and responded to by others' (2018, 110). In their isolation and in being 'acted upon' by a host of agents other than themselves, they become vulnerable to ceasing to be 'the source of recognized validity claims,' which can only be parsed with respect to a shared public framework in the world. Their capacities for responsibility and agency are increasingly diminished in this web of circumstances. In a sense, our interviewees exemplify Arendt's prescient warning that those who are stateless in a world organized around state and nation foremost are persistently in jeopardy of losing their place in anything like what we might describe as a public sphere. That is, given the communicative nature of freedom and agency itself, they are in constant peril of 'losing their place in the world' (Benhabib 2018, 110).

While those we interviewed obviously have not lost their capacity for action or for formulating their own views, those capabilities were nonetheless sharply circumscribed in practice and were especially tenuous and dependent on the right actions and good will among many actors who had no special rationale or incentive to guard them apart from a normative claim in the abstract that our interviewees themselves could not articulate.

Taken as a whole, our sample of individuals mark each day in a scenario of continuing and prevailing precarity. This is not to say that our interviewees have lost or can lose their agency, but it is to remark that its exercise is hedged about in just the ways captured above by the beliefs, norms, and behaviors of actors far beyond the ken of our respondents even to imagine, let alone to act to seek to control. Our interlocutors pass each day in a sort of netherworld in which their grasp on the public sphere, always tenuous, can be made still more feeble, by actions taken by actors of whom they are utterly unaware.

Searching for an analogy for this reality, we are reminded of the English novelist Charles Dickens's fascination concerning the implications for individual lives of choices taken elsewhere or on the spur of the moment by actors whose 'rights' to such grave implications may be few or none, but whose choices, nonetheless, may set an individual's life course in specific directions (Douglas-Fairhurst, 2011, 270–281). We think of our interviewees in just such terms. Their agency is intact to be sure, but their wherewithal to act in the world, in the public sphere as highlighted above, is ever at issue and ever subject to enervation. As Arendt put this paradox when considering the origins and possibility of human rights when considering the experience of the Holocaust, 'the right to have rights, or the right of every individual to belong to humanity, should be guaranteed by humanity itself. It is by no means certain whether this is possible' (Arendt 1979, 296–297).

Conclusions

We offer four principal conclusions and a caution. First, our sample of refugees was extremely isolated socially and geographically. While nominally advantaged in terms of employment because they could get work in their chosen occupation when many refugees could not, albeit on whatever terms made available to them, compared to a share of their peers who cannot work, at least legally, they knew very little about their situations and rights. That fact, coupled with their isolation, and for many, their illiteracy, made it extremely difficult for members of this group to exercise their agency in any meaningful way.

Secondly, as a group and as individuals, accordingly, events happen to these individuals or life befalls them. Put differently, it is difficult for us to contend that their active engagement in the public sphere was in any way securing or shifting the boundaries of the lives they were prosecuting.

Third, their relative powerlessness, predicated foremost on their enervated agency, had bred for many the sense of anomie and dissociation from the broader world that portended Arendt's warning of a slipping away from the public sphere and into a condition of worldlessness. We were struck that only others, as least as our interviewees reported their life conditions to us, could wrest them from that positionality. In our view, that represents a very parlous condition indeed, given Arendt's appropriate remark concerning the potential abyss that is the exercise of human freedom. Fourth, we find ourselves wondering if a more active UN presence for this group might mitigate some of the harsher edged factors now shaping their agential possibility. Yet even as we might hope that UNHCR might find ways and means to support and educate this group more strongly, especially its adults, we wonder whether state sovereignty as well as its progeny, the fact that governments can and do provide whatever resources and remit they wish to that body, will ever permit it so strong a rights-oriented presence. Finally, one caution: Our encounter with this very exposed group has reminded us of the severe limits and fragility of the international human rights regime. However, one believes that enterprise is sustained, it seems clear that hatred and alterity are its sworn enemies, and these are both ever healthy in humanity and at something of an apogee worldwide as we write.

Table 1: Interviewee Characteristics

INTERVIEWEE	GENDER	AGE	FAMILY SIZE	LITERACY	RIGHTS AWARENESS
1	Male	41	5	Illiterate	None
2	Female	33	5	Unknown	None
3	Male	29	4	Unknown	None
4	Male	56	8	Unknown	'Not much'
5	Female	36	7	Illiterate	None
6	Female	25	5	Unknown	None
7	Female	28	7	Illiterate	'Hear the news'
8	Female	31	8	Illiterate	'Not much'
9	Female	34	8	Illiterate	None
10	Female	22	8	Illiterate	None
11	Female	52	8	Unknown	'Not much, hear the radio news'
12	Male	56	8	Unknown	'Unsure'
13	Male	40	6	Unknown	'No need to know'
14	Male	43	6	Unknown	None
15	Male	39	8	Illiterate	None
16	Male	35	6	Illiterate	'Not much, hear the radio news'

Appendix 1: Interview Questions

1. Can you share with us your age, family composition and occupation?

2. We are very interested in how you came to live in Ma'an. Can you share with us briefly how you happened to come to Jordan – why you left Syria – and when and came to live as you are now living? How much time do you generally spend in Ma'an and Al-Ghor each year?

3. Assuming you (and your family, if relevant) chose to come to Jordan, can you describe what factors you considered and which among those was most significant in persuading you to come to Jordan, rather than say, for example, Germany or Lebanon, perhaps?

4. Do you see yourself staying in Jordan permanently? Why? Or why not?

5. If you hope to remain, do you currently see yourself as a member of Jordanian society? Why or why not?

6. a. If you see yourself as a member of Jordanian society, why is that so?

7. b. If not, do you think that such could occur with time? Are there any specific obstacles to such occurring in your view? What would you say are the most important of those?

8. Do you feel you are able to express your views and opinions about what the Jordanian government does and what its laws are as those affect you as a refugee?

9. As a resident of Jordan are you aware of laws in the country, specifically affecting refugees? If so, could you share what those are and what they mean for you in your daily life?

10. Do you participate in debates or discussions about public issues that are important to you at home or in public? For example, in school, mosque, a community group, or church?

11. Do you do so with other Syrian refugees? How about with native Jordanians?

12. Do you ever choose not to participate in debates or discussions about these subjects with any groups or individuals?

13. Why/why not?

14. Do you think the Jordanian Government is establishing better living conditions for refugees? Why or why not? Are there laws or government policies that affect refugees in Jordan that you would like to change? If so, can you share what those are, please?

15. What do you know about ideas such as human rights documents, such as the 1948 Universal Declaration of Human Rights that govern refugee rights as a matter of international law? If you know something of these principles and laws, would you say they are supporting you during this period of life outside your native country? Why? If not, why do you think they are not doing so?

References

Arendt, Hannah. 1979. *The Origins of Totalitarianism, 3ʳᵈ edition*. New York: Harcourt, Brace, and Jovanovich.

Balibar, Etienne. 2014. *Equaliberty: Political Essays*. Translated by James Ingram. Durham: Duke University Press.

Benhabib, Seyla. 2011. *Dignity in Adversity: Human Rights in Troubled Times*. Cambridge: Polity Press.

Benhabib, Seyla. 2018. *Exile, Statelessness, and Migration: Playing Chess with History from Hannah Arendt to Isaiah Berlin*. Princeton: Princeton University Press.

Countryeconomy.com. 2022. "Syria-Literacy rate." Accessed 18 April, 2022. https://countryeconomy.com/demography/literacy-rate/syria.

Douglas-Fairhurst, Robert. 2011. *Becoming Dickens: The Invention of a Novelist*. Cambridge, Mass: The Belknap Press of Harvard University Press.

Gündogdu, Ayten. 2015. *Rightlessness in an Age of Rights. Hannah Arendt and the Contemporary Struggles of Migrants*. Oxford: Oxford University Press.

Statista. 2022. Jordan: Literacy Rate from 2007 to 2018, total by gender. Accessed17 April 2022. https://www.statista.com/statistics/572748/literacy-rate-in-jordan/

The New Arab. 2022. 95% of Jordanians say, 'too many refugees in Jordan' amid economic strain, UN survey finds, 15 July 2021. https://english.alaraby.co.uk/news/un-poll-finds-hardening-attitudes-toward-refugees-jordan

8

Egypt and the Syrian Refugee Crisis

DINA RASHED

The 2011 uprising against the regime in Syria soon transformed to a full-fledged civil war, leading to one of the worst humanitarian crises and the displacement of millions of Syrians across the globe. As of June 2021, there are 6.7 million Syrian refugees around the world, constituting twenty seven per cent of total refugees globally (UNHCR 2022b), of which 5.7 million are hosted across the MENA region in Turkey, Lebanon, Jordan, Iraq and Egypt (UNHCR Operation Data Portal n.d.). Syrian refugees constitute the largest group of refugees in Egypt; as of April 2022, there are 141,303 persons (UNHCR Operation Data Portal n.d.) representing about 50 per cent of total registered refugees in the country (UNHCR Egypt 2022).

In 2022, Egypt ranked fifth in host countries for displaced Syrians in the MENA region, following Turkey, Lebanon, Jordan and Iraq. While not sharing a border, Syria and Egypt had shared a unique political history with their short-lived union between 1958–1961. In this chapter, I argue that Egypt's policies towards the Syrian refugee crisis have been shaped by considerations for domestic stability and economic capacity. Like Syria, Egypt experienced mass protests in 2011, but the respective political paths of the two countries have diverged significantly. While Egypt's political turmoil resulted in regime change in 2011 and again in 2013, Syria has not experienced a regime change and slipped into civil war aided by foreign intervention from regional and international powers to its warring parties. To the Egyptian state, spillover effects from neighboring conflicts remain a clear and present danger and that fact has impacted policies regarding entry regulation of displaced persons, including Syrian refugees. Economically, the Egyptian government has worked to restore macroeconomic stability and provide appropriate services to its citizens, yet the side effects of following neoliberal international prescriptions have affected living conditions for both

Egyptian citizens and Syrian refugees, as well as the state's policies towards them.

This chapter first reviews Egypt's legal framework on refugees. I then discuss the political context of the Syrian and Egyptian uprisings and how it influenced Syrians' influx into the country. The third section addresses the socio-economic experiences of Syrian refugees in Egypt. The chapter concludes with an analysis of how these experiences have been a mix of challenges and opportunities to both refugees and their host communities.

This chapter's analysis is guided by reports and statistics of international organizations working with and around refugees. Unfortunately, because of the social distancing and restrictions on mobility and close interactions caused by the COVID-19 pandemic, many of the annual and biannual reports were not updated. I have sought to rely on the latest available information about the status of refugees in Egypt.

Egypt's Responsibility towards Refugee from Laws to Practices

The Legal Framework

Egypt was one of two Arab states participating in the drafting committee of, and later a signatory to, the 1951 Convention Relating to the Status of Refugees (UNHCR 2010). While the Government of Egypt (GoE) acceded to the Convention and its 1967 added Protocol only in May 1981, the state's responsibility towards refugees was referenced in Egyptian constitutions since 1953 (Sadek 2016). Article 5 of the Constitutional Declaration of February 1953 acknowledged the right of asylum in Egypt. This right was reiterated in the 1971 constitution. The 2012 constitution affirmed the protection of refugees and asylum-seekers in Article 57, prohibiting the extradition of political refugees. The current constitution of 2014 stipulates granting protection to refugees subjected to persecution in article 91 (Elshokeiry 2016, 13).

Under these conventions and constitutional frameworks, Egypt has committed to abide by the non-refoulement principle. However, the administration of asylum activities including Reception, Registration, Documentation and Refugee Status Determination (RSD) are carried out by United Nations High Commissioner for Refugees (UNHCR) Cairo office at the request, and on behalf, of the government. UNHCR assists governments in finding solutions for refugees including settlement in the host country, transition to a third country or repatriation (UNHCR 2013). The UNHCR interviews persons of concern through its RSD process and provides a yellow refugee card to those who fall under the refugee status. The card is stamped by the Ministry of Foreign Affairs and the Refugee Affairs section of the Ministry of Interior's Department of Migration and Citizenship. The UNHCR works in close collaboration with Egyptian authorities to ensure that all persons of concern are protected (UNHCR 2013, 7).

Refugees in Egypt

The experiences of refugees in Egypt have varied over time and have been shaped by both the political relationship between Egypt and the country of conflict, as well as the health of the Egyptian government's purse. Palestinian refugees are considered the oldest group of Arab refugees, arriving in the aftermath of the 1948 War, and enjoying a wide range of benefits including the right to own properties, study at Egyptian universities and work. In the following years, conflicts in the MENA region increased the number of displaced persons and refugees. Through the 1950s and until the 1990s, government policies fluctuated in the level of service they provided for non-Palestinian refugees. But in 1996, Presidential Decree 8180 gave refugees a renewable three-year temporary residency permit to be issued by the Ministry of Interior (Elshokeiry 2016, 13) and the state's provision of public services was extended to displaced persons from neighboring Arab countries. Although Egypt made a reservation to article 22, section 1 of the Refugee Convention, thereby denying refugees the right to be admitted to public schools, the Egyptian Minister of Education (MoE) issued Ministerial Decree No. 24/1992, allowing the children of recognized refugees to attend public schools (Sadek 2016). At different times, the decree allowed children of Sudanese, Libyan, Iraqi and later Syrian asylum-seekers and refugees to access Egypt's public educational system.

Syrian Refugees in Egypt post 2011 Uprisings: The Political Context

Both Syria and Egypt were grounds for mass protests in 2011 but each country experienced a distinct trajectory. The January 2011 Egyptian Uprising led to a regime change and the ouster of President Mubarak in February of the same year to be followed by another mass protest that ousted President Mohamed Morsi in 2013 with the state – backed by the military – regaining much of its strength since then. Syria on the other hand, has experienced a protracted civil war. Despite support to anti-regime factions from Western and Arab countries at the onset of the civil war, Russian and Iranian political and military backing to Syrian President Bashar al-Assad (r. 2000–) has prevented the fall of his regime. Syria's lack of strong state institutions, the fragmentation of the military and plethora of armed actors in an ethnically divided society all provided favorable conditions that shifted the Syrian Uprising to an ongoing conflict zone.

The ebb and flow of Syrian refugees' movement into Egypt has followed not only the civil war, but also the political change in Egypt. The Egyptian administration that came to power with the election of President Mohamad Morsi (r. 2012–2013), a Muslim Brotherhood leader, welcomed the influx of Syrians fleeing the conflict as refugees, asylum-seekers, and residency-seekers. On 15 June 2013, Morsi announced the breaking off of diplomatic ties with the Syrian regime, promised financial aid to the Syrian rebels, and pledged support from both Egyptian society and military. He expressed his plans to work with other countries, including Turkey and Saudi Arabia, and the Red Crescent, in cooperation with civil society organizations, to coordinate Egypt's assistance to rebels in Syria and Syrian refugees residing in Egypt. While stressing his rejection of western political or military interference in the conflict, President Morsi called on the international community to implement a no-fly zone over the conflicted country (Mohsen 2013). The announcements came as he faced strong domestic opposition to his rule. The influence of the Muslim Brotherhood on his policies came under fire from non-Islamist opposition that had mobilized against and successfully ousted Mubarak a year earlier (Ahram Online 2013), as well as Islamist Salafi groups who felt marginalized by the Muslim Brotherhood's monopolization of power (Hendawi and Michael 2013). At the same time, many Egyptian activists, politicians and state officials were alarmed by how the Syrian Uprising had shifted to sectarian violence and cautioned against taking sides that can be too costly to Egypt (Witte 2013). Mass protests against Morsi and the Muslim Brotherhood broke out on 30 June 2013. Courted by the military as well as other state and society institutions, the protests led to the ouster of Morsi from power on 3 July 2013 and the overt return of the military to power (Hanna 2013).

In the following months, Egypt's governmental policies on open borders to Syrians shifted as the interim government of Judge Adly Mansour (2013–14) tightened its grip on border security. Policies on entry included re-instating some restrictions that the Egyptian government had lifted in 2012. In July 2013, Syrian nationals were asked to secure a visa before entry and those already in the country have been asked to renew their residency permits in a timely fashion. Despite announcements by Egyptian Ministry of Foreign Affairs at the time that these requirements were related to 'current and temporary' security conditions (Kortam 2013), these measures remain in place till the time of writing this chapter. However, some Syrians are still allowed to enter on the basis of family reunification (UNHCR Egypt 2020b), and the government continues to work with UNHCR on the registration of refugees and asylum-seekers.

The Syrian Refugees in Egypt post 2011 Uprisings: The Socio-Economic Context

Unlike other neighboring MENA countries, Egypt does not confine Syrian refugees to living in camps. Syrian refugees and asylum seekers, as well as those on visitor or student visas, are free to reside, intermingle and travel freely within the country. They tend to concentrate geographically in the major cities of Cairo, Alexandria, and Damietta. They have access to many public services especially education and health on equal footing with Egyptians. While enjoying freedom of movement and residency, the refugees face social and economic hardships resulting from their displacement as well as the impact of the economic structural adjustment policies that the Egyptian government continue to implement. According to the Egyptian Central Agency for Public Mobilization and Statistics (CAPMAS), almost one-third of Egyptians live below the national poverty line (A.Moneim 2020), and earlier estimates show that 67 per cent of Syrian refugees in Egypt are extremely poor and in need of financial assistance (UNHCR Egypt 2020b). With the devaluation of the Egyptian pound in 2016 and again in 2022, inflation and soaring consumer prices has taken its toll on both Egyptian citizens and Syrian refugees.

The sustainable development goals of the government's 2030 Vision, which was announced in 2016, aim to couple macroeconomic stabilization policies with safety net programs, such as *Takaful and Karama*. Since 2016, the UNHCR and other international agencies working with Syrian refugees have aimed to align assistance efforts with the government's *Takaful and Karama* projects in order to improve the quality of life for refugees and their host communities. These efforts include partnering with government ministries to streamline aid and establish a 'one-refugee' policy. The 'one refugee' approach is a Response Plan for Refugees and Asylum-Seekers from sub-Saharan Africa, Iraq, Yemen, and 50 other countries that was launched in 2018, and revised in 2019 by UN and other international and national non-governmental organizations in collaboration with the government. The response plan aimed to continue addressing the needs of refugees and asylum-seekers (UNHCR Egypt 2019).

As a relief partner, the World Food Program (WFP) has been especially active in extending cash assistance as well as food for children in primary schools. While WFP extends support to all refugees in Egypt, Syrian refugees have received a significant portion of its relief efforts. Since 2019, WFP has supported 78,000 Syrian refugees out of 117,000 total aid recipients. This amounts to 36 per cent of the Syrian refugee community receiving monthly humanitarian cash assistance, and 58 per cent receiving food vouchers. The WFP provides monthly cash-based transfers (CBT) of EGP 400 (equivalent to

USD 24) to support nutritional needs of Syrian pregnant and lactating women on the condition of regular medical check-ups for themselves and their child at participating health centers. Similarly, beneficiaries targeted through livelihood support activities receive monthly household assistance of EGP 2,000 upon completion of the training courses (UNHCR Egypt 2020b, 51–53). In addition, WFP's National School Feeding Programme, a key social safety net, has provided nutritious meals to school children. It also engaged in capacity building activities for their teachers through various trainings on nutrition, emergency preparedness and positive discipline as well as renovating school facilities to encourage children to attend schools (United Nations 2019).

Many displaced Syrians who moved to Egypt since the start of the conflict are white collar professionals who are trained in accounting, engineering, medical, legal, and education professions. However, governmental regulations of work and residence permits, which are often contradictory and ambiguous, limit their ability to secure appropriate employment opportunities, thereby increasing their sense of insecurity.

While asylum-seekers and refugees have the right to wage earning employment and self-employment in Egypt, these rights are governed by Egypt's domestic employment legislation, which puts a 10 per cent quota of foreign labor (UNHCR Egypt 2020b, 43). The government also requires work permits and regulates their issuance through the Ministry of Manpower (MoM) prior to work. Refugees seeking employment have to qualify with the MoM's terms, which included qualifications and experience, and the employer's need for such. Article 11 of Ministerial Resolution 390 of 1982 issued by the Ministry of Manpower, requires proof on the part of the employer that no Egyptian national is available to do the same work before permits may be issued. In addition to these requirements, refugees need to pay annual permit fees (UNHCR 2013). The ability to find stable work is further complicated by the government's regulation of refugees' residency. According to the Ministry of Interior's Decree No. 8180 of 1996, refugees generally receive a three-year temporary residency permit. Such permits are renewable if the refugee 'remains of concern to UNHCR' (Sadek 2016). However, this decree is not being implemented, because of another ministerial regulation that limits refugees to only six-month renewable residency permits.

With short-term residencies and constraints on the issuance of work permits, many resort to the informal economy. Syrian refugees living in Egypt primarily work in three main economic sectors: Food (restaurants and food processing), furniture production, and textile (ready-made garments). (UNOCHA 2017, 91). UN reports show that 80 per cent work mainly in the informal food service and therefore face high worker turn-over and a lack of required skilled workers (International Labor Organization 2018).

In terms of education, the Egyptian government allows Syrian refugees to attend public schools on equal footing with Egyptian nationals. This access is extended to all stages and types of education, including vocational and technical schools, as well as higher education institutions. For the academic year 2018/2019, the Ministry of Education (MoE) reported that approximately 42,300 Syrian students, both registered and not registered with UNHCR, were enrolled in public schools. In addition, an estimated number of 6,800 Syrian youths attended Egyptian public universities and higher education institutes. While enrollment rates are high – about 90 per cent of refugee children are enrolled in the school system per UNHCR survey of 2019 – Syrian refugee children face the same challenges facing Egyptian school children in particular overcrowded classrooms, limited resources, and long distance to schools. In addition, Syrian children face the challenges of dialect (UNHCR Egypt 2020b, 23–30).

The UNHCR has been working with the MoE to improve the education services provided to children with special needs from both the refugee and the host communities. These initiatives allow Syrian children with disabilities to have access to inclusive schools close to areas of residency, in addition to specialized private schools that meet their educational and care needs. These children receive special education grants to cover school fees, transportation, and other specialized services.

Due to the dire economic situation facing many refugee families, some children drop out of school to help contribute to family income. A 2019 survey by UNHCR found that 10 per cent of all Syrian refugee children were not enrolled or are attending school less than three times per week. Disability, general poverty, child labor, distance to available schools or overcrowded classrooms in public schools were among the key reasons indicated by families for refugee children to drop out of school (UNHCR Egypt 2020b, 4). In a way to remedy some of these challenges, the Egyptian government has agreed to allow Syrian community schools to operate. These schools host approximately 7,300 refugee children and they employ about 2,000 Syrian teachers (UNOCHA 2017, 91). These community schools allow refugee children to be taught the Egyptian curriculum and be officially enrolled in local public schools while being taught by Syrian teachers, which eases the dialect gap. In many ways, these community schools provide both education and counseling opportunities to children and youth, and employment to adult refugees. In these schools, children receive psycho-social support providing a much-needed service to traumatized children. However, these schools charge fees that while less than what is charged by private Egyptian schools can be a burden to destitute refugee families (Allam 2016, 39). In many cases, UNHCR provides financial support to cover some of these fees. The UNHCR gives education grants to approximately 55,000 Syrian refugee boys, girls, and youth upon enrollment in kindergarten classes, primary, and secondary education, and providing proof of regular attendance. These education grants are distributed according to the school year, school type, and the grade of the student, and are meant to help with school fees, uniforms, books, and transportation to schools. Children from destitute families who are unable to afford their school fees, even after receiving such grants, are offered additional means between US$ 100–147 on a case-by-case basis (UNHCR Egypt 2020b).

Other efforts focus on transferring Syrian educational and professional certifications under Egypt's current law and practice, as well as vocational training to Syrian refugees (UNOCHA 2017, 91). Since 2014, UNHCR in cooperation with other international and local organizations have been working with the Egyptian Ministry of Education to support training of teachers and social workers, construction and upgrading of classrooms, and Water, Sanitation and Hygiene (WASH) facilities, as well as provision of teaching and learning materials. These capacity-building measures in areas with the highest concentrations of Syrian refugees, aim to improve educational services offered to their children, and children of their host communities. Such efforts support a school-based reform model that provides stakeholders, such as teachers, social workers, students, parents and community leaders, with a voice and opportunities to improve the education process in their districts.

Refugees' access to higher education is more challenging as the Ministry of Higher Education (MoHE) requires secondary school certificates for admission to colleges and universities and continues to accept Syrian diplomas regardless of the year they were obtained. While the government allows displaced Syrians, irrespective of their legal status, or access to education, the biggest challenge is the financial burden especially as the government faces surmounting challenges to its ability to provide for its own citizens. As of January 2016, the MoHE issued a decree specifying that only Syrian refugees who obtained their secondary school certificates from an Egyptian public school will be granted access to universities on the same footing as Egyptians. Syrian refugee youth with a secondary school certificate from Syria need to pay 50 per cent of the foreign student fee reaching over US $2,500 annually. All other Syrian youth with a secondary school certificate obtained outside of Egypt or Syria need to pay the full fee charged to non-Egyptian students on an annual basis. While resources to assist Syrian refugees in higher education exist, their supply remains very limited compared to the demand. The Albert Einstein German Academic Refugee Initiative (DAFI) is one resource that continues to provide scholarships for tertiary education to refugee youth of all nationalities. The total number of Syrian refugees benefiting from this scholarship for academic year 2019–2020 reached 500. In addition, UNHCR continues to support through scholarships four students enrolled in the Egypt Japan University of Science and Technology in Burg El Arab, Alexandria. Approximately 2,400 higher education students need such support. For the 2019–2020 academic year, UNHCR received over 1,000 applications for the DAFI Scholarship – while only 150 slots are available.

Syrian refugees have access to the national health care system. Decree 601/2012 by the Ministry of Health and Population (MoHP) has allowed Syrian refugees' access to the health care system on equal footing to Egyptians. Since 2012, primary health care was particularly enhanced through various partnerships and signed memoranda between the government and international organizations in particular UNHCR, UNICEF, UNFPA, and WHO to establish resilience plans (UNHCR Egypt 2020b, 33). The resilience projects aim to alleviate the austere conditions facing both the refugees and their host communities and enhance the health care service provided to them. More attention is given to children and adolescent, reproductive and mental health as well as emergencies and referral care management.

The Egyptian Red Crescent, in cooperation with the UNHCR, provides Syrian families with cash assistance grants. In 2015, about 15,500 refugees received such grants, 12,000 of whom were Syrian refugees. Refugee families that are not currently receiving food or cash assistance and are large-sized, single-headed households or households with members suffering from a medical condition are the main recipients of these cash assistance grants (Sadek 2016).

In 2018, Egypt adopted the National Health Insurance Law, which stipulates that refugees can enjoy health insurance services within specifically devised insurance schemes (Law 2/2018 on Comprehensive Health Insurance Scheme). In addition, refugees from all nationalities, including Syrian refugees, were included in the nationwide presidential initiative "100 Million Health" for hepatitis C screening and treatment as part of enhancing universal health coverage in 2019. This national initiative has been part of the WHO-led Global Action Plan for Healthy Lives and Well-being for All.

Despite these efforts, Syrian refugees still face some financial burdens related to health care. Out-of-pocket expenses, which are estimated to be at 30 per cent of medical care and apply equally to citizens and refugees alike, high medicine high prices, and hospital care costs are some of the big burdens (UNHCR Egypt 2020b, 33–34). The majority of Syrian refugees in Egypt (about 67 per cent) are considered vulnerable, and a 2018 World Health Organization assessment of health status and health needs of displaced Syrians in Egypt showed that 82 per cent reported a family member's need for medical services with 48 per cent relying on the public health sector, 18 per cent on private health facilities and 12.7 per cent on non-governmental organizations. The main factor determining refugees' choice has been the affordability of those services (UNHCR Egypt 2020b, 33–34).

Syrian Refugees in Egypt: Challenges and Opportunities

Egyptian policies towards refugees have been greatly influenced by both the state's political objectives and financial ability. Unlike other countries that share borders with Syria, Egypt has been able to control the influx of Syrian refugees through some measures, in particular rules of entry and exit. This has mitigated the 'hosting fatigue' that is more visible in other countries such as Jordan, Lebanon, and Turkey, as they deal with the fallout from the Syrian refugee influx for decades (Sullivan and Hawkins 2019, 246).

The unstructured movements that ensued following the Arab Uprisings, coupled with failure to secure borders in several Arab countries has led to an increase in illegal migration across the Middle East as well as from the region to neighboring European countries. This made Egypt a country of origin, a country of transit and a country of destination for illegal migration (Reda 2019). The permeable borders posed security threats to Egypt on two levels. On one level, it allowed the influx of not only peaceful refugees, but also militant groups that trickled from the country's eastern and western borders with attempts to build bases on Egyptian soil. On another level, refugees, including Syrians, used Egypt as a stop on their illegal migration to European countries (Walker 2014).

Western opposition to the overt intervention of the Egyptian military into politics and removal of an elected president in 2013 strained the relationship between the new Egyptian regime and Western donors. This prompted President Abdel Fattah al-Sisi (r. 2014-) to pay special attention to improving relations in areas of cooperation, of which border security issues remains an important issue. Since 2016 Egyptian Law-enforcement authorities have taken strong measures on both counter trafficking and counter smuggling, and succeeded in limiting illegal entry into, and exit out of, the country. The Sisi regime's policies proved successful in curtailing violent extremism spillover from neighboring conflict areas and establishing itself as a trusted partner to European countries across the Mediterranean in the fight against illegal migration. By cracking down on smuggling gangs on the western and northern Mediterranean borders (ElMoly 2015), international partners have supported Egyptian efforts to curb activities of criminal migration networks and domestic laws' attention to protection of victims. In 2018, officers from the UN's International Organization of Migration lauded the state's crackdown on state officials accused of helping smuggling networks (Reda 2019). Other policies included providing employment opportunities and social welfare to Egyptian provinces with a history of illegal youth emigrating. The policies were praised for bringing levels of illegal immigration to almost zero at the beginning of 2020 (Al-Youm 2020; CGTN Africa 2020).

In addition to state policies, several national and international NGOs work to improve refugees' living conditions, their professional training and relationships with host communities. These organizations include UNHCR and ILO which provide employment training. Syrian NGOs have helped connect business entrepreneurs from both countries. The Syrian Business Association in Egypt has assisted refugees to establish businesses, providing guidance and counseling on official regulations, market trends, and asset management. Syrian businesses have partnered with Egyptian counterparts to minimize bureaucratic red tape and allow for smooth operation in accordance with Egyptian governmental rules (Startup Scene 2017).

In addition, Syrians themselves have launched initiatives focused on assisting refugees with school registration, access to health and housing, and employment skills. *Khatwa* or Step, is one initiative founded by Syrian university students to explain the process of university and K-12 school registration. By acting first as an information resource and later as an intermediary between the displaced population and Egyptian authorities, *Khatwa* managed to make registration less strenuous. Other initiatives have collaborated with *Terre des hommes* to provide psychological support and career advancement skills to displaced Syrians. This refugee-to-refugee service has been effective in reaching out to groups while understanding the daily pressures and challenges they face. *Fard*, or an Individual, is another civil society organization focused on providing solutions to socio-economic problems – especially in housing and protection, childcare, and income generation for women who work from home. Care is also another active organization that has focused on engaging with issues related to sexual and gender-based violence by providing educational seminars and psychological support to traumatized women (Allam 2016, 115–22).

Institutions in the higher education field have been also active in reaching out to the Syrian refugee community. In 2019, the Arab Academy for Science Technology, and Maritime Transportation (AASTMT), partnered with UNHCR to launch vocational training courses in linguistics, business management and entrepreneurial skills for Syrian refugees and youth from host communities (UNHCR Egypt 2020b, 53). The Sawiris Foundation for Social Development, a private philanthropy, has also partnered with UNHCR in 2020 to provide aid to Syrian refugees and families (UNHCR Egypt 2020a).

While the country at large remains hospitable to foreign nationals fleeing conflict, much of the status of incoming displaced persons relies on their financial outlook. Like Iraqi refugees and displaced persons who fled Iraq following the US invasion in 2003, Syrians who moved to Egypt since 2011 feature many educated and established entrepreneurs who injected capital into the Egyptian market. The presence of displaced Syrians bears positive consequences to both the fleeing community and their host country on the economic level. Many Syrian refugees and asylum-seekers arrive in Egypt with prior work experience, vocational expertise or strong higher education records and therefore can contribute substantially to the Egyptian economy (International Labor Organization 2018). By some estimates, the total capital invested by Syrians and their Egyptian partners between 2011 and 2019 has been estimated at nearly $800 million, though this is likely an underestimate as Syrian businesses frequently do not register or partner with Egyptians and register under an Egyptian name. Ranging from large factories to microenterprises in diverse sectors – including garment and textiles, food industry, and IT firms – these businesses employ Egyptians and Syrians.

While facing challenges to securing long-term residency permits amid the visa regulations, Syrian entrepreneurs still managed to start economic activities, with many catering to the needs of the Egyptian market (Noureldin 2019). The Egyptian market has been an attractive place for Syrian business due to its size, supply chain, and a pre-existing Syrian business community (e.g., there is a Syrian Business Association and multiple Syrian-managed NGOs). In addition, Egyptian society has been welcoming to Syrian business and products (UNOCHA 2017, 91). The Egyptian economy has also benefited from international aid earmarked for refugees living in Egypt. Since it started assisting refugees from Syria in 2013, WFP Egypt has supported the Egyptian economy by injecting US $172.4 million through cash-based transfers (CBT), the voucher program, local food procurement and other expenditures (UNHCR Egypt 2020b, 52). Despite funding challenges imposing the prioritization of WFP's humanitarian assistance to the most vulnerable refugees starting in August 2021, WFP reached over 125,000 refugees and asylum seekers with cash assistance to secure their basic food needs. WFP was able to re-launch unconditional nutrition cash assistance for about 3,500 pregnant and lactating refugee women in the last quarter of 2021, following a one-year halt due to funding shortages (World Food Programme 2021).

Gender-related issues remain a concern for displaced populations. Syrian women and young girls continue to bear the brunt of the civil war in their country. A study by the Arab Women Organization in 2016 has documented the challenges that females face in the Arab world, including Syrian refugees. In addition to problems of displacement, impoverishment and loss of homes, women face issues of physical and sexual-based violence during their flight and many times during their temporary residence in host countries. Others suffer from increasing issues of domestic abuse when husbands are unable to protect and/or provide for the family. Younger women are wed off at a younger age to decrease the financial burden on the family and/or to delegate the process of social and physical protection to another person (Allam, 2016). In Egypt, displaced Syrian women have highlighted their problem with verbal harassment and protection in city streets, a problem that they note was uncommon in Syrian society. Egyptian women have been equally facing this challenge in the past decades. One of unintended consequence of this problem has been Syrian women's break out of social norms that previously limited their voice in public space. Some women reflecting on this problem highlighted that living in Egypt allowed them to stand up for themselves and break a seal of shyness to fend for themselves on the street (Allam 2016).

On the economic level, an ILO study found that female participation in the foodservice industry, which is the dominant economic activity of Syrian refugees, is very limited. Most Syrian women prefer to work from their homes to avoid harassment at work and on the street, and long commutes (International Labor Organization 2018). Syrian women note that they were not used to working in Syria as men were the breadwinners of their households (Allam 2016). With changes in their economic status after displacement, many women find themselves pushed to the workforce to make ends meet. In that regard, their engagement in the textile and garment-making sector seems to be more favorable due to the sector's flexibility to their needs, in particular the ability to work from home.

Conclusion

While the life of refugees in Egypt is far from ideal, Syrians have received relatively better treatment compared to other refugees in the country. Historically, the Egyptian government has been more hospitable to Arab refugees compared to other nationals. As a legal expert notes, the baseline for granting asylum is everybody, then the government gives to nationalities on the basis of them being Arabs, they are seen as brothers or sisters (Elshokeiry 2016). In addition to governmental policies, assistance given to Syrians Refugees by international organizations working in Egypt has been bigger compared to other refugees. This can be explained by the dire conditions under which Syrians fled their country. One example is the winter assistance, a one-time grant distributed among the most vulnerable refugees registered with UNHCR to purchase basic items as a means to overcome the coldest months of winter in Egypt. In 2016, UNHCR assessed that a total of 85,000 vulnerable Syrian refugees needed assistance during the winter months. In coordination with UNICEF, UNHCR provided cash grants to some 61,000 Syrian refugees and 8,500 African and Iraqi refugees, and about

24,000 Syrians with children under 18 were assisted by UNICEF. While African and Iraqi beneficiaries received EGP 200 per person, Syrian refugees received EGP 300 per person (UNHCR Egypt 2016).

Reports from international organizations have shown that there is improvement in their living conditions. Some estimates had shown that 67 per cent of Syrian refugees in Egypt are extremely poor and in need of financial assistance (UNHCR Egypt 2020b). However, more recent reports show that poverty levels are less prevalent among Syrian refugees (UNHCR 2022a, 9).

The number of Syrian refugees in Egypt will continue to be impacted by the political conditions of the civil war and the ability of the fleeing population to repatriate. However, the economic conditions will also play an important factor in their residency situation. To the extent that displaced Syrians will be able to find employment opportunities, a hospitable environment for their businesses, and uninterrupted education for their children, Egypt will continue to be a favored destination.

References

Ahram Online. 2013. Morsi's Syria Stance Influenced by US: Egyptian Opposition, 16 June 2013. https://english.ahram.org.eg/ NewsContent/1/64/74123/Egypt/Politics-/Morsis-Syria-stance-influenced-by-US-Egyptian-oppo.aspx

Al-Youm, Al-Masry. 2020. Illegal Immigration from Egypt to Europe down to Almost Zero: IOM Chief, *Egypt Independent*, 19 January 2020, sec. Egypt. https://egyptindependent.com/illegal-immigration-from-egypt-to-europe-down-to-almost-zero-iom-chief/

Allam, Rabha. 2016. Wade'e al-Laje'aat wa al-Nazehat fi al-Dewal al-Arabia [The Status of Female Refugees and Displaced in Arab Countries]. Arab Women Organization. http://elibrary.arabwomenorg.org/AWOPublications. aspx?ContentID=21064

A.Moneim, Doaa. 2020. Egypt's Poverty Rate Declines to 29.7%: CAPMAS - Economy - Business." *Ahram Online*, 3 December 2020. https://english. ahram.org.eg/NewsContent/3/12/396107/Business/Economy/ Egypt%E2%80%99s-poverty-rate-declines-to--CAPMAS.aspx

CGTN Africa. 2020. IOM Chief Hails Egypt's Role in Tackling Illegal Immigration, *CGTN Africa* website, 19 January 2020. https://africa.cgtn. com/2020/01/19/iom-chief-hails-egypts-role-in-tackling-illegal-immigration/

ElMoly, Ibrahim. 2015. Eyes on the Sea: Syrian Refugees Flee Egypt. *Jadaliyya* (blog). 2 November 2015. https://www.jadaliyya.com/Details/32643

Elshokeiry, Nadine. 2016. Egypt's Post 2012 Response to the Syrian Refugee Crisis: A Theoretical Critique of Practical Approaches. Issue 1, 2016. PPAD Working Paper Series. Cairo, Egypt: School of Public Affairs and Global Policy, the American University in Cairo. https://doi.org/10.13140/RG.2.2.35003.82726.

Hanna, Michael Wahid. 2013. Blame Morsy. *Foreign Policy* (blog). 8 July 2013. https://foreignpolicy.com/2013/07/08/blame-morsy/

Hendawi, Hamza, and Maggie Michael. 2013. Mohamed Morsi's Final Days—the inside Story. *The Guardian*, 5 July 2013, sec. World news. http://www.guardian.co.uk/world/2013/jul/05/morsi-final-days-egypt-president

International Labor Organization. 2018. Market Systems Analysis for Syrian Refugees in Egypt. Report. *Market Systems and Value Chain Analysis*. International Labor Organization. http://www.ilo.org/empent/areas/value-chain-development-vcd/WCMS_649835/lang--en/index.htm

Kortam, Hend. 2013. New Requirements for Entry of Syrians. *Daily News Egypt*, 10 July 2013. https://dailyfeed.dailynewsegypt.com/2013/07/10/new-requirements-for-entry-of-syrians/

Mohsen, Manar. 2013. Egypt to Aid Syrian Rebels. *Daily News Egypt*, 15 June 2013. https://dailyfeed.dailynewsegypt.com/2013/06/15/egypt-to-aid-syrian-rebels/

Noureldin, Ola. 2019. Syrian Immigrants Spur Economic Revival. *AmCham* (blog). April 2019. https://www.amcham.org.eg/publications/business-monthly/issues/280/April-2019/3843/syrian-immigrants-spur-economic-revival

Reda, Lolwa. 2019. Egypt's Legal Framework Supports Efforts to Stop Human Trafficking: IOM Egypt Chief. *Egypt Today*, 26 February 2019, sec. News. https://www.egypttoday.com/Article/1/65282/Egypt's-legal-framework-supports-efforts-to-stop-human-trafficking-IOM

Sadek, George. 2016. Refugee Law and Policy: Egypt. Web page. United States: Library of Congress. https://www.loc.gov/law/help/refugee-law/egypt.php

Startup Scene. 2017. Did You Know That Syrian Refugees Have Contributed Over $800 Million to the Egyptian Economy? Startup Scene website. 15 May 2017. http://thestartupscene.me/MenaEcosystems/Syrian-Refugees-Contributed-800-Million-Egyptian-Economy

Sullivan, Denis J., and Allyson Hawkins. 2019. Migrants and Refugees: Crisis Responses from the Middle East, the Balkans, and the EU. *Horizons: Journal of International Relations and Sustainable Development*, no. 13: 240–49.

United Nations. 2019. Canada and WFP Support Social Inclusion of Syrian Refugees in Egypt through Education | World Food Programme. United Nations World Food Programme. March 18, 2019. https://www.wfp.org/news/canada-and-wfp-support-social-inclusion-syrian-refugees-egypt-through-education

UNHCR. 2010. *Convention and Protocol Relating to the Status of Refugees*. Geneva, Switzerland: United Nations High Commissioner for Refugees. https://www.unhcr.org/protection/basic/3b66c2aa10/convention-protocol-relating-status-refugees.html

UNHCR. 2013. Information for Asylum-Seekers and Refugees in Egypt. Egypt: United Nations High Commissioner for Refugees Regional Representation in Egypt. https://www.refworld.org/docid/5267a1d9b.html

UNHCR. 2022a. 3RP Regional Strategic Overview 2022. United Nations High Commissioner for Refugees. https://data.unhcr.org/en/documents/details/90787.

UNHCR.2022b Figures at a Glance. UNHCR. 16 June 2022. https://www.unhcr.org/figures-at-a-glance.html

UNHCR Egypt. 2016. Egypt UNHCR Operational Update January 2016. UNHCR Egypt. https://www.unhcr.org/protection/operations/5548c50f9/egypt-unhcr-operational-update.html

UNHCR Egypt. 2019. Egypt Regional Refugee & Resilience Plan (3RP) 2019-2020. UNHCR Egypt. https://data2.unhcr.org/en/documents/details/69672

UNHCR Egypt. 2020a. Partnering with GFF 2020, Sawiris Foundation & UNHCR Partner to Support Refugee Children in Egypt 2021/22. *UNHCR Egypt* (blog). 25 October 2020. https://www.unhcr.org/eg/16283-partnering-with-gff-2020-sawiris-foundation-unhcr-celebrate-their-collaboration-announce-2021-2022-commitment-to-refugee-children-in-egypt.html

UNHCR Egypt. 2020b. Regional Refugee & Resilience Plan in Response to the Syria Crisis: Egypt (2020/2021). UNHCR Egypt. https://reliefweb.int/report/egypt/egypt-3rp-regional-refugee-resilience-plan-response-syria-crisis-20202021

UNHCR Egypt 2022. UNHCR Egypt Monthly Statistical Report. UNHCR Egypt. https://www.unhcr.org/eg/wp-content/uploads/sites/36/2022/06/Monthly-Statistical-Report_April_2022.pdf

UNHCR Operational Data Portal. N.d. Situation Syria Regional Refugee Response. Accessed 21 June 2022. https://data.unhcr.org/en/situations/syria

UNOCHA. 2017. Jobs Make the Difference: Expanding Economic Opportunities for Syrian Refugees and Host Communities: Egypt, Iraq, Jordan, Lebanon, Syria, Turkey. United Nations Development Programme (UNDP), the International Labour Organization (ILO) and the World Food Programme (WFP). https://www.jobsmakethedifference.org/full-report. https://reliefweb.int/attachments/9d57f5ea-6b87-3fbd-80d7-b90e9870f488/compressed_12312313123UNDP_JOR_FINAL_Low%20Res.pdf

Walker, Peter. 2014. Migrant Boat Was 'deliberately Sunk' in Mediterranean Sea, Killing 500, *The Guardian*, 15 September 2014, sec. World news. http://www.theguardian.com/world/2014/sep/15/migrant-boat-capsizes-egypt-malta-traffickers

Witte, Griff. 2013. New Wave of Foreigners in Syrian Fight. *Washington Post*, 21 June 2013, sec. World. https://www.washingtonpost.com/world/new-wave-of-foreigners-in-syrian-fight/2013/06/21/e32d9d58-d9b8-11e2-b418-9dfa095e125d_story.html

World Food Programme. 2021. "Annual Country Report: Egypt." World Food Programme. https://www.wfp.org/operations/annual-country-report?operation_id=EG02&year=2021#/22309

9

National Responses to the Syrian Refugee Crisis: The Cases of Israel and Cyprus

ERICA MARTIN AND YANNIS A. STIVACHTIS

The Syrian refugee crisis began in March 2011, when the Arab Spring reached Syria's borders and the Assad regime violently countered protesters demanding social justice and democracy. After more than 11 years of civil unrest and chaos, the Syrian conflict has created the world's largest refugee population. To date, that war has resulted in the displacement of approximately 13.2 million people, including 6.6 million refugees, 6.2 million internally displaced people, and 140,000 asylum seekers (Ghadbian 2021, 52–55; Kapusnak 2014, 209–210). The Syrian refugee flows have sparked a dangerous rise in exclusionary populism, right-wing nationalist movements, and national security concerns (Alecou and Mavrou 2017, 1–2; Filc 2018, 124–131). Anti-immigration and anti-asylum seeker sentiments have continued to rise in affected countries (Moscovitz 2016, 140–143; Trimikliniotis and Demetriou 2011, 2–3). This escalation has stemmed from concerns arising from perceived threats to national security caused by Syrian 'outsiders,' which has resulted in their 'othering'. It has also arisen from post-9/11 perceived linkages between Islam and terrorism that have framed refugees from the Middle East as possible 'terrorists' and 'security threats' (Moscovitz 2016, 145–147; Trimikliniotis and Demetriou 2011, 24). The rising salience of these sentiments has allowed various far-right political parties, including in Israel and Cyprus, to gain political power and recognition during the past decade. These have adopted harsh immigration policies and othered and excluded immigrants from Syria (Baider and Kopytowska 2017, 216–219; Charalambous and Christoforou 2018, 452–455; Fischer 2020, 971–973; Ariely 2021, 1089–1091).

Israel and Cyprus are located at the geographic intersection of multiple cultures, making these two states destinations for refugees as they travel to seek permanent asylum in Europe (Trimikliniotis 2013, 441–445; Yaron et al. 2013, 145–147). Unfortunately for asylum seekers, both Israel and Cyprus do not have accommodating asylum policies and are ranked amongst the worst countries in the world for refugee integration and acceptance into civil society (Trimikliniotis and Demetriou 2011, 18–20; Kalir 2015, 581). This chapter examines how political actors have sought to securitize Syrian refugees in Israel and Cyprus and how the governments of those states have responded to those efforts and companion nativist claims directed at the displaced.

The Israeli Response to the Syrian Refugee Crisis

National security is a predominant concern in Israeli politics and policy and that has been so since the state's establishment in 1948 (Yaron et al. 2015, 145–146; Ziegler 2015, 175–176). After the Holocaust, the Israeli leaders viewed themselves as morally obliged to provide a haven for Jews from around the world, thus prompting the nation's aspiration to create an ethnocentric, Jewish majority state as the only way to preserve its identity (Zeedan 2019, 3–4; Kalir 2015, 580–583; Paz 2011, 8–10). The 1950 *Law of Return* sought to realize that goal, stating that any Jew could apply and automatically be granted citizenship in Israel without length of residency or language requirements (Hercowitz-Amir et al. 2017, 6; Afeef 2009, 3). This policy approach has produced a strong sense of ethno-nationalism within the country's population and has also made immigration a hotly contested issue, as ethnically different refugee and asylum-seekers have been perceived widely as potentially disrupting the integrity and security of the Jewish majority state (Hercowitz-Amir et al. 2017, 6–7; Kalir 2015, 580–583).

Indeed, refugees and asylum seekers are viewed in the general population as a possible threat to Jewish identity (Hercowitz-Amir et al. 2017, 6–7). Israelis distrust and marginalize Middle Eastern asylum seekers and refugees due to their nation's historical conflict concerning Palestine (Hercowitz-Amir et al. 2017, 6–7; Ziegler 2015, 175–176). Although specially targeted asylum seekers and immigrants are not subject to this policy, including the Alawites and the Druze, these populations are quite small and permitted for very specific reasons, which we treat below (Yaron et al. 2013, 147–152; Ziegler 2015, 175–176; Theodorou 2016; Halabi 2013, 265–270; Myhill 2011; Weinblum 2019, 699–700). To date, the Israeli government has not accepted any Syrian refugees and it has likewise offered limited humanitarian assistance to displaced Syrians in the name principally of preserving its national security (Kapusnak 2014 209–210; Boms and Karolina 2019, 683–687; Lewis 2018; Sales 2015).

Israel's ongoing securitization of non-Jewish immigration is deeply rooted in the nation's ongoing conflict in Palestine (Paz 2011, 8–10; Kalir 2015, 585–588). The latter began with the establishment of the Jewish state in 1948, which displaced 750,000 Palestinians and aggravated pre-existing tensions. The Israeli-Palestinian conflict remains a serious security issue in Israel due to multiple wars and armed conflicts concerning unresolved territorial and resource claims. The Israeli government has characterized Palestinians as a collective threat to the country's Jewish identity and national security and has long enacted and enforced legislation to prevent such individuals from entering its territory except under strictly regulated conditions (Ziegler 2015, 176; Paz 2011, 8–10). The 1945 *Prevention of Infiltration Law*, for example, stated that any 'infiltrators' caught entering Israel illegally with the intention to cause harm, and who were nationals of an enemy country, which included Lebanon, Egypt, Syria, and inhabitants of Palestine, would be deemed enemies of the state and could be sentenced to up to five years in prison (Kalir 2015, 587; Yaron et al. 2015, 145–146).

The word 'infiltrators' in the 1945 *Prevention of Infiltration Law* is now often employed to describe all asylum seekers and refugees, even though the term had been used originally to describe interlopers with malicious intent (Kalir 2015, 587; Yaron et al. 2015, 145–146). Put differently, the Israeli government has adopted policies that have resulted in the 'Palestinianization' of all refugee groups, with the result that all refugees, especially those from nations in the Middle East, are viewed through the lens of the Israeli-Palestine conflict, and a priori defined as members of opposition groups aiming to destroy Israel (Duman 2015, 1236–1237). Israel is also concerned that allowing some refugees and asylum seekers into the country could provide a legal mechanism for Palestinians to return *en masse* (Duman 2015, 1238; Paz 2011, 8–10). In this sense, and with that fear foremost in mind, Israel's anti-immigration stance can be interpreted as a self-preservation strategy. In summary, Israel's securitization of the refugee issue, based on a desire to preserve the Jewish identity of the country, has been used to discriminate against, delegitimize, and 'other' Syrian refugees.

Israeli Policies and Attitudes on Immigration

Although successive Israeli governments have either enacted or vigorously enforced legislation prioritizing Jewish immigrants, including the 1950 *Law of Return* and the 1945 *Prevention of Infiltration Law*, Israel has nonetheless also sought, at least nominally, to harmonize its domestic laws and actions with international legislative mandates concerning refugees and asylum seekers (Kalir 2015, 587; Yaron et al. 2015, 145–146; Hercowitz-Amir et al. 2017, 6–7; Afeef 2009, 3–4). One such mandate is the 1954 *UNHCR Convention Relating to the Status of Stateless Persons*, which states that signatory nations will honor 'international law with regard to the establishment of Refugee Status Determination processes and the treatment of refugees' (Yaron et al. 2015, 149–150). Nonetheless, Israel has not incorporated this mandate into its national law and has not translated its international obligation into Hebrew, meaning the Israeli government has essentially ignored its obligation. In addition, Israel has failed to honor several additional Convention provisions, including Article 26, by adopting its 'North to Hadera, South to Gedera' policy, which prevents asylum seekers from moving freely within the nation. Israel also failed to honor Article 33 of the Convention in its now withdrawn 'Hot returns' policy, in which its military and officials engaged in refoulement of asylum seekers, that is, their forced return to their countries of origin (Yaron et al. 2015, 149–150). In short, while Israel has ratified multiple international mandates addressing universal refugee and asylum seeker rights, its governments have rarely followed those policies, and instead, have implemented initiatives designed to maintaining a mainly religious and to a lesser extent a linguistically homogeneous Jewish population (Kalir 2015, 580–587; Yaron et al. 2015, 149–150; Hercowitz-Amir et al. 2017, 6–7; Afeef 2009, 3–4).

Right-wing Israeli political groups have promoted negative attitudes concerning refugees and asylum seekers based on their embrace of nativist sentiments and fear of the 'other' (Orr and Ajzenstadt 2020, 144–145; Duman 2015, 1237–1238). These groups have branded refugees and asylum seekers as 'infiltrators,' 'terrorists,' and 'criminals' in efforts to delegitimize their rights, racialize them, and frame them as a threat to the Israeli state and population (Moscovitz 2016, 150–156; Duman 2015, 1237–1244). Right-wing political groups have garnered surprising support for these claims among journalists and political leaders alike (Yaron et al. 2013, 147–154). Israeli media often frame refugees and asylum seekers as 'dehumanized entities' (Tirosh and Klein-Avraham 2019, 382). In addition, such individuals are often used as scapegoats for other social and economic problems, including increasing crime, rising unemployment, and limited access to social services (Orr and Ajzenstadt 2020, 143–148).

While many parties and officials have tended to treat refugees in these terms, some groups are portrayed as greater threats than others. These include Eritrean and Sudanese Darfuri asylum seekers (Yaron et al. 2015, 147–154; Hercowitz-Amir et al. 2017, 6–7). Israel experienced an influx of 50,000 such asylum seekers between 2005 and 2013 and in response to international pressures the Israeli Government granted a share of them Temporary Group Protection in accordance with its obligations under the 1954 *UNHCR Convention* (Yaron et al. 2015, 147–154; Hercowitz-Amir et al. 2017, 6–7; Weinblum 2019, 701–702). Many Sudanese Darfuri and Eritreans have experienced severe hardships while residing in Israel, including an inability to find stable work, living in a permanent state of poverty as a result of protracted unemployment, and enjoying quite limited access to health care (Kalir 2015, 585–590). Alongside political and economic marginalization, some in the Israeli media have also socially constructed the Eritreans and Sudanese Darfuris as 'infiltrators' and participants in 'criminal' networks (Orr and Ajzenstadt 2020, 149–152). Overall, these individuals have been popularly systematically criminalized and racialized and therefore are further categorized as public health and safety threats (Orr and Ajzenstadt 2020, 149–157; Weinblum 2019, 699–702). Furthermore, right-wing politicians and some media sources have accused these individuals of being economic migrants (even though a majority have been denied access to steady employment) and therefore not 'true' asylum seekers (Orr and Ajzenstadt 2020, 149–157; Weinblum 2019, 701–702).

The 'Good' Immigrants

In contrast to an overarching negative depiction of refugees and asylum seekers, government officials and party leaders have portrayed some migrant groups in 'positive' or 'neutral' terms, including, as noted above, the Alawites, a small Shia sect, and the Druze, also an outgrowth of Shia Islamicism, but whose members no longer consider themselves Muslim (Hercowitz-Amir et al. 2017, 6–7; Afeef 2009 3–4; Myhill 2011; Rathauser 2019; Eglash 2015; Halabi 2013, 265–270; Zeedan 2019, 1–5). The Alawites' village, Ghajar, was originally located in the Golan Heights, but after Israel occupied that territory during the 1967 Six Day War, the Alawites agreed to become Israeli citizens (Rathauser 2019; Rathauser 2019; Myhill 2011). The Alawites have maintained a distinctive identity within Israel and are often the subject of popular discrimination (Shmuel et al. 2017, 69–70).

The other exception to Israel's generally severe approach to immigration and refugees is the Druze community which, like the Alawites, is a sect with no theological or territorial objections to the Jewish state (Eglash 2015; Halabi 2013, 265–270; Zeedan 2019, 1–5). As a result, Israel has formally granted members of the Druze community citizenship (Eglash 2015; Halabi 2013, 265–270; Zeedan 2019, 1–5). Israel granted the Druze the right to serve in the nation's military in 1956 and they were the only group, besides Jews, accorded that right at the time. Compulsive military conscription was a huge turning point in the Druze's ethnicization and officially separated them from other members of other Arab minorities in Israel (Halabi 2013, 269–270; Zeedan 2019, 1–5). Israel formally designated the Druze as a separate ethnic category for purposes of citizen identification, further distinguishing them from perceived 'bad Arabs' (Halabi 2013, 269). Although the Druze have always been disadvantaged socioeconomically compared to the broader Jewish population, they share strong emotional and political ties with that population.

They are also in a much better position politically, economically, and socially relative to other ethnic groups in Israel (Saguy et al. 2019, 673).

Impact of the Syrian Refugee Crisis in Israel

Syria and Israel have formally been at war throughout the latter state's existence. Consequently, Israeli leaders perceive Syria as a key political and national security threat (Kapusnak 2014, 207–209). Since the 1973 Yom Kippur War, and prior to the 2011 Syrian Civil War and ensuing mass displacement, the Syria-Israel border had remained relatively stable in practice in recent years, if not accepted formally by Syria. However, relations between Israel and Syria had not been politically stable during the years leading up to the civil war due to the Assad regime's involvement in various proxy conflicts aimed at unsettling and nettling Israel (TOI Staff 2015; 'Israeli-Palestinian Conflict').

Given Israel's generally unwelcoming policies toward non-Jewish asylum seekers and refugees, it is not surprising that the nation's government has not granted asylum to any Syrian Civil War refugees (TOI Staff 2015). In fact, Israeli officials stated that they would not allow any 'infiltrators,' 'illegal migrants,' or 'terrorists,' into their territory, claiming that Israel was too small and did not have the demographic or geographic capacity to manage an influx of Syrian refugees (Sales 2015). Despite not accepting Syrian refugees, Israel did supply food, medical supplies, and fuel to Syria's displaced in the form of 'Operation Good Neighbor' (Boms and Karolina 2019, 684; Eglash 2018). However, it should also be said that Israeli leaders justified that effort as a means by which to protect the Israeli-Syrian border from asylum seekers and ISIS terrorists, to support the Druze community, and to remain on good terms with the international and European Union communities (Boms and Karolina 2019, 683–687).

Cyprus and the Syrian Refugee Crisis

Syrian refugees and asylum seekers seeking succor or passing through Cyprus have found themselves enmeshed in social, economic, and political conditions unleashed by the 1974 *de facto* division of the state, and the multiple crises facing Cypriot government officials (Charalambous 2018, 25–27; Trimikliniotis and Demetriou 2011, 2–10; Hajisoteriou 2020, 31–32). Right-wing political groups have pressed anti-immigration agendas and have typically othered would-be refugees and asylees in Greek-Cypriot society. However, certain immigrants have been accorded special standing in Cyprus, including wealthy individuals specifically (Rakopoulos and Fischer 2020; Charalambous 2018, 33–38; Milioni et al. 2015, 175–179; Charalambous and

Christoforou 2018, 452–455). Overall, the Cypriot response to the Syrian refugee crisis has been marginal at best, as the nation has accepted only a small number of refugees and otherwise intentionally limited the government resources available to such individuals (Alecou and Mavrou 2017 1–2; Fischer 2020, 970–971).

Historical Developments Shaping Securitization Politics of Cyprus

During the 1960s and 1970s, the two largest ethnic communities in Cyprus, the Greek-Cypriots and the Turkish-Cypriots, became embroiled in ethnic violence (Charalambous and Christoforou 2018, 452–455; Charalambous 2018, 31–33; Drousiotou and Mathioudakis 2019, 22–31). Those tensions reached a breaking point in 1974 when a Greek junta-instigated coup led to a Turkish invasion of the island's northern region, which split the nation into two separate territories and displaced thousands of people (Charalambous and Christoforou 2018, 452–455; Charalambous 2018, 31–33; Drousiotou and Mathioudakis 2019, 22–31). The unresolved and continuing tensions between Turkish and Greek Cypriots, in conjunction with the unsettled issue of the country's potential reunification have been at the heart of what is now often called the 'Cyprus problem' (Trimikliniotis and Demetriou 2011, 2–10).

The 'Cyprus problem' has served as a major political framework to reinforce nationalist sentiments amongst the Greek-Cypriot population against Turkish Cypriots, alongside any groups perceived to be unfamiliar 'others,' which have included refugees and asylum seekers (Charalambous and Christoforou 2018, 452–455; Charalambous 2018, 31–39; Drousiotou and Mathioudakis 2019, 22–31).

Greek Cypriot decisions on what constitutes citizenship in the Republic have primarily been employed to marginalize and discriminate against Turkish-Cypriots, as well as refugees and asylum seekers (Trimikliniotis and Demetriou 2011, 2–10). The Greek Cypriot population exhibits a strong sense of ethno-nationalism. Those individuals tend to believe they are the island's 'true' inhabitants and to view others as interlopers as a result. This perception has played a large role in the othering of Turks and other groups in Cyprus. This nativism has been heightened by the existence of the UN controlled 'Green Line,' which Greek Cypriots perceive as the division between an 'inferior' Turkish culture and a 'superior' Greek one. Many asylum seekers have illegally crossed the 'Green Line' into the Republic of Cyprus, thus further stigmatizing the division of the two territories and Turkish-Cypriots in the process, even if/when those crossing illegally into the Republic are not Turkish Cypriots (see Charalambous 2018, 31–39).

Another critical turning point in the securitization of migrants and refugees in Cyprus arose from the Republic's 2004 accession into the European Union (Fischer 2020, 965; Kadianaki et al. 2018, 408). Cyprus joined the EU with the goal of solving the 'Cyprus problem' and of increasing its economic prosperity in the wake of multiple economic crises. Many of the country's goals for its membership were never realized, however, with the EU unable to resolve the 'Cyprus problem' and economic concerns continuing to plague the nation as well (Fischer 2020, 965–966).

The Cypriot government was required to adopt some of the EU's immigration policies to become a member of that group. Those included providing asylum seekers the 'right to asylum' and allowing refugees and migrants access to social services. These stipulations forced the Republic to provide intercultural education and social security services for those groups in its legislation. Joining the EU also turned Cyprus into an attractive initial destination for asylum seekers, with the country acting as a gateway to other, more prosperous European Union nations. Although formally Cyprus' Union membership has required the Republic to relax its most onerous requirements concerning refugees and asylees, the country's government continues to undermine those individuals' access to basic services by othering them in public rhetoric, discriminating against them in practice, and by a failure to encourage their social integration into Cypriot society (Fischer 2020, 964–974; Kadianaki et al. 2018, 408).

An Overview of Immigration in Cyprus

Cyprus had historically been a country of net out migration until the 1990s, when mass tourism brought many employment opportunities to the island. That growth also drew the attention of would-be immigrants (Trimikliniotis and Demetriou 2011, 2–10). The rapid uptick in tourism created economic development and labor shortages, prompting policymakers to shift their stance toward immigration in 1991 to allow for low-skill temporary laborers to enter the state (Trimikliniotis and Demetriou 2011, 2–10; Trimikliniotis 2013, 445–446). These individuals were supposed to work in Cyprus temporarily and although they received the same employment terms as other Cypriots, they were restricted to positions in specific sectors unappealing to the nation's citizens and were otherwise discriminated against socially and politically (Trimikliniotis 2013, 453–456; Alecou and Mavrou 2017, 6–9). As a result, the labor migrants had little opportunity to integrate into Cyprus' society (Alecou and Mavrou 2017, 6–9).

As a general proposition, Cyprus is notorious for its restrictive refugee policies, which have included inhumane detention policies, excessively bureaucratic support processes, and a very low probability that asylum applicants would be granted that status. Overall, Cyprus is ranked amongst the least successful nations in the world in the long-term integration of foreigners (Fischer 2020, 964–974; Milioni et al. 2015, 156–157).

All of this said, and perhaps paradoxically, depending on their classification, some migrants are not as marginalized politically, socially, and economically as others, and are even able to join the social elite (Trimikliniotis 2013, 453–456; Trimikliniotis 2018, 20–24). Immigrants in Cyprus are generally categorized as either subaltern migrants, who are laborers willing to work in otherwise undesirable temporary jobs, or elite migrants, who are highly skilled and/or wealthy business people (Trimikliniotis 2013, 447). The latter group is treated much differently than subaltern migrants. Indeed, an investigation in 2020 revealed that these individuals, primarily from Eastern Europe, were bypassing Cypriot immigration processes altogether to purchase 'golden passport' citizenship applications directly from government officials. The only requirement to receive a 'golden passport' was that applicants invest millions of dollars into high-end real estate located on the island. Although this 'golden passport' practice has *officially* ended according to government officials, its existence demonstrates Cyprus' preference for certain types of immigrants and an elitist mentality concerning who could be eligible to enter that class (Rakopoulos and Fischer 2020).

After Cyprus' accession, the state experienced an increase in EU citizens exercising their right to free movement into and out of the country and, as noted, an overall increase in labor migrants and immigrants. Those trends coupled with the 2009-2013 economic crisis, prompted right-wing politicians and media outlets in the Republic to mount an anti-immigration campaign (Trimikliniotis 2013, 447–450). Right-wing populism grew in Cyprus alongside the weaponization of immigration and the use of asylum seekers and refugees as scapegoats for economic and other social problems, including rising crime and unemployment rates (Milioni et al. 2015, 33–38).

Elements of the Greek-Cypriot media as well as rightist political and social groups have cited economic concerns to frame asylum seekers and refugees as 'welfare exploiters,' 'job stealers,' and 'burdens'. Moreover, these same organizations and officials have portrayed asylum seekers and refugees as threats to the national and collective identity and labeled them 'barbarians,' 'terrorists,' and 'invaders' (Baider and Kopytowska 2017, 216–219; Kadianaki et al. 2018, 408–409). Due to the political, economic, and social hardships faced by asylum seekers and refugees in Cyprus, many such individuals actively seek other options. As such, many asylum seekers view Cyprus as an 'accidental,' as opposed to a 'final' destination, perhaps ugly evidence of the relative success of Cyprus's deterrence policies (Fischer 2020, 966–967).

In summary, asylum seekers, refugees, and labor migrants are disenfranchised politically, economically, and socially in Cyprus, except for a few very wealthy individuals. As a group, they are popularly portrayed as threats to the nation's economic and national security as well as to its identity.

The Educational Exclusion of Migrant Populations

Asylum seekers and refugees are poorly integrated into Cyprus' civil society generally and especially within the Greek-Cypriot public-school system (Charalambous et al. 2013, 79–80; Theodorou 2014, 255–256). Intercultural education is a relatively new phenomenon in Cyprus and began to be offered only when the nation was admitted to the Union (Charalambous et al. 2013, 82–88). Prior to 2004, education in the Republic was largely framed by the 'Cyprus problem' and included a curriculum focused on maintaining an ethnocentric viewpoint of the Greek-Cypriot identity, maintaining a strong Hellenocentric national identity, and reproducing negative representations of Turkish-Cypriots (Charalambous et al. 2013, 82–88). Although intercultural education has been introduced into the Cypriot education system, it has yet to be fully integrated in practice, and there is still a strong Greek-Cypriot ethnocentric narrative and negative association of the 'other' being dispensed in Cypriot classrooms (Theodorou 2014, 255–256).

Asylum seeker and refugee children confront exclusion and an overall lack of integration in the Cypriot public education system, including language barriers and a focus on assimilation rather than accommodation (Lambri et al. 2020, 6; Michalinos 2012, 195–196). Additionally, some Greek-Cypriot children in Cyprus are affected by othering narratives and the 'Cyprus problem,' when they express tolerance toward asylum seeker and refugee children (Michalinos 2012, 198–199). The rhetoric and reality surrounding children's integration and inclusion in education is connected to debates on citizenship and economic development as popularly contextualized within the 'Cyprus problem' (Trimikliniotis and Demetriou 2011, 13–16).

Impact of the Syrian Refugee Crisis in Cyprus

The Syrian Civil War affected Cyprus via an increased volume of asylum applications entering the nation's Asylum Services System (Fischer 2020, 966–967). In fact, in 2017, Cyprus received the greatest number of such applications, 1,762, from Syrian refugees among EU nations, but accepted only 21 of those (Fischer 2020, 966–967). During the past decade, Cyprus has accepted a limited number of temporary asylum seekers from Syria, but its overall asylum rejection rate is one of the highest in Europe, reaching 51.18% in 2018 (Fischer 2020, 966–967). Moreover, applications that Cyprus has accepted required an average of 18–24 months to process to decision (Drousiotou and Mathioudakis 2019, 22–31).

Conclusions

Israel and Cyprus have many similarities when it comes to their political, economic, and social responses to asylum seekers and refugees. Both countries are examples of how refugees and asylum seekers can be portrayed and thereafter perceived as threats to a country's military, societal, political, and economic security regardless of whether they innately represent such threats in fact. Both Israel and Cyprus have mandated that refugees and asylum seekers may only temporarily be granted asylum. Despite nominal obeisance to international and EU agreements, each has also enacted policies designed to make it difficult for these groups to access the social services they need to survive. In both states, asylum seekers and refugees have been widely pilloried and 'othered' by right-wing political groups claiming that they threaten the identity of the dominant ethnic group, the Jews in Israel and the orthodox Greek Cypriots in Cyprus. These groups have employed negative rhetoric and descriptors such as 'infiltrators' and 'barbarians' to dehumanize and delegitimize these displaced individuals.

Asylum seekers and refugees have also popularly been blamed for causing social and economic problems in both states, including rising crime rates and undue and undeserved use of state-sponsored fiscal sources and welfare services and supports. Middle Eastern asylum seekers and refugees have been singled out for special opprobrium in Israel because of fears inhering in its long-lived conflict with neighboring nations and Palestinians. A similar dynamic has unfolded in Cyprus rooted in its long-standing conflict with Turkey. Cyprus and Israel have each granted certain migrant groups exceptions to their otherwise punitive policies. For Cyprus, that group has been those who possess wealth and promise to invest some share of it in the Republic. Israel has meanwhile accorded the Druze and Alawites similar special standing in its refugee policy. These exceptions notwithstanding, most asylum seekers and refugees in Israel and Cyprus are routinely racialized, ostracized, and kept separate from civil society. Finally, neither of these states has sought to engage in meaningful integration efforts for the few they have elected to support.

References

Afeef, Karin Fathimath, and Office of the United Nations High Commissioner for Refugees. Evaluation and Policy Analysis Unit. 2009. *A Promised Land for Refugees? Asylum and Migration in Israel*. New Issues in Refugee Research, No. 183. Geneva: UNHCR.

Alecou, Alexios, and Josefina Mavrou. 2017. "Refugees in Cyprus: Local Acceptance in the Past and Present" *Social Sciences* 6, no. 4: 111. https://doi.org/10.3390/socsci6040111

Ariely, Gal. 2021. Collective Memory and Attitudes Toward Asylum Seekers: Evidence from Israel. *Journal of Ethnic and Migration Studies* 47 (5): 1084–1102. https://doi.org/10.1080/1369183X.2019.1572499

Avraamidou, Maria, Irini Kadianaki, Maria Ioannou, and Elisavet Panagiotou. 2019. Representations of Europe at Times of Massive Migration Movements: A Qualitative Analysis of Greek-Cypriot Newspapers during the 2015 Refugee Crisis. *Javnost-The Public* 26 (1): 105–19.

Baider, Fabienne and Kopytowska, Monika. Conceptualising the Other: Online discourses on the current refugee crisis in Cyprus and in Poland. Lodz Papers in Pragmatics 13, no. 2 (2017): 203-233. https://doi.org/10.1515/lpp-2017-0011

Boms, Nir, and Zielińska Karolina. 2019. Changing Borders in a Changing Region: The Civilian Dimension and Security Predicament along the Syrian-Israeli Border. *Israel Affairs* 25 (4): 675–98. https://doi.org/10.1080/13537121.2019.1626090.

Charalambous Giogos. 2018. Constructing 'the People' and Its 'Enemies' in the Republic of Cyprus: A Country of Populist Frames but Not Fully Fledged Populism. *Cyprus Review* 30 (2): 25–41.

Charalambous, Giorgos, and Panos Christoforou. 2018. Far-Right Extremism and Populist Rhetoric: Greece and Cyprus during an Era of Crisis. *South European Society and Politics* 23 (4): 451–77. https://doi.org/10.1080/13608746.2018.1555957

Charalambous, Panayiota, Constadina Charalambous, and Michalinos Zembylas. Old and New Policies in Dialogue: Greek-Cypriot Teachers' Interpretations of a Peace-Related Initiative through Existing Policy Discourses. *British Educational Research Journal* 40, no. 1 (14 February 2013): 79–101. https://doi.org/10.1002/berj.3030.

Drousiotou, Corina, and Manos Mathioudakis. Rep. *Country Report: Cyprus*. Cyprus Refugee Council, 2019. https://asylumineurope.org/wp-content/uploads/2020/04/report-download_aida_cy_2019update.pdf

Duman, Yoav H. 2015. *Infiltrators Go Home!* Explaining Xenophobic Mobilization against Asylum Seekers in Israel. *Journal of International Migration and Integration* 16 (4): 1231–54. https://doi.org/10.1007/s12134-014-0400-2.

Eglash, Ruth. Thousands of Syrians Are Fleeing toward Israel's Border, Posing a New Challenge. *The Washington Post*. WP Company, 2 July 2018. https://www.washingtonpost.com/world/middle_east/israel-in-dilemma-over-thousands-of-syrians-fleeing-fighting-toward-its-borders/2018/07/02/af85631a-7dd6-11e8-b0ef-fffcabeff946_story.html

Filc D. (2018) Political Radicalization in Israel: From a Populist Habitus to Radical Right Populism in Government. In: Steiner K., Önnerfors A. (eds) *Expressions of Radicalization*. Palgrave Macmillan, Cham. https://doi.org/10.1007/978-3-319-65566-6_5

Fischer, Leandros. 2020. Gramscian Perspectives on Citizenship: Snapshots from the Experience of Regional Migrants in the Republic of Cyprus. *Citizenship Studies* 24 (8): 959–78. https://doi.org/10.1080/13621025.2020.1768222.

Ghadbian, Najib. The Syrian Refugee Crisis and the International Community. *Middle East Policy* 28, no. 1 (6 June 2021): 51–69. https://doi.org/10.1111/mepo.12543.

Hajisoteriou C. 2020. Migration Policies and Education Responses to Migration in Cyprus: From Intercultural Policy Discourses to 'Trivialised' Multicultural Practices. *Cyprus Review* 32 (1): 31–62.

Halabi, Rabah. Invention of a Nation: The Druze in Israel. *Journal of Asian and African Studies* 49, no. 3 (9 June 2013): 267–81. https://doi.org/10.1177/0021909613485700.

Hercowitz-Amir, Adi, Raijman, Rebeca, and Davidov, Eldad. 2017. "Host or Hostile? Attitudes Towards Asylum Seekers in Israel and in Denmark." Info:Doi/10.1177/0020715217722039. http://www.zora.uzh.ch/id/eprint/139368/1/Hercowitz-Amir_Raijman_Davidov_IJCS_Final_Version_Submitted.pdf

Israeli-Palestinian Conflict. Global Conflict Tracker. Council on Foreign Relations, 13 October 2021. https://www.cfr.org/global-conflict-tracker/conflict/israeli-palestinian-conflict

Kadianaki, I., Avraamidou, M., Ioannou, M., & Panagiotou, E. (2018). Understanding media debate around migration: The relation between favorable and unfavorable representations of migration in the Greek Cypriot press. *Peace and Conflict: Journal of Peace Psychology, 24*(4), 407–415. https://doi.org/10.1037/pac0000285

Kalir, Barak. 2015. The Jewish State of Anxiety: Between Moral Obligation and Fearism in the Treatment of African Asylum Seekers in Israel. *Journal of Ethnic and Migration Studies* 41 (4): 580–98. https://doi.org/10.1080/136918 3X.2014.960819.

KAPUSŇAK, Ján. Israeli Response to the Syrian Crisis and New Security Environment on the Israel-Syria border. In Peter Bátor, Róbert Ondrejcsák. Panorama of Global Security Environment 2014. Bratislava: Centre for European and North Atlantic Affairs, 2014. s. 207-218. *Panorama of Global Security Environment 2014*. ISBN 978-80-971124-9-3.

Lambri Trisokka, Leslie Gautsch, Christoforos Mamas. 2020. 'Feeling at home away from home?' Social participation of refugee students in Cyprus: A mixed methods case study design, *Journal of Refugee Studies*, feaa124, https://doi.org/10.1093/jrs/feaa124

Lewis, Ori. 2018. Israel Will Not Accept Any Syrian Refugees on Its Territory: Defense Minister. *Reuters*. Thomson Reuters, 29 June 2018. https://www.reuters.com/article/us-mideast-crisis-syria-israel/israel-will-not-accept-any-syrian-refugees-on-its-territory-defense-minister-idUSKBN1JP10E

Michalinos, Zembylas. 2012. The politics of fear and empathy: emotional ambivalence in 'host' children and youth discourses about migrants in Cyprus, *Intercultural Education*, 23:3, 195-208, DOI: 10.1080/14675986.2012.701426

Milioni D.L, Spyridou L.-P, and Vadratsikas K. 2015. Framing Immigration in Online Media and Television News in Crisis-Stricken Cyprus. *Cyprus Review* 27 (1): 155–86.

Moscovitz, Hannah. 2016. The Mainstreaming of Radical Right Exclusionary Ideology: Israeli Parliamentary Discussions Over Asylum. *Journal of Political Ideologies* 21 (2): 140–59. https://doi.org/10.1080/13569317.2016.1150138.

Myhill, Prof. John. The Alawites and Israel. Begin-Sadat Center for Strategic Studies. Bar-Ilan University, 4 May 2011. https://besacenter.org/the-alawites-and-israel/

Noam, Tirosh and Inbal Klein-Avraham. 2019. Memoryless, *Journalism Studies*, 20:3, 381-400, DOI: 10.1080/1461670X.2017.1383857

Orr, Zvika, and Mimi Ajzenstadt. 2020. Beyond Control: The Criminalization of African Asylum Seekers in Israel. *International Review of Sociology* 30 (1): 142–65. https://doi.org/10.1080/03906701.2020.1724369.

Paz, Yonathan, and Office of the United Nations High Commissioner for Refugees. Policy Development and Evaluation Service. 2011. *Ordered Disorder: African Asylum Seekers in Israel and Discursive Challenges to an Emerging Refugee Regime*. New Issues in Refugee Research, Research Paper; No. 205. Geneva, Switzerland: UNHCR, Policy Development and Evaluation Service.

Rakopoulos, Theodoros, and Leandros Fischer. In Cyprus, the Golden Passports Scheme Shows Us How Capitalism and Corruption Go Hand in Hand. *Jacobin*, 11 October 2020. https://www.jacobinmag.com/2020/11/cyprus-golden-passports-citizenship-corruption

Rathauser, Ben. Ghajar, Home of the Israeli Alawites. *The Jerusalem Post,* JPost.com, 13 April 2019. https://www.jpost.com/israel-news/culture/ghajar-home-of-the-israeli-alawites-586566

Saguy, Tamar, Danit Sobol-Sarag, Samer Halabi, Katherine Stroebe, Emile Bruneau, and Siwar Hasan-Aslih. 2019. When a Sense OF 'WE' Is Lost: Investigating the Consequences of a Lost Common Identity Among Druze in Israel. *Social Psychological and Personality Science* 11, no. 5: 667–75. https://doi.org/10.1177/1948550619884562

Sales, Ben. As Europe Takes in Migrants, Israel Tries to Keep Them Out. *Jewish Telegraphic Agency*, 8 September 2015. https://www.jta.org/2015/09/08/israel/as-europe-grapples-with-migrant-crisis-israel-considers-its-own

Shmuel, Shamai, Shemali Ali, Gorbatkin Dennis, Chativ Nadim, Elachmad Halil, and Ilatov Zinaida. 2017. Identity and Sense of Place of GHAJAR Residents Living in Border Junction of Syria, Israel and Lebanon. *Mediterranean Journal of Social Sciences*, 1, 8, no. 4-1, 1 July: 61–72. https://doi.org/10.2478/mjss-2018-0074.

Theodorou, Angelina E. "5 Facts about Israeli Druze, a Unique Religious and Ethnic Group." Pew Research Center. Pew Research Center, March 21, 2016. https://www.pewresearch.org/fact-tank/2016/03/21/5-facts-about-israeli-druze-a-unique-religious-and-ethnic-group/

Theodorou E. (2014) Constructing the 'Other'. In: Vega L. (eds) Empires, Post-Coloniality and Interculturality. The CESE Series. SensePublishers, Rotterdam. https://doi.org/10.1007/978-94-6209-731-5_16

TOI Staff. "Poll Shows Few Israelis Willing to Take in Syrian Refugees." The Times of Israel, September 7, 2015. https://www.timesofisrael.com/poll-shows-few-israelis-willing-to-take-in-syrian-refugees/

Trimikliniotis, Nicos and Demetriou Corina. 2011. Tolerance and Cultural Diversity Discourses in Cyprus. ACCEPT-PLURALISM, 2011/01, 1. Overview National Discourses, Background Country Reports. Retrieved from Cadmus, European University Institute Research Repository, at: http://hdl.handle.net/1814/19789

Trimikliniotis, Nicos. 2018. *Report on political participation of mobile EU citizens: Cyprus*, [Global Governance Programme], GLOBALCIT, Political Participation Reports, 2018/12 Retrieved from Cadmus, European University Institute Research Repository, at: http://hdl.handle.net/1814/59408

Trimikliniotis, Nicos. 2013. Migration and Freedom of Movement of Workers: EU Law, Crisis and the Cypriot States of Exception *Laws 2*, no. 4: 440–468. https://doi.org/10.3390/laws2040440

Weinblum, Sharon. 2019. Conflicting Imaginaries of the Border: The Construction of African Asylum Seekers in the Israeli Political Discourse, *Journal of Borderlands Studies*, 34:5, 699–715, DOI: 10.1080/08865655.2018.1436001

Yaron, Hadas, Nurit Hashimshony-Yaffe, and John Campbell. 2013. 'Infiltrators' or Refugees? An Analysis of Israel's Policy Towards African Asylum-Seekers. *International Migration* 51 (4): 144–57. https://doi.org/10.1111/imig.12070.

Zeedan, Rami. The Role of Military Service in The Integration/Segregation of Muslims, Christians and Druze within Israel. *Societies* 9, no. 1 (8 January 2019): 1–15. https://doi.org/10.3390/soc9010001

Ziegler, Reuven. 2015. No Asylum for 'Infiltrators': The Legal Predicament of Eritrean and Sudanese Nationals in Israel. *Journal of Immigration, Asylum and Nationality Law* Vol. 29, No. 2, P. 172–191.

10

The Critical Role of Turkey in the Management of the Syrian Refugee Crisis

DIMITRIS TSAROUHAS

The role of Turkey in the management of the Syrian refugee crisis is long-running and multifaceted. It also has important political implications, both in terms of Turkey's domestic political scene and regarding its external relations with Syria as well and countries in the wider region and beyond. Moreover, the crisis has had a direct effect on European Union (EU)-Turkey relations in the light of the agreements reached between the two sides in 2015–2016 and their implementation since. When the Syrian Civil War began in 2011, few predicted that it would morph into a regional conflict and affect both domestic politics and the foreign policies of multiple states in the region and beyond. Turkey is undoubtedly one of the countries mostly influenced by it, partly by default (it shares a 900 km long land border with Syria) and partly by design, that is, due to conscious decisions made by its leadership. Turkey has been active in the Syrian refugee crisis and its decision to open its borders to refugees from that nation became well known worldwide. A decade later, 3.64 million Syrian refugees are officially registered in the country (UNHCR 2021) and questions arising from the current situation are multiple. Will Turkey opt for the integration of those refugees, or does its government view them as temporary residents? How is the presence of such a large and visible minority affecting Turkish politics? Finally, to what extent does Turkey's stance on the issue, and the Syrian crisis more generally, influence its relations with the European Union (EU)?

This chapter offers tentative answers to these questions. To do so, I begin with a few theoretical considerations premised on the Europeanization thesis and its application to Turkey. The section thereafter discusses Turkey's legal and institutional context on the matter prior to the crisis, before focusing on a watershed moment in the refugee crisis, namely the EU-Turkey agreement of 2015 and its implications. The third section outlines the domestic political challenges that policy makers and parties confront at present, before concluding with an overall assessment of the country's role in managing the Syrian refugee issue.

My main argument is that Turkey has sought to cope with the crisis in two distinct ways and over two identifiable phases. During the first phase, which lasted roughly until 2015, Turkey sought to reap political benefits from the Syrian crisis. It did so by welcoming an influx of millions of Syrians and seeking to manage the situation by upgrading its domestic infrastructure to do so, both legally and institutionally, with the support of external actors and especially the EU. All the while, Turkish government leaders believed that Assad's regime would soon collapse, placing Ankara in a prime position to influence the future of Syria. The fact that this expectation did not materialize weighed heavily in subsequent developments. In the second period, post-2015, and as the crisis became endemic, Turkey's government confronted a threat and an opportunity. On the one hand, the nation's ability to manage the crisis fell, as the number of Syrians residing in the country remained very high and opposition parties began offering an effective political narrative that cornered the government and articulated the frustration of large swathes of the population set against Syrian migrants. During this second period, Turkey's government began losing control of the discourse regarding Syrian migrants and refugees, a process that became a potent electoral threat.

On the other hand, Turkey sought during this period to reap the benefits of its earlier activism on the issue and benefit from the lack of coordination among EU member states concerning it. The EU-Turkey agreements of 2015 and 2016 are a potent example of the EU's reliance on Turkey to help to manage the crisis on Europe's behalf. That fact gave the Turkish government leverage over EU affairs and allowed it to extract concessions (political and financial) from the Union. In theoretical terms, this case analysis of Turkey's behavior during the crisis confirms the validity of the 'instrumental Europeanization' thesis (Aybars et al. 2019; Fougner and Kurtoğlu 2015), which suggests that Turkey will seek to adjust to EU norms and policies only to the extent that such action aligns with its national priorities. In this view, EU-Turkey relations manifest a transactional character (Dimitriadi et al. 2018) and remain robust only in those policy areas where the two parties derive direct, immediate material benefits from cooperation.

Turkey and Europeanization: Two Stories

Turkey's relations with the EU go back to the 1960s. After submitting its membership application in 1987, Turkey signed a Customs Union (CU) agreement with the Union and trade relations between the two sides flourished as a result (World Bank and European Union 2014). Turkey's goal of EU membership appeared more likely following the 1999 EU Summit in Helsinki that offered the country EU candidate country status. By the mid-2000s, Turkey's economy was growing, its politics had become more stable and Tayyip Erdoğan and his Justice and Development Party (AKP) dominated the nation's governance.

The Europeanization process, which guided the accession into the EU of Central and East European states in the recent past (Schimmelfennig and Sedelmeier 2004; Grabbe 2006) and had been heavily influential in Southern Europe's incorporation into the Community, was now creating expectations for Turkey (Tocci 2005). Schimmelfennig and Sedelmeier (2005) have argued that the mechanisms of Europeanisation in candidate countries are evident in two dimensions: the hard mechanism refers to *acquis* implementation while the second, soft mechanism relates to pressures to internalize the EU's normative codes of conduct and 'appropriate' policy behavior. During the early 2000s, in both domestic and foreign policy, Turkey implemented a series of far-reaching political, judicial, and economic reforms. These appeared to confirm the 'stick and carrot' approach, also known as conditionality policy, through which the EU entices members to adopt rules and policies in line with its own. While important challenges remained in several policy areas, not least civil-military relations (Duman and Tsarouhas 2006) and social policy (Manning 2007), Turkey's strategic direction appeared to confirm that a combination of material incentives and normative alignment would eventually result in the country joining the EU.

The impact of Europeanization on Turkey was limited from the start. Indeed, although accession negotiations began in 2005, they never gathered steam. The immediate cause was the Cyprus problem. Turkey refused to extend its Customs Union provisions with the EU to the Republic of Cyprus (Eralp 2009) and its failure to resolve the problem through UN mediation in 2004 meant that its accession process was marred by a major diplomatic spat with an EU member (Cyprus had joined the EU in 2004). As with Cyprus, timing did not prove helpful to Turkey either. The nation's EU accession talks began at a time when 'enlargement fatigue' was becoming evident among Union member governments. EU public opinion was on average negative concerning the prospect of Turkey's accession and several member states, including France, Germany, and Austria, publicly voiced a desire to develop alternatives to full Turkish membership. At the same time, the Turkish government adopted a 'double standards' argument, accusing the Union of opposition to Turkey's accession due to its predominantly Muslim population. In due course, Turkey froze and then reversed EU-aligned legislation, distancing itself from the EU *acquis*. Indeed, the limits of Europeanization (Nutcheva and Aydin-Düzgit 2011; Tsarouhas 2016) were revealed in 2016, during which the Turkish government gradually dropped its EU-related aspirations and openly contradicted EU policies by reversing earlier reforms. The EU lost its ability to act as an anchor to Turkey's reform drive and the lack of a credible accession prospect reinforced Turkey's shift away from the EU. The Eurozone economic crisis tainted the EU's image in the country further, while the Arab Spring facilitated Turkey's attempts to establish itself as a regional power in the Middle East (Öniş 2014).

The validity of the Europeanization framework has come under intense scrutiny because of rising Euro-skepticism in EU member states, the rise of illiberal tendencies inside and outside the EU as well as the multiple crises the Union has confronted, not least Brexit and the migration and refugee crisis. Turkey's relationship has followed this trajectory and a large literature on 'De-Europeanization' has emerged. This scholarship has demonstrated that in various policy areas, ranging from the rule of law (Saatçioğlu 2016) to media freedoms (Yilmaz 2016), Turkey's policies and practices have moved away from the EU *acquis*.

I argue that, although Turkey's estrangement from the EU is evident in recent years in the case of the Syrian refugee and migration crisis, a longitudinal perspective reveals a sort of 'instrumental Europeanization' stance aimed at using the crisis for political benefit on a transactional, interests-first basis. Methodologically, I use primary and secondary sources as well as semi-structured interviews conducted with policy officials representing Turkish and international organizations, the details of which can be found at the end of the chapter.

Turkey's Policies on Migration and Asylum

Turkey's first legislative initiative in refugee law dates to 1934 when the nation passed its Settlement Law. The Law was quite restrictive: it mandated that only those of 'Turkish culture and descent' would be eligible to receive refugee status. The EU membership process led to realignment in Turkey's legislative framework regrading refugees, but later statutes maintained the ethnic descent criterion, especially for the purposes of settlement in the country (*Iskan Kanunu* 2006).

In 1951, the landmark Geneva Convention offered a definition of who may be regarded as a refugee and established the principle of non-refoulment, prohibiting states from returning refugees to states where they could face torture and other forms of prosecution due to their race, ethnicity, nationality or views (UNHCR 2010). A 1967 protocol broadened the definition of refugee and obliged states to comply with the Convention's provisions without time limitations (UNHCR 2010). Turkey has signed these key documents; however, its government stipulated that a right to asylum in Turkey could be granted only to those arriving from Europe. The direct consequence of this provision has been that the Turkish government views refugees arriving from elsewhere in the world, as occurred in the aftermath of the Iraq war in the 1990s and more recently because of the Syrian conflict, as 'guests,' with no asylum claim right. Such individuals are therefore expected to depart from the country at some point in the future. After the end of the Cold War and the beginning of the first Gulf War, as well as the earlier Iraq-Iran war of 1980–1988, people fleeing conflict in the Middle East (and further East) started arriving in Turkey. The country became a transit spot for those whose final destinations were further west, while others sought to settle in the nation (Tsarouhas 2019). The legal and regulatory framework of the country was inadequate to deal with this new reality. In the circumstances it confronted following these conflicts, Turkey ceased to be a country of emigration to safer and more prosperous western nations. It was therefore imperative that the country's government craft new initiatives to deal with that changing reality.

In 1994, Regulation 69/1994 offered temporary protection status to refugees. Those whose status was approved became entitled to resettlement in third countries. This was the first instance in which Turkey defined refugees (stemming from Europe) and asylum-seekers (stemming from elsewhere in the world) by use of national legislation (Kaya 2009). However, the big legislative changes to consolidate various instruments on refugee status occurred in the 2000s due to two factors: first, Turkey's EU accession talks, and second, the Syrian crisis and agreements with the European Union. Legislative alignment with the EU *acquis* is a major precondition for accession, and the Turkey's National Action Plan (NAP) for Asylum and Migration adopted in 2005 pointed to Turkey's willingness to proceed with alignment.

In 2006, an Implementation Directive issued by Turkey clarified the legal status of refugees and asylum-seekers. However, the geographical limitation was maintained resulting in a two-tier asylum and migration system: the first, referring to Europeans, arose from Turkey's approximation to the West during the Cold War. The second, addressing non-Europeans, was the product of an influx of Iraqi Kurds after 1988 and the first Gulf war (Kirişçi 2012). Nevertheless, this did not automatically mean dropping the geographic limitation that only offered asylum to people stemming from Europe. The NAP identified two conditions for lifting that limitation. First, that EU members commit to burden-sharing and second, legislative changes to prevent a rapid rise in refugees entering the country (National Action Plan 2005).

EU-Turkey Relations and the Syrian Crisis: The First Phase

Turkey began receiving Syrian refugees following the onset of the civil war in Syria in the spring of 2011. The government established an open-door policy for (what it labeled as) its 'guests' from Syria fleeing prosecution (Erdoğan 2014, 66). In the early days of the conflict, Turkey's refugee policy was premised on two assumptions. The first was a belief that the Syrian Civil War would not last long and Syrian President Assad would flee from power, opening opportunities for Turkey to play a decisive role in a post-Assad Syria. Second, Turkey's leaders believed that Syrians coming to Turkey would soon be able to return to their homes and that, therefore, there would be minimal need to integrate and accommodate them into Turkish society. Both assumptions were underpinned by Turkey's changing approach towards the Middle East during the 'Arab Spring' revolt. In an earlier era, the nation's government had sought to normalize and desecuritize relations with countries in the region, notably Syria, to fulfill the 'zero problems with neighbors' doctrine espoused by Ahmet Davutoğlu, advisor to Erdoğan and later Prime Minister. By the time the Arab Spring occurred, however, and in line with Davutoğlu's ambitious 'Strategic Depth' approach to Turkish foreign policy, the government sought to maximize diplomatic gains by positioning itself as a protagonist in the Middle East (D'Alema 2017, 10). Turkey's policymakers saw themselves as leaders of the indispensable country that other peoples and elites, including those of the EU, would need to look to for guidance, inspiration, and support. Turkey's approach to the Syrian Civil War was at least partly shaped by its expectations about what a post-conflict Syria would look like.

It is in 2011 that relations with the EU became important. Both Ankara and Brussels were committed to Assad's overthrow. Their cooperation concerning the Syrian crisis was instrumental in character from the start. Nonetheless, Turkey's agenda appeared not to clash with Europe's yet. Moreover, the mass exodus of Syrians via Turkey to Europe had yet to materialize. Further, although strains in EU-Turkey relations had already appeared, Ankara's senior policy makers maintained rhetorical commitment to EU membership, and the Union was happy to encourage cooperation with a key ally. In sum, in 2011, Turkey's politics in dealing with the Syrian crisis pointed to generosity and solidarity; its capacity to deliver sustainable protection, however, was limited and its relations with key EU member states very complicated.

In 2013, Turkey's adoption of the Law on Foreigners and International protection (LFIP) was a major step forward in the nation's refugee policy, constituting the first ever integrated national law concerning asylum in Turkey's history. (Suter 2013). The statute created a new body to deal with the issue of migrants and refugees, the General Directorate for Migration Management (GDMM). International actors were key in the process: the United Nations High

Commission for Refugees (UNHCR) played a considerable role in drafting the effort (Çorabatir 2016, 7), while the EU congratulated Ankara on its passage, and pointed to the salience of the Visa Liberalization Roadmap in achieving further progress (European Commission 2014). The new law was very much in line with EU legislation and asylum procedures, such as provisions regarding 'safe third countries' and 'first-country-of asylum' (Çorabatir 2016, 7). It defined several categories of foreigners for the first time, and was explicit regarding the terms of entry, stay, and exit in the country (Soykan 2012). Moreover, the formation of the GDMM meant that tasks regarding the management of migration would now fall under the authority of that body instead of the country's General Directorate for Security. The new law also offered refugees and asylum seekers access to specified social services (*Yabancilar ve Uluslararasi Koruma Kanunu* 2013).

In 2014 and in line with its emphasis on EU-inspired reforms, Turkey issued a Temporary Protection Regulation to offer Syrians healthcare and education opportunities in accord with the Geneva Convention (Makovsky 2019). Further, Syrian nationals were given biometric ID cards, the opportunity to work legally in Turkey (many were involved in the informal economy already), and to access psychological support services, a crucial service to individuals frequently suffering from post-traumatic stress disorder and other mental health issues. On the other hand, the implementation of these reforms has not proceeded without difficulty. Bureaucratic hurdles to gain access to those services, including ID cards, have meant that most Syrian refugees in Turkey have been unable to benefit from available support structures (Interview 2).

There has been a discernible effect on Turkey's public administration regarding migration and asylum as a result of the reforms mentioned above. The government has cooperated with NGOs in crisis management to an unprecedented degree, not least because of the central role those organizations have played in project management and capacity building (Interview 1). Moreover, the UNHCR and the International Organization for Migration (IOM) have also been directly involved, reinforcing the ability to run relevant projects smoothly, in cooperation with local government and especially municipalities. (Interviews 1, 2 and 4). One of the obstacles Turkey faces however, is its centralized state administration structure: coordination with 'on the ground' municipal authorities remains subject to a top-down relationship with central government officials holding the upper hand in allocating resources (Interview 4).

The progress that Turkey has made notwithstanding, it is worth pointing to deficiencies that persisted throughout the 2010–2015 reform era. First, the 2013 Law did not grant equal protection to all groups entering the country, relying instead mostly on a 2001 EU Directive outlining temporary protection

(Çorabatir 2016, 7). Second, the new legislative framework did not include the right to work for Syrian refugees. Instead, individuals had to apply for work permits under a cumbersome and heavily bureaucratic process, which drove most into the underground economy (Kirişçi et al. 2018). Given the sheer number of Syrians in Turkey, these difficulties have had important consequences, as most refugees are unable to sustain decent living standards and remain part of the informal economy. They are also in effect subject to the Turkish government's willingness (or not) to satisfy their demands, resulting in a high level of vulnerability. Finally, Turkey has not lifted the geographic limitation provision mentioned earlier. A credible interpretation of that decision offered by Kirişçi (2012, 75) argues that this decision resulted from Ankara's fears of doing so without securing its EU membership first.

The Second Phase: EU-Turkey Agreements and instrumental Europeanization

2015 was a game-changing year in terms of Turkey's role in the Syrian crisis. The government's approach changed quite quickly as a result of the fact that the crisis now spilled over to its European neighbors. Large masses of people moved westward from Syria and put enormous pressure on EU governments to accept them as migrants and/or refugees. In most EU countries, right-wing populists saw a golden opportunity to proclaim an 'invasion' against 'native cultures,' and European governments were forced to act quickly to reduce the immigration-related pressures they faced. Germany recognized both the magnitude of the problem and the significance of Turkey as a country able to help it fend off those pressures, putting pressure on other member states to reach an agreement with Turkey. As a result, the EU and Turkey reached a series of crucial agreements. Turkey and the Union adopted a Joint Action Plan (JAP) in late 2015 and an EU-Turkey Statement followed in early 2016. Both agreements are crucial in understanding the central role Turkey has played during the Syrian migration crisis as well as the changing relations between Ankara and the EU.

The JAP resulted from the realization in Brussels, expressed in concrete terms through a September 2015 decision by the European Council, that Turkey could play a key role in stemming the flow of refugees heading towards Europe. It was also an EU candidate country and therefore the ability of Brussels to entice Ankara to comply with its demands was relatively high. What is remarkable about the JAP in retrospect was the EU's willingness to ignore Turkey's de-alignment with the EU legislative and political framework. Although cooperation between the two sides had proceeded smoothly since 2010 on migration issues, Turkey had started, as I noted above, to 'de-Europeanize' by the early 2010s.

In line with the agreement, a new EU accession chapter was opened for Turkey (chapter 17 on Economic and Monetary Policy). Further, Ankara would now be able to cooperate with FRONTEX, the EU border guard force, which would be deployed in the Aegean Sea, and to receive financial assistance to continue housing Syrians in its territory (European Commission 2015). The EU agreed to provide additional funds to assist Syrians regarding education and employment opportunities.

Perhaps more significantly, Turkey was able to land a bigger prize: the EU committed itself to enhancing the country's capacity to meet the identified criteria (benchmarks) to enable visa-free travel for Turkish citizens to the EU, a scheme Brussels has been implementing with neighboring countries and which aims at softening the Union's image in the region. Talks with Ankara had begun in 2013 and the country was making steady progress in meeting the 72 criteria that the EU demanded it meet to participate in the initiative, some of which were technical and others more political. For Turkey, achieving visa-free travel had always been the ultimate reward, even more important than full EU membership and its associated obligations. That is because freedom of movement is prized highly by the Turkish population, offering lucrative employment opportunities in European countries and the chance to visit countries such as Germany or the Netherlands, where large Turkish minorities reside.

The EU-Turkey Statement of March 2016 was more significant than the JAP. Turkey agreed in that pact to allow Syrian nationals to gain formal employment in the country. The Turkish government also committed to curbing the illicit trade of smugglers who transported desperate people under dangerous sea conditions across the Aegean Sea to EU member Greece. But the key aspect of the agreement was an effort to stanch the flow of migrants crossing from Turkey via Greece to EU territory. To do so, the Union and Turkey agreed on a 'one-in, one-out' formula. Irregular migrants that had crossed to Greece would now be returned to Turkey and would stay there; in return, the EU agreed to resettle Syrians from Turkey, based on certain criteria and up to a maximum of 72,000 individuals (European Council 2016). This rather artificial number proved not only inadequate, given the scale of human suffering at the time, but also unrealistic given the deep divisions within the Union's nations concerning the subject. The EU admitted that such a solution was far from perfect and claimed that cooperation with Turkey had become a necessity to manage the unfolding extraordinary circumstances. The scant attention paid to human rights in the EU-Turkey statement, and Ankara's track record on the subject, heightened criticism of the agreement (Haferlach and Kurban 2017). Finally, the Statement reenforced provisions already present in the JAP. The Union agreed that Ankara was now entitled to further financial assistance of €3 billion, to negotiations to open another chapter toward accession (the chapter in question was 33 of the *acquis* on financial and budgetary provisions), and to continuing dialogue to accelerate and confirm the visa liberalization process.

For political elites in the EU, and especially those of countries who had welcomed Syrian refugees in 2015 (such as Germany, Sweden and Greece) there is little doubt that the agreement with Turkey has worked well. In 2018, the European Commission released a report on the second anniversary of the EU-Turkey Statement and presented data on developments. Arrivals on the Aegean Sea islands from Turkey had dropped by 97% in two years; daily, this meant an average of about 80 a day, compared to more than 3000 during 2015 (European Commission 2018; Interviews 2–4, 6–7). Further, the Commission underlined that the resettlement of Syrian refugees to member states was continuing apace and that support provided to Greece had allowed the latter to manage the crisis more effectively. Finally, the Commission underscored how its financial aid to Turkey had enabled hundreds of thousands of Syrian children to attend school, 1.2 million people to obtain access to healthcare and hundreds of new schools to be constructed in Turkey (European Commission 2018).

Instrumental Europeanization and the Limits to EU-Turkey Cooperation

Turkey's political turmoil

By the time Turkey negotiated its agreements with the EU, facts on the ground in Syria had changed and the spill over of the crisis had reached major Turkish cities as well. Domestic political developments had accelerated and Turkey was caught in a spiral of violence and instability. As a result, its policy stance, both foreign and domestic, was upended. Its crucial role in tacking the crisis remained, but electoral calculations and growing signs of authoritarianism meant that the partnership with Europe became less a matter of pragmatic cooperation and more of an expedient instrument, or even a bargaining chip (Kaya 2021) to be used at will.

During the Syrian Civil War ISIS had used the power vacuum and chaos in Syria (and neighboring Iraq) to extend its influence and achieve territorial gains. To stop ISIS, the United States and other allied forces worked alongside the Kurdish militia YPG, which fought successfully against ISIS, but is also linked with the PKK in Turkey, an organization depicted as terrorist not only by Ankara, but also by its western allies. A peace process in Turkey that involved the government and the HDP, the Kurdish-dominated political party represented in Parliament, ended in failure in 2015. In that year and for a prolonged period, Turkey was rocked by successive terrorist attacks, mostly carried out by ISIS, including the killing of hundreds of innocent civilians in Ankara and a mass shooting at an Istanbul nightclub on New Year's Eve in 2016. The combination of heightened tensions concerning the 'Kurdish problem,' terrorism and growing nationalism led to a swift securitization of Turkish society and the growth of already existing anti-western sentiment.

Things only worsened when alleged followers of the Islamic preacher Fettulah Gülen infiltrated the state and attempted to carry out a *coup d'etat* in the summer of 2016. The Turkish Parliament was bombed by Turkish air pilots, a first in the nation's history, and tanks were rolled out on the Bosphorus bridge, a scene that most Turks had believed belonged to the past. Eventually the plotters were arrested and mass support for the civilian government restored Erdoğan as the elected President. However, the 2016 coup attempt changed Turkey: the government moved quickly to declare a state of emergency to 'cleanse' the state of conspirators and fellow travelers of the alleged masterminds. In the process, hundreds of thousands of civil servants, and private sector employees lost their jobs and associated rights. The army, police, media, judiciary, and academia all saw alleged conspirators imprisoned or accused of cooperation with the putschists. Whilst the Turkish government called on the European Union to support its anti-terrorist measures to address what it saw as the trauma of 15 July 2016, the EU condemned the coup attempt but also called for respect for democratic institutions and a quick return to the rule of law (IKV 2016).

Second, EU-Turkey acrimony increased further ahead of the controversial 2017 Turkish referendum to change the country's Constitution and political structure towards a Presidential system. As domestic Turkish politics and the associated tensions among different segments threatened to spill over to EU member states with a large Turkish population, President Erdoğan accused Germany and the Netherlands of restricting freedom of speech by prohibiting or curtailing campaign events ahead of the referendum. Turkey's belligerent rhetoric, characterizing German and other officials as 'Nazis', heightened already escalating tensions between Turkey, leading EU countries and the Union (Pierini 2018). Turkey's decision to undertake close economic, political and even military cooperation with Russia, beginning in 2016, drove the EU and Turkey further apart concerning how to deal with the Syrian crisis, an issue that had united them until then. The EU also objected to what the Turkish government called stringent 'anti-terrorist' legislation as preventing visa-free travel with Union countries. Gaining the right to visa-free travel has been a long-cherished goal of every Turkish government since the EU ceased the practice following the 1980s coup, when the army took over for three years, but also managed to cause long-lasting damage to Turkish democracy through the introduction of an illiberal Constitution in 1982 (Kirişçi 2014). The issue remains high on Turkey's agenda, as this is written, but the EU Council remains reluctant to grant Turkey that right, aware of the sharp domestic criticism that such a step would likely elicit.

The Syrian Crisis and its repercussions

Heightened political instability in Turkey has combined with the non-resolution of the Syrian crisis to lead to increasing tensions regarding the integration and accommodation of millions of refugees. The Turkish government is ambivalent regarding the extent to which it wishes to integrate Syrian refugees into the country (Interviews 2 and 3). Some major civil society stakeholder groups, such as some trade unions, argue that informal employment by refugees undercuts minimum wage legislation and penalizes Turkish workers as a result (Interview 6). Integration has also becomes become more difficult because Syrians now constitute a majority in certain cities along the country's southern border and form majorities in certain neighborhoods in the country's 17-million-person metropolis, Istanbul. The once welcoming attitude of the Turkish people has turned to increasing anger, as it is becoming increasingly clear that most Syrians intend to stay in the country even after a political solution is reached in Syria (Makovsky 2019). Worryingly, the issue is no longer a matter of displaying solidarity to those fleeing conflict. When President Erdoğan raised the prospect of granting citizenship to Syrians in 2016, the opposition vociferously opposed such a plan and a popular backlash forced Erdoğan to backtrack. Although about 95,000 Syrians had been granted citizenship by early 2021, the government now claims that eventually all Syrian refugees will return home, a rather unlikely prospect given the conditions in their home nation (Makovsky 2019). Humanitarian organization representatives argue that the ambiguous status of Syrians in Turkey cannot continue as they are (interview 6-8), although it is equally clear that awarding full citizenship rights to all of them is politically untenable. Incidents of violence between Syrian refugees and locals, sometimes resulting in deaths and widespread urban violence, have been on the increase, especially in the western urban centers where cultural misunderstandings and differences are as deep as those between Syrians and EU member state citizens (International Crisis Group 2018). Public opinion polls suggest that most Turks see Syrian refugees as neither willing nor able to integrate into Turkish society.

The 2019 local elections provided a political platform for open discussion of the issue of Syrian migrants and refugees. Opposition parties sought to capitalize on growing popular discontent and supported more restrictive treatment of Syrians in the country. The governing AKP responded to those claims by promising to deliver on a more stringent approach and thus appease its critics. In October 2019 Turkey engaged in a military operation in Syria with the ostensible aim of resettling more than a million Syrians in a safe zone there (*Deutsche Welle* 2019). This, however, occurred after the political damage had been done. In the March 2019 local elections, the opposition won almost all of the major cities, including the key battleground of Istanbul and the capital Ankara. In Istanbul, in particular, the country's largest city and major financial, commercial, and artistic center, the AKP disputed the first round's results and forced a runoff. Its second defeat, larger in scale, confirmed increasing citizen discontent with government policies, including those addressing the Syrian issue. Metropolitan cities in Turkey are major sources of political patronage, able to distribute goods such as employment and benefits to millions of citizens and voters. In that sense, the result is significant in the medium to long-term in terms of the opposition parties, principally the center left Republican peoples' Party (CHP) to drum up support ahead of national elections.

Caught between growing domestic discontent and its obligations towards the EU, the Turkish government decided to ease a share of that pressure by taking unilateral action. In February 2020, 33 Turkish soldiers were killed in Syria by government-backed rebels. In a swift response, Turkey announced that its western borders with Greece were now open, inviting migrants and/or refugees to leave the country and pass on to EU territory (Evans and Coskun 2020). This unilateral action met with a severe response by Greece; Athens sealed the border and pushed back people caught between the two countries. The resulting human misery is a stain on the reputation of both governments, but also a symbolic expression of the unresolved dilemmas that the Syrian war and resultant migration crisis has created. Greece summoned high ranking EU officials to the Greek-Turkish border and capitalized on their expression of solidarity towards a member state, vowing to prevent a repetition of the 2015 crisis (Politico 2020). The outbreak of the COVID-19 pandemic has inevitably eased the crisis, but no long-term solution has been found and the ongoing Greek-Turkish dispute regarding their bilateral relations has found another platform through which to find expression.

Conclusion

Turkey has played a critical role in the Syrian crisis. During the first years of the civil war in Syria, its role was widely (and rightly) celebrated: Turkey conducted a huge humanitarian effort, and millions of desperate people found refuge in the country. Although Turkey continues to host record numbers of Syrian refugees, its motives and policy stance have now become much more complicated. Moreover, in recent years Turkey has become part of the crisis, not least through its incursion into northern Syria and the stationing of Turkish troops inside Syrian territory. Ankara's activism, while justified in the name of the fight against terror, has concerned many of its allies worried about its intentions, due to the fact that it is now Turkey, along with Russia, that largely controls Syria's future political trajectory. The absence of a permanent solution to the Syrian crisis allows Turkey to maintain its leverage *vis-á-vis* western states, but it has come with a high degree of uncertainty and an inability to extricate itself from a long-standing conflict.

In theoretical terms, this chapter has argued that close analysis of Turkey's role in the Syrian crisis provides further empirical proof of the aptness of the 'instrumental Europeanization' thesis. From 2010 to 2015 and despite the emergence of tendencies to distance itself from the EU in other policy areas, Turkey benefited greatly from the legal and institutional expertise of international organizations (primarily the EU) in handling the Syrian crisis. The upgrading of its institutional infrastructure paved the way for the 2015 and 2016 refugee-related agreements with the EU and made Turkey popular regarding its readiness to show compassion to desperate civilians. However, the second phase has been less benign. Turkey's domestic political scene became inextricably linked to the ongoing crisis in Syria, not least due to the Kurdish issue, and a wave of political instability was followed by increasing authoritarian tendencies by the ruling party and government. Domestic opposition to the long-term hosting of millions of refugees has grown as the crisis has gone on and relations with the EU have likewise grown progressively more tense. The agreements reached between these two parties remain formally in place, but the transactional, interest-based character of their relations highlights the limits of Turkey's Europeanization process.

List of Interviews

- International Organization for Migration (IOM) Project Development and Implementation Unit. 13 October 2016, Ankara.
- International Organization for Migration (IOM) Project Coordinator, 14 October 2016, Ankara.
- International Organization for Migration (IOM) Program Officer, 14 October 2016, Ankara.
- Confederation of Progressive Turkish Trade Unions (DISK) Istanbul Regional Representative, 8 December 2016, Istanbul.
- Support Life Foundation (Hayata Destek Vakfi) Program Manager, 9 December 2016, Istanbul.
- Support Life Foundation (Hayata Destek Vakfi) Protection Expert 1, 9 December 2016, Istanbul.
- Support Life Foundation (Hayata Destek Vakfi) Protection Expert 2, 9 December 2016, Istanbul.
- Support to Life Foundation (Hayata Destek Vakfi) Protection Expert 3, 9 December 2016, Istanbul.
- Istanbul Development Foundation (IKV) Secretary General, 12 December 2016, Istanbul.

References

Aybars, Ayşe Idil, Paul Copeland and Dimitris Tsarouhas. 2019. Europeanization without substance? EU–Turkey relations and gender equality in employment. *Comparative European Politics* 1, no. 5: 778–796. https://doi.org/10.1057/s41295-018-0125-2

Aydin-Düzgit, Sanem and Alper Kaliber. 2016. Encounters with Europe in an Era of Domestic and International Turmoil: Is Turkey a De-Europeanising Candidate Country? *South European Society & Politics*, 21, no.1: 1–14.

Balamir Çoskun, Bezen and Selin Yildiz Nielsen. 2018. *Encounters in the Turkey-Syria Borderland*. Newcastle Upon Tyne: Cambridge Scholars Publishing.

BBC News. Erdogan threatens to scrap EU-Turkey migration deal. 16 March 2017.   https://www.bbc.com/news/world-europe-39294776

Çorabatir, Metin. 2016. The evolving response to refugee protection in Turkey: assessing the practical and political needs. Washington, D.C.: Migration Policy Institute.

D'Alema, Francesco. 2017. The evolution of Turkey's Syria Policy. *Istituto Affari Internazionali* (IAI) Working Papers 17, 28 October 2017. https://www.iai.it/en/pubblicazioni/evolution-turkeys-syria-policy

Dimitriadi, Angeliki, Ayhan Kaya, Basak Kale and Tinatin Zurabishvili. 2018. EU-Turkey Relations and Irregular Migration: Transactional Cooperation in the Making. FEUTURE Online Paper No.16, https://feuture.uni-koeln.de/sites/feuture/user_upload/FEUTURE_Online_Paper_No_16_D6.3.pdf

Deutsche Welle. 2017. Angela Merkel rules out upper limit on refugees. 12 September 2017. https://www.dw.com/en/angela-merkel-rules-out-upper-limit-on-refugees/a-40459431

Deutsche Welle. 2019. Syria: what does Turkey's 'resettlement' plan mean? 1 November 2019.   https://www.dw.com/en/syria-what-does-turkeys-resettlement-plan-mean/a-51082589

Duman, Özkan and Dimitris Tsarouhas. 2006. 'Civilianization' in Greece versus 'Demilitarization' in Turkey: A Comparative Study of Civil-Military Relations and the Impact of the European Union. *Armed Forces & Society* 32, no. 3: 405–423. https://doi.org/10.1177/0095327X05282122

Eralp, Atila. 2009. Temporality, Cyprus Problem, and EU-Turkey Relationship. EDAM Discussion Paper Series 2009/02, July.

Erdemli, Özgül. 2003. Chronology: Turkey's Relations with the EU. *Turkish Studies* 4, no.1: 4–8.

European Commission. 2014. Report from the Commission to the European Parliament and the Council: On Progress by Turkey in Fulfilling the Requirements of its Visa Liberalization Roadmap. COM 2014/0646 final. Brussels: European Commission.

European Commission. 2015. EU–Turkey Joint Action Plan. MEMO 15/8560. Brussels: European Commission.

European Commission. 2018. EU-Turkey Statement: Two Years On. Brussels: European Commission. https://ec.europa.eu/home-affairs/sites/homeaffairs/files/what-we-do/policies/european-agenda-migration/20180314_eu-turkey-two-years-on_en.pdf

European Council. 2016. EU-Turkey Statement. Brussels: European Council. https://www.consilium.europa.eu/en/press/press-releases/2016/03/18/eu-turkey-statement/#

Evans, Dominic and Orhan Coskun. 2020. Turkey says it will let refugees into Europe after its troops killed in Syria. *Reuters*, 27 February 2020. https://www.reuters.com/article/us-syria-security-idUSKCN20L0GQ

Fougner, Tore and Ayça Kurtoğlu. 2015. Gender policy: a case of instrumental Europeanization? In Aylin Güney and Ali Tekin (eds), *The Europeanization of Turkish Public Policies: a scorecard*, 143–163. London: Routledge.

Grabbe, Heather. 2006. *The EU's Transformative Power: Europeanization through Conditionality in Central and Eastern Europe*. New York: Palgrave MacMillan.

Haferlach, Lisa and Dilek Kurban. 2017. Lessons Learnt from the EU-Turkey Refugee Agreement in Guiding EU Migration Partnerships with Origin and Transit Countries. *Global Policy* 8, no.4: 85–94.

Heraclides, Alexis. and Gizem Alioğlu Çakmak. (eds) 2019. *Greece and Turkey in Conflict and Cooperation: from Europeanization to de-Europeanization*. London and New York: Routledge.

IKV. 2016. The Day After: Turkey's Recovery following the failed coup attempt. *Publication No 287*. Istanbul: Economic Development Foundation.

International Crisis Group. 2018. Turkey's Syrian Refugees: Diffusing Metropolitan Tensions. *Europe Report No 248*. Brussels: International Crisis Group.

Iskan Kanunu [Settlement Law]. 2006. Law No. 5543/19. http://www.mevzuat. gov.tr/MevzuatMetin/1.5.5543.pdf

Kanter, James and Tim Arango. Turkish Leader says EU should do more about Syria. *The New York Times*, 5 October 52015. https://www.nytimes. com/2015/10/06/world/europe/turkey-erdogan-syria-european-union-refugees. html

Kaya, Ayhan 2009. Reform in Turkish Asylum Law: adopting the EU Acquis? Robert Schuman Centre for Advanced European Studies, CARIM Research Reports 2009/16. http://cadmus.eui.eu/bitstream/handle/1814/11849/CARIM_ RR_2009_16.pdf;jsessionid=77E4437E3332349ABA3BF C18004E4E71?sequence=2

Kaya, Ayhan. 2021. Migration as a Leverage Tool in International Relations: Turkey as a Case Study. *Uluslararasi İlişkiler*, 17, no.68: 21–39.

Kirişçi, Kemal. 2012. Turkey's New Draft Law on Asylum: What to Make of it? In *Turkey, Migration and the EU: Potentials, Challenges and Opportunities*, Hamburg Institute of International Economics 5: 63–83.

Kirişci, Kemal. 2014. Will the readmission agreement bring the EU and Turkey together or pull them apart? CEPS Commentary, 4 February 2014. https:// www.ceps.eu/system/files/KK%20EU-Turkey%20readmission%20agreement. pdf

Kirişçi, Kemal, John Brandt and Murat Erdogan. 2018. Syrian refugees in Turkey: beyond the numbers. Brookings Institution, 16 June 2018. https:// www.brookings.edu/blog/order-from-chaos/2018/06/19/syrian-refugees-in-turkey-beyond-the-numbers/

Makovsky, Alan. 2019. *Turkey's Refugee Dilemma: Tiptoeing towards Integration*. Washington, DC: Center for American Progress.

Manners, Ian. 2002. Normative Power Europe: a contradiction in terms? *Journal of Common Market Studies* 40, no.2: 235–258. https://doi.org/10.1111/1468-5965.00353

Manning, Nick. 2007. Turkey, the EU, and Social Policy. *Social Policy and Society* 6, no.4: 491–501. https://doi.org/10.1017/S1474746407003831

National Action Plan. 2005. Turkish National Action Plan for the adoption of the EU Acquis in the field of asylum and migration" http://www.madde14.org/images/0/03/Uepeng.pdf

Öniş, Ziya. 2014. Turkey and the Arab Revolutions: boundaries of regional power influence in a turbulent Middle East. *Mediterranean Politics* 19, no.2: 203–219.

Ozcurumez, Saime and Nazli Şenses. 2011. Europeanization and Turkey: studying irregular migration policy. *Southeast European and Black Sea Studies* 13, no.2: 233–248.

Pierini, Marc 2018. *The 2018 Turkey Regress Report*. Brussels: Carnegie Europe.

Saatçioğlu, Beken. 2016. De-Europeanisation in Turkey: the case of the rule of law. *South European Society & Politics* 21, no.1: 133–146. https://doi.org/10.1080/13608746.2016.1147994

Schimmelfennig, Frank and Ulrich Sedelmeier. 2004. Governance by conditionality: EU rule transfer to the candidate countries of Central and Eastern Europe. *Journal of European Public Policy* 11, no.4: 661–79. https://doi.org/10.1080/1350176042000248089

Soykan, Cavidan. 2012. The New Draft Law on Foreigners and International Protection in Turkey. *Oxford Monitor of Forced Migration* 2, no.2: 38–47.

Stamouli, Nektaria, and Herszenhorn, David. 2020. EU leaders deploy to help Greece seal Turkish border." *Politico*, 3 March 2020. https://www.politico.eu/article/eu-leaders-deploy-to-help-greece-seal-turkish-border/

Stein, Aaron. 2014. For Turkey, it's all about regime change in Syria. *Al Jazeera* Opinion, 8 October 2014. https://www.aljazeera.com/indepth/opinion/2014/10/turkey-it-all-about-regime-chan-201410785656887159.html

Suter, Brigitte. 2013. Asylum and Migration in Turkey: an overview of developments in the field, 1990-2013. MIM Working Paper Series 13, no.3. https://www.mah.se/upload/Forskningscentrum/MIM/Publications/WPS%2013.3%20Brigitte%20Suter%20final.pdf

Tocci, Natalie. 2005. Europeanization in Turkey: trigger or anchor of reform? *South European Society & Politics* 10, no.1: 73–83. https://doi.org/10.1080/13608740500037973

Tsarouhas, Dimitris. 2016. Social Policy in the EU and Turkey: the limits of Europeanization. In Çiğdem Naş and Yonca Özer, eds., *Turkey and the European Union: Processes of Europeanization*, 161–179. London: Routledge.

Tsarouhas, Dimitris. 2018. Turkey: identity politics and reticent Europeanization. In Mike Mannin and Paul Flenley (eds), *The European Union and its eastern neighbourhood: Europeanisation and its twenty-first-century contradictions*, 126–38. Manchester: Manchester University Press.

Tsarouhas, Dimitris. 2019. Turkey and the European Migration Crisis: Apprehensive Cooperation. In Alexandra Prodromidou and Pavlos Gkasis (eds), *Along the Balkan Route: the impact of the post-2014 'Migrant Crisis on the EU's South East Periphery,'* 28–42. Berlin: Konrad Adenauer Foundation.

Turkish Heritage Organization. 2016. "Turkey's Role in the Refugee Crisis." THO Factsheet. https://www.turkheritage.org/en/publications/factsheets/humanitarian-aid/turkeys-role-in-the-refugee-crisis-2493

UNHCR. 2010. Convention and Protocol relating to the status of refugees. Geneva: UNHCR.

UNHCR. 2021."Syria regional refugee Response—Total Persons of Concern by Country of Asylum. https://data2.unhcr.org/en/situations/syria

Yabancilar ve Uluslararasi Koruma Kanunu. 2013. Law on Foreigners and International Protection. 11 April 2013. *Resmi Gazete* [Official Gazette], No. 28615. http://www.mevzuat.gov.tr/MevzuatMetin/1.5.6458.pdf

Yilmaz, Gözde. 2016. Europeanisation or de-Europeanisation? Media freedom in Turkey (1999–2015). *South European Society & Politics* 21, no.1: 147–161.

11

From Transit Country to Destination: The Road to Refugee and Asylum Seekers' Integration in Greece

ALEXANDRA PRODROMIDOU AND FAYE VERVERIDOU

Although the EU is not a novice recipient of migration waves, due to the *sui generis* format of its multi-governance system, combining supranational with state level policy making, it lacks an effective common policy that could be implemented at the supranational level. The EU migration regime is the result of interactions among an array of different actors including EU institutions, EU member states, states belonging to the Schengen Zone and non-state actors (D'Amato and Lucarelli 2019). The paradox of an applied common European immigration and asylum policy lies in the fact that although under the Treaties, the EU is competent to develop a common procedure, EU level provisions remain only complementary to state level immigration law, as EU member states retain the right to adopt only the more favorable regulations to their national interests, as well as, to control the volumes of admissions of third country nationals (TNCs) (Strumia 2016).

Migration was long perceived as a secondary concern for the EU. In fact, migration governance has been largely viewed as a security issue mainly in response to internal and external challenges to EU security including the migrant 'crisis' and its often undermining implications for the implementation and functioning of the Schengen Accord, as well as terrorist attacks on European soil (Ceccorulli and Lucarelli 2017). For example, although the topic of migration is not perceived nor discussed as a security threat *per se* in the European Union Global Strategy (EUGS) (European Union External Action 2019) or in any previous EU migration related document, like the

European Security Strategy of 2003 (European Council 2009), in the EUGS, migration is most frequently mentioned in reference to 'foreign policy objectives (including internal repercussions), geographical areas and the purported values of the European Union' (Ceccorulli and Lucarelli 2017, 84). As a result, migration governance has revolved around deterrence of irregular migration and protection of the EU's external borders, rather than integration.

Greece has been at the forefront of the 'migrant crisis' as it lies along one of the main migratory routes to the EU. The combination of a prolonged period of strict economic austerity measures, political and social turmoil dating back to the signing of the first Memorandum of Understanding (MoU) in 2010, and an insufficient migration policy left the country severely ill-equipped to deal with rising numbers of irregular migrants, the majority of whom crossed from Turkey to Greece via the Aegean Sea. Initially a transit country, after the signing of the EU-Turkey Statement (European Council 2016) in March 2016, Greece became a destination country. Indicatively, according to official statistics, the numbers of asylum applications in the country went up by 236.4 per cent immediately after the agreement came into force in April 2016 in relation to asylum applications submitted in 2015 (Ministry of Interior 2016).

Even though the state has undoubtedly always been central in decision-making, after 2014 the role of the UNHCR has equally been pivotal in the coordination of activities accommodating the needs of asylum seekers, as well as, in supervising housing programs. Alongside the UNHCR, several international nongovernmental organizations (INGOs) dealing with migration related issues became involved in migration governance in Greece, together with local non-governmental organizations (NGOs) which were created driven by demand and availability of funding mainly from the EU. INGOs and national NGOs have been offering services to mixed flows of migrants in Greece spanning from medical on-site assistance, informal education, building of labor skills, assistance with state bureaucracy, legal advice and interpreters, to name but a few. The imminent departure of the UNHCR from the country and the end of international funding signifies that national NGOs, which are central to migration governance, will struggle to survive. In the current transitional period, the state is called in to fill in these gaps. Thus, one of the catalysts that defines the format and the quality of the state's response to refugee and asylum seekers' integration in Greece is the way the state is taking over supervision and coordination of the operations and integration programs from the departing organizations, while, at the same time, attempting to address the gaps in their administration.

We examine the legislative evolution in Greek integration law within the framework of EU policy, before and after the post-2014 migrant 'crisis' caused by the Syrian conflict as Greece moved from a transit to a destination country.

We contend that while there has been an attempt to create a normative and policy framework for integration, a critical policy implementation gap still exists.

Methodology

During the last decade, literature on migration policies and response in Greece has been voluminous. In the post-2014 environment, social scientists have concentrated their research efforts on different facets of migration with regards to social integration, such as the intersection of economics, healthcare, and the migration 'crisis' (Kentikelenis 2018, 61–62; Papadakaki et al. 2017, 128–134), links between health and social integration (Rapp et al. 2018, 48–53); accessibility of services (Fouskas et al 2019, 13–28); and pathologies in the housing and education schemes (Kourachanis 2018, 1153–1167), among others.

Legal scholars have so far appeared to be intrigued by more 'legalistic' aspects of the phenomenon. Queries related to the legal status of refugees, the harmonization of immigration law with EU prerequisites (Karamanidou 2021, 89-117), the legitimate character of detention measures (Koutsouraki 2017, 85–106), or specific subgroups of migrants who merit special treatment, such as unaccompanied minors (Kovner et al. 2021), have been regularly revisited in the Greek legal environment. While there is literature that provides legal analysis of the relevant laws, and empirical studies that employ primary data collection methods to identify barriers to migrant integration, socio-legal approaches that combine doctrinal and empirical research to identify gaps and necessary reforms in the Greek integration system are rather scarce (for an example, see Leivaditi et al. 2020).

Yet, there is value in adopting a two-pronged, socio-legal methodology in this case. On the one hand, the doctrinal legal approach is appropriately suited to the analysis of legal norms, the contribution of pertinent case law, and the understanding of the interplay of multilevel legal bodies (Cryer et al. 2011). Rooted in realism, the doctrinal legal approach seeks to provide an objective and accurate picture of the phenomenon under study, one that stands independently from the individual's understanding of the world and in opposition to a phenomenological or a social constructivist approach, which would be concerned more with the reported experiences of the relevant actors (Bryman 2012). However, a doctrinal approach does not yield insights into the practical implementation of the regulatory framework, as it does not entail the employment of any empirical methods (Dobinsons and Johns 2007). Thus, an additional non-doctrinal, socio-legal perspective was deemed suitable in order to identify the extent to which the Greek legal and policy framework on migrant integration is reflected in practice, and to allow for recommendations on law and policy reforms. The combination of the two approaches provides a holistic perspective of law as it focuses on both its 'internal' and 'external' aspects (Hart 2015; van Aeken 2011).

We address this gap by investigating Greek legislation and policies concerning integration of beneficiaries of international protection and asking whether that normative framework has been implemented. To this end, we combined desk research on the legal framework of migrant integration with data collected through in-depth interviews with professionals working in the field. The first part of the methodology included identification and analysis of relevant policies of EU and national legal and policy documents pertaining to migrant integration, in order to offer an understanding of the evolution of the normative framework on integration at the national scale and the EU fundamental principles on treatment of applicants and beneficiaries of international protection. This inquiry focused on three sectors of integration policy: housing, access to health, and employment. Part of adult education is included in housing through the language programs. Interculturalism and education for minors has not been included.

The second part of the methodology entailed six in-depth, online, semi-structured interviews with experts working on organizations that have played an instrumental role in migration management and integration in the country. The interviews took place between August and November 2020, and their duration ranged from 45–60 minutes. Two of them were carried out in Greek, upon the preference of those interviewees. In compliance with the General Data Protection Regulation, the interviewees remained anonymous. The selection of participants was based on the principle of purposive sampling (Bryman 2012), in accordance with two criteria, impact and diversity. Thus, the list of prospective interviewees was narrowed according to the continuity of service provision in the field of migration and the established partnerships at national and EU level, as well as their operation on a different scale (national-international-local) and through a variety of services in the areas of employability, housing, and psychosocial support.

The Evolution of Greece's Integration governance within the EU framework

The EU's integration policy in relation to migration governance has been developing steadily, over the years, since the Maastricht Treaty in 1992 with the abolition of internal borders in the EU and implementation of the Schengen Agreement in 1995. It was then that consensus for common policies on both adopting a common asylum and immigration framework, as well as strengthening policies against irregular migration were developed (Garcés-Mascareñas and Penninx 2016). In Table 1 below, a chronology of EU migrant integration policies can be seen.

The current normative framework in Greece bears the clear imprint of EU integration legislation, but this was not always the case. As Triandafyllidou has remarked, Greece was a 'latecomer in regularisation policies' for non-nationals, who were long viewed as a threat to the national identity (Triandafyllidou 2009, 162; Triandafyllidou 2001). The first Immigration Law, enacted in 2001 (Law 2910/2001), bears little resemblance to the relevant EU legal documents (Mavrodi, 2005); it was, however, the first step towards the development of a national migration framework, which gradually became oriented towards a more positive inclusive approach of legally residing TNCs.

The first account of social integration in national legislation is found in Law 3386/2005, viewed in scholarship as the first act to treat migration as a long-term phenomenon (Anagnostou 2016). In Article 65, social integration is defined as the 'proportionally equal participation' of migrants in the economic, social, and cultural life of the country, premised on the conferral of rights and the obligation to respect the founding values of the Greek society. Set out in article 66 par. 4, dominant parameters of integration are the certified knowledge of the Greek language, history and culture, access to the labor market and participation in Greek society.

The definition was revisited under a different light in the Immigration and Social Integration Code (Law 4251/2014). This law marked the first attempt to codify national migrant legislation in harmonization with the EU *acquis* and remains the main legal act regulating the integration of migrants in the country today. Pursuant to art. 128 para. 1,

> Social integration policy aims at the smooth adaptation of third country nationals into the Greek society and the recognition, on behalf of the Greek society, of the possibility for an equal participation in the economic, social, and cultural life of the country. During their integration process in the Greek society, third country nationals obtain rights and obligations, like Greek citizens (Law 4251/2014).

The new provision shared few commonalities with the one it was drafted to replace. The definition still lacked the key element of mutuality that permeates the European principles, demanding adaptation only on behalf of TCNs. On a positive note, however, it explicitly equates their rights and obligations with those of Greek citizens. In general, the Code facilitates the legal sojourn of migrants in the country by simplifying the procedure for issuance of residence permits, enabling access to work, and upholding respect for cultural identity, non-discrimination, gender equality, and children's rights.

Prior to the insertion of the Immigration Code, an evolved understanding of the concept of social integration appeared in the text of the first National Integration Strategy adopted in 2013. Although Law 3386/2005 was still in force, the strategy endorsed the Council of Europe's definition of social integration, describing it as a 'dynamic, two-way process of mutual accommodation by all immigrants and residents of Member States' (Hellenic Ministry of Migration Policy 2013). Along similar lines, the ensuing National Integration Strategy, developed in July 2019, envisions integration as a dynamic procedure founded upon mutuality and multiculturalism aims (Hellenic Ministry of Migration Policy 2019a). Building upon the European multicultural model of social integration, it embraces the idea of open society, promotes interaction and social cohesion, and spells out rights and obligations that fall under the same restrictions imposed on the native national population (Hellenic Ministry of Migration Policy 2019a).

The update of the national integration scheme with the adoption of a new policy was highly anticipated; yet, the new Strategy was received with skepticism by civil society. At the stage of public consultation, several complaints were voiced regarding the fact that the document was drafted without prior consultation with civil society actors and migrant associations in the country. This not only deprived the latter of the opportunity to put forward instrumental suggestions, but it also clashed with the new strategy, which explicitly placed political representation among the axes of social integration. Coupled with the fact that the first strategy of 2013 established a bad precedent by remaining largely ineffective, serious concerns emerged regarding the practical implementation of the new regime. Similar doubts were raised due to the absence of a timeframe, as well as an action plan, which traditionally accompanies strategic documents. The document was further criticized for encouraging a single understanding of TCNs, instead of adopting tailored policies for different subgroups of migrants according to a set of criteria, such as age, duration of sojourn, or country of origin (Report of public consultation on the National Integration Strategy 2019).

Despite its weaknesses, the strategy has been a welcome addition to a rather limited body of legal documents that address integration. Perhaps most importantly, the new strategy posits that social integration is a complex concept that unfolds on two levels: the reception of applicants of international protection, and the integration of beneficiaries of international protection, as well as migrants (National Integration Strategy, 2019). In other words, the integration of TCNs does not commence at the moment that international protection is being granted but much earlier, at the moment of arrival in Greece. The document also lays out the axes of integration policy, which include access to fundamental services (such as housing, adequate information, healthcare); integration in education; access to the labor market, interculturalism, civic participation; and a small number of policies dedicated to the key role of the local administration and the adoption of special measures for vulnerable groups of TCNs. This classification agrees with the dominant understanding of social integration in the literature as a multi-faceted phenomenon (Ager and Strang 2008).

Finally, the second half of 2019 constituted a benchmark in migration governance in Greece. Following the elections of July 2019, a new government was formed by the conservative party 'New Democracy' which had been pushing for a tougher and more securitized agenda on migration for years. Only days after 'New Democracy' came to power, the operation of the Ministry for Migration Policy ended and all its competences were transferred to the Ministry for Citizen's Protection. In the four-point plan presented by the Prime Minister in October 2019, securitization of borders was listed among the objectives to enhance the overburdened asylum system, to strengthen the cooperation of public authorities and to relieve pressure on the islands. Integration was left out of this list (Bourdaras 2019).

The shift towards a stringent stance on migrants was also reflected in Law 4636/2019, which established a uniform regime on the status of applicants and beneficiaries of international protection in the country. In a glimpse, the new act accelerates first instance and appeals procedures; it establishes constraints to healthcare access for asylum seekers; it adopts punitive measures for families with children who do not attend school; and it extends conditions of detention. With regard to integration, perhaps the most important change was the introduction of a grace period of six months for the exit of recognized beneficiaries from the accommodation facilities, which was further reduced to one month in March 2020 (Article 114 Law 4674/2020). The document was denounced, almost unanimously, by both NGOs and international agencies for posing a severe threat to the protection of the fundamental rights of the persons falling under its scope (UNHCR 2019). In the same vein, the role of NGOs in the field of migration was redefined with the configuration of a new online registration system, which established onerous certification procedures and provided new grounds for the cooperation with the State (Law 4662/2020). The Expert Council on NGO Law has twice condemned this system for being incompatible with European standards, especially for violating the right to free association (Expert Council on NGO Law 2020a; Expert Council on NGO Law 2020b).

Integration Pillars

Housing

The 2019 framework foresaw three different forms of housing for asylum seekers: in reception premises at the national borders (this was particularly the case when the EU-Turkey agreement was in place); in accommodation centers, managed by state authorities, NGOs or international organizations guaranteeing adequate conditions of living; and private houses, apartments or hotels available within the frame of funded housing programs (Article 56 Law 4636/2019). As the housing environment is currently shaped in Greece, the first two forms described in the provision refer to RICs, the Reception and Identification Centers, as well as the 32 accommodation sites dispersed throughout the mainland. Despite state and private efforts for the upgrade of living standards through site management support (SMS), accommodation in camps is routinely considered an unfavorable housing scheme for the protection of asylum seekers (Kourachanis 2018).

Beyond the in-site accommodation, the two main housing programs in place for several years, FILOXENIA and ESTIA I (Emergency Support to Integration and Accommodation Program), were exclusively reserved for asylum seekers. In what has been characterized as a novelty at the global level by experts, ESTIA I entailed the practice of direct apartment rentals in dispersed areas within urban centers to accommodate vulnerable asylum seekers.

Refugees are entitled to housing on the same terms and conditions as TNCs legally residing in the country (Art. 34 Law 4636/2019). One may conclude that the provision shapes a more inclusive framework compared to asylum seekers. However, this is not the case. Until recently, refugees were allowed to remain in accommodation sites or apartments of ESTIA I, even after having obtained their residence permit. Law 4636/2019 ended this tolerant stance, by stipulating that refugees are obliged to leave the accommodation structures within 6 months from the moment of recognition of their asylum status. In 2020, this deadline further shrank to one month, a decision taken unrelated to the COVID-19 pandemic. Under this light and taking into account that no social housing policy exists in Greece, refugees may only benefit from the "HELIOS" program, which provides financial assistance to promote independent living and integration of refugees in the social web.

Physical and mental health

Against the post-2014 humanitarian crisis backdrop, amendments were introduced in the national normative framework concerning access to healthcare. In response to the country's label as a 'welfare state,' Article 33 Law 4368/2016 included a vision of universal health coverage, which enables all vulnerable social groups to fully access the public healthcare system and receive nursing and medical treatment free of charge. Both asylum seekers and refugees are explicitly classified as vulnerable individuals under this provision, contrary to irregular migrants who remain outside the scope of this provision, as they are only entitled to emergency healthcare.

The newly established Law 4636/2019, in Art. 31 par. 1, placed refugees on equal footing with Greek nationals with regard to healthcare access, which effectively verified the need of a social insurance number (AMKA) in order to be able to receive treatment in the public healthcare sector. For asylum seekers, this has not been equally straightforward. Although Law 4368/2016 granted free healthcare access, there was no clarification as to whether this group is eligible for obtaining AMKA. A Joint Ministerial Decision later in 2016 established an alternative document, the Foreigner's Health Care Card (KYPA), for those vulnerable groups clustered in Article 33 Law 4368/2016 who did not qualify for an AMKA. However, the KYPA system was never implemented, and asylum seekers continued to apply for AMKA to gain access to the national health system.

In July 2019, the new government revoked the circular regulating the procedure to issue AMKA to non-nationals. Pending a new regime that would not be introduced until 6 months later, this executive action meant that asylum seekers were banned from access to public health facilities, a practice that was condemned by national and international actors as a clear violation of their fundamental right to health (among others, Amnesty International 2019). Finally, a new state institution provided for unlimited access to public healthcare for asylum seekers with the issuance of a Temporary Insurance and Foreigner's Healthcare Number (PAAYPA), valid until the Asylum Service's decision on their application (Art. 55 Law 4636/2019 and Art. 15 of the Ministerial Decision 717 (OGG B' 199/31.01.2020). Notably, the same law deals not only with access to healthcare, but also encompasses safeguards for the healthy living conditions of these populations.

Employment

According to Art. 71 Law 4375/2016 in its original form, asylum seekers are entitled to access to wage employment and service or work provision, provided they have obtained a valid asylum card. This marked a significant advance along the road to integration; unlike the previous regime, a work permit is no longer required and Greek nationals were no longer legally prioritized over foreign employees. However, the provision was soon amended by Art. 53 Law 4636/2019, which introduced a six-month time limit, from the moment of application submission, for asylum seekers to gain 'effective access' to the labor market. This new restriction was met with severe criticism for hindering, instead of facilitating, self-sustainment of individuals seeking international protection (Greek Ombudsman, 2019). For refugees with a valid residence permit, the limitation does not apply; access to wage and self-employment is granted without a work permit, on the same terms as for Greek nationals (Art. 69 Law 4375/2016 and Article 27 Law 4636/2019), with an exception regarding working in the public sector.

In essence, every individual who wishes to enter the Greek labor market, regardless of the type of employment they may pursue, needs to have a tax registration number (AFM) and a national security number (AMKA) or PAAYPA, for asylum seekers. Hence, in revoking the asylum seekers' entitlement to AMKA in the second half of 2019 and prior to the insertion of the PAYYPA regime, the state effectively hampered access not only to healthcare, but also to employment for this population.

Equal treatment with Greek nationals is also granted in access to vocational training, internships and consulting, as well as the recognition of foreign diplomas and other qualifications (Articles 29 and 54 Law 4636/2019 for beneficiaries of international protection and asylum seekers, respectively). In the event that supporting documents cannot be provided, beneficiaries are permitted to participate in programs aimed at assessing their skills, in compliance with EU Directive 2005/36/EC on the recognition of professional qualifications (transposed by the Presidential Decree 38/2010). For asylum seekers who reside in Reception and Identification Centers (RICs) or temporary accommodation sites, vocational training and consulting may also be provided within the premises of those structures as a measure to foster social integration (Art. 15 of the Ministerial Decision 23/13532/2020 - Official Gazette B' 5272/30.11.2020).

Gaps in Migrants' Integration Governance and Policy Implementation: A View from the Field

General comments on integration

Asylum seekers appear to have more access to services than refugees:

> If you think in a logical way, you expect as an asylum seeker to have some rights and access to different things, but generally there is this idea that when you are a recognized refugee, you have more access and more rights. From what I understand

> from the population we see every day, it is more difficult to be a recognized refugee than an asylum seeker (Athena, 6 November 2020).

> The logic of the Greek government is that since someone is a recognised refugee, they have access to the same services provided to a Greek citizen. So why would they provide you with more cash assistance and more accommodation, when they are not providing the other citizens the same? (Kostantinos, 7 October 2020).

The concept of integration has been inherently linked to the concept of dependent living of refugee populations, creating expectations for the provision of assistance indefinitely

> Generally, there was a concept in the whole system and in beneficiaries' minds that they will stay in the program forever. However, at some point, the law changed. [...]This was not explained to the beneficiaries at the start, that this is something temporary (Danae, 24 August 2020).

> The most important thing is for these people to understand that they will not remain under the umbrella of international protection forever. At some point, they will have to start leading their lives here (Andreas, 17 September 2020).

Language lessons are neither mandatory during the first stage of integration nor available at all temporary placements. There is a need for language courses to become mandatory from the reception stage onward, both to aid integration and to encourage self-reliance among program beneficiaries.

> To become a beneficiary of the HELIOS program, one needs to attend language lessons. I think it's too late to start considering this after one becomes a recognized refugee. Learning the language needs to be a condition from the start of the ESTIA program (Danae, 24 August 2020).

> It should have been mandatory to take Greek or English courses from the very beginning. One needs to be able to find a way to communicate (Anna, 1 September 2020).

> Teenagers at the age of 15-18 [...] cannot even answer to which school they go to. [...] They cannot do their homework at

all because their level of Greek language is not just primary, it is non-existent (Stella, 13 October 2020).

I believe there is a very limited number of Greek language classes offered right now. There is not enough support in this area for free. [...] Additionally, the classes offered are only for beginners. To achieve a more advanced level of speaking the language, beneficiaries need to pay privately (Athena, 6 November 2020).

There is a need for more organized training to identify skills and abilities of refugees and asylum seekers:

There should be more educational programs, in order to give beneficiaries the opportunity to learn some type of skill; or properly interview them, in order to understand what they can offer back to you, what are their skills and abilities (Anna, 1 September 2020).

Housing

Although the vast majority of the interviewees referred to housing as one of the most important pillars of integration, in practice integration is not treated as a primary goal at the first stage of reception: 'The ESTIA's goal is first and foremost to accommodate and then integrate. Integration is applied as a secondary goal only' (Danae, 24 August 2020). As the ESTIA program was a novel migration governance tool, the implementing organizations are the only ones with the know-how of its effective operation.

The Ministry wishes to involve actors that can bring the know-how in several aspects of migrant integration (Stella, 13 October 2020).

The government said that they wanted to include new and inexperienced NGOs in accommodation programs. This means that they will not have the necessary 'know-how' to avoid past mistakes. The handover needs to be done keeping this in mind to avoid repetition of the same mistakes (Kostantinos, 7 October 2020).

In its original release, the ESTIA II program was designed with a sharp decrease in the budget. In this light, concerns have been raised regarding the quality of services and capacity of the state and the few NGOs that expressed willingness to participate, to accommodate the needs of beneficiaries.

> The budget set by the Ministry doesn't even come close to the UNHCR's one. As a result, NGOs refrain from applying to continue with ESTIA II [...] In Thessaloniki there are about 1,000 houses under ESTIA. 60%-70% of them are not managed by any organization now (Andreas, 17 September 2020).

> For the NGOs that are going to remain in the program, as the budget is a lot smaller than before, they need to reduce the staff a lot. So there is a question regarding the quality of the program (Danae, 24 August 2020).

HELIOS poses challenges with regard to housing for refugees. These stem from the limited personal scope of HELIOS to previously self-accommodated asylum seekers; the lack of proper documentation, of the limited understanding of the accommodation procedures and of the financial capacity of refugees to rent apartments on their own; and the reluctance on the part of homeowners to have non-nationals as renters.

> There are specific conditions to enter the program, such as having a housing contract, which means that the beneficiaries must have the money in order to pay for a deposit, which in some cases is more than one month's rent in advance. The organizations are trying to help them find and book houses [...] but there is an issue with covering the expenses for the upfront rents on the side of the refugees (Danae, 24 August 2020).

> Self-accommodated asylum seekers becoming refugees turn mostly into homeless people. They are considered by the government as self-sustained people, so they [are believed to] have no need of an integration program such as HELIOS (Danae, 24 August 2020).

Health

In the field of health, the major threat that migrants have been faced with since the beginning of 2020 has been the COVID-19 pandemic, not as a health issue *per se*, but rather as a matter of accessing services and being able to benefit from on-site help due to prolonged and repetitive lockdowns.

The pandemic has caused severe delays and suspensions in the provision of services.

> [...] Everything got delayed so everything that was going already slowly, it stopped at that point. [...] The moment the prevention measures started, it made most of the public sector shut down. In the sense that hospitals were not accepting visitors anymore, even for the slightest thing, schools were closed for the students, public service offices that could provide assistance, such as those offering social security numbers, were closed, NGOs were mandatorily informed that they were not allowed to receive more than a certain limit of people per day (Konstantinos, 7 October 2020).

The shift in the operation of organizations in the field had both a negative and a positive effect on the delivery of services to beneficiaries.

> The office was closed; we were working from home. We did not have direct contact with the beneficiary, to see each other and understand what exactly their needs are. This has been a huge problem, especially in the domain of housing (Andreas, 17 September 2020).

> We had to change certain activities to limit physical contact with the beneficiaries due to covid-19, which also decreased the amount of information that we obtained but increased the amount of workload. [...] Since things are happening remotely, things sometimes are more efficient, as many NGOs have found a way to limit or even completely take out a task that was very time-consuming (Konstantinos, 7 October 2020).

Access to health services for regular check-ups and non-COVID related conditions has been especially hard during the pandemic.

> The hospitals are running at full capacity right now, so you cannot make appointments. It is very difficult. The other day, I obtained an appointment at the hospital, and I was very happy. The only thing that's working in the hospital is the emergency shift. Everything is really impacted during this period. [...] It's

> very difficult to arrange an appointment to the doctor at the present, because the number of available appointments is down by 50% of what they used to be. Some of the hospitals are not now even accepting new appointments (Athena, 6 November 2020).

For refugees and asylum seekers, the situation becomes even more cumbersome due to the shortage of interpreters in healthcare facilities.

> Some of the hospitals operate with translators, but not all of them. There are only specific ones that are supported by METAdrasi and there are very few hospitals this period who are getting this support (Athena, 6 November 2020).

Employment

Access to the labor market for asylum seekers and refugees is mostly limited to professions related to interpretation. 'There are not actually a lot of jobs available for this population, other than cultural mediators and interpreters. Maybe if they studied, they might find relevant employment' (Danae, 24 August 2020). Access to local labor market/local industries can be key to integration within the community.

> In Veroia, for example, where they have fields with peaches and factory, they ask beneficiaries to learn how to use the machines in the factory and start working there. It had a very good impact in the society of Veroia, they felt very embraced and welcome there (Anna, 1 September 2020).

Expectations on employment need to take into account the cultural and societal background of the populations.

> If you have a single mother with five underage children, how will this woman, who never worked in her life because her society raised her to be like that, how would you get her a job? There was a huge (effort) to train these women and get them to make money on their own. And for them, it was too much of a responsibility (Anna, 1 September 2020).

Conclusions

The current Greek integration policy has been developed based on EU migrant integration policies pertinent to the broader concept and regulations of migration governance, adapted to the specificities of the Greek legal framework. Due to the securitization of migration governance both at the EU and national level, priority has been set on deterrence of illegal migration, rather than the integration of refugees and asylum seekers into Greek society. In the post-2014 context, inevitably the focus of national and supranational legislative efforts partly shifted away from deterrence of irregular migration, and towards the entry, stay and integration of applicants and beneficiaries of international protection. Nonetheless, the advent of "New Democracy" to power in 2019 reinstated a more securitized agenda on migration governance favoring border controls in order to enhance the overwhelmed asylum system and relieve pressure on the islands, while overlooking the development of integration policies.

The national integration strategy and subsequent legal documents have conceptualized 'integration' as a two-step process, consisting of the reception of people pending a decision on their asylum application, and the integration of those who have been recognized as beneficiaries of international protection. Sadly, despite the undeniable value of the introduction of a social integration scheme, the numerous concerns that emerged at the adoption of the new regulatory and policy framework have, by and large, been confirmed in practice. The views from the field attest to the existence of an insufficient integration scheme, both in law and in practice. At a normative level, there are evident pathologies in the domestic legislation, such as the 6-month deadline for exit of recognized refugees introduced by the Law 4636/2019 or the new registry for NGOs. At a policy implementation level, several gaps have been identified with regards to the unbalanced accommodation schemes, the poor employment opportunities and the interruption of services provision in healthcare and other sectors due to the pandemic.

One of the major problems inherent in the implementation of the national integration policies is the creation of aid-dependency in the first stage of reception, which is followed by an abrupt shift to self-sustainment in the second stage of integration of refugees. In essence, asylum seekers are introduced into a system of assisted integration with no prerequisites for receiving financial support, access to services and accommodation. This inevitably gives rise to false expectations of a prolonged situation of support by the State or the civil society actors, which clashes with the reality following a positive decision on the asylum application. As a result, recognized refugees are expected to ensure their survival with their own means, let alone provide for their integration as well.

Finally, the change in the role of the third sector in integration governance in Greece enhances the policy implementation gap in integration. INGOs and NGOs have been central in migration management in Greece since 2014.

Nonetheless, their role is gradually diminishing, either by being excluded from consultations on policies or by not taking part in new programs due to budgetary decreases. This leads to concerns that precious 'know-how' is lost, especially when it comes to accommodation programs. Likewise, services offered by INGOs and NGOs including, but not limited to, interpreters, psychological support and legal advice, need to be provided by the state soon, as there is an evident gap in such support now. This indicates that the transition of Greece to a destination nation for refugees and asylum seekers is a rather complex, long-term process, which needs drastic changes to bridge the policy implementation gap in integration, including safety nets when it comes to housing or integration into the labor market, as well as close cooperation between the state and the third sector.

Table 1

1997/1999	**The Treaty of Amsterdam:** Integration of migrants from non-EU countries becomes affected by EU policies for the first time
2004	**The Common Basic Principles for Immigrant Integration Policy in the EU:** A milestone for the development of a common immigration policy
2009	**The European Website on Integration:** Launch of an online source of information for sharing information and best practices
2010/2012	**Agreement on a Common set of Integration Indicators:** A basis for EU monitoring and coordination. The 2012 update encompassed employment, education and social inclusion
2014	**The Asylum, Migration and Integration Fund:** It replaces three previous financing instruments. 20 per cent of its budget is dedicated to integration through calls for proposals
2016	**The Action Plan on the Integration of TNCs:** A framework to support national policies and a map of concrete measures that the Commission will implement
2017	**The Skills Profile Tool for TNCs:** A tool to map qualifications, professional aspirations, and to suggest next steps
2020	**The Action plan on Integration and Inclusion (2021–2027):** Following up on the New Pact on Migration and Asylum, which highlighted the importance of integration, the Action plan aims at inclusion by building on multi-stakeholder partnerships, including the host communities and the private sector, providing funding and modernizing access to services by using digital tools.

Interviews

- Andreas. Interview by Faye Ververidou and Alexandra Prodromidou. Online. 17 September 2020.
- Anna. Interview by Faye Ververidou and Alexandra Prodromidou. Online. 1 September 2020.
- Athena. Interview by Faye Ververidou and Alexandra Prodromidou. Online. 6 November 2020.
- Danae. Interview by Faye Ververidou and Alexandra Prodromidou. Online. 24 August 2020.
- Konstantinos. Interview by Faye Ververidou and Alexandra Prodromidou. Online. 7 October 2020.
- Stella. Interview by Faye Ververidou and Alexandra Prodromidou. Online. 13 October 2020.

Glossary of Terms

Applicant of international protection: Any third-country national or a stateless person who has made an application for protection from a Member State, in respect of which a final decision has not yet been made and who can be understood to seek refugee status or subsidiary protection status (Art. 2(h) and (i) of Directive 2011/95/EU-Recast Qualification Directive). Although narrower in scope in the EU legal framework, the term 'asylum seeker' is used to describe all applicants of international protection for the purposes of this report.

Beneficiary of international protection: Any person who has been granted refugee status or subsidiary protection status (Art. 2(b) of Directive 2011/95/ EU (Recast Qualification Directive)

Irregular migrant: Any person whose movement takes place outside the laws, regulations, or international agreements governing the entry into or exit from the State of origin, transit, or destination (IOM 2019).

Person eligible for subsidiary protection: A third-country national or a stateless person who does not qualify as a refugee but in respect of whom substantial grounds have been shown for believing that the person concerned, if returned to his or her country of origin or of former habitual residence, would face a real risk of suffering serious harm and is unable, or, owing to such risk, unwilling to avail himself or herself of the protection of that country Serious harm consists of: (a) death penalty or execution; or (b) torture or inhuman or degrading treatment or punishment of an applicant in the country of origin; or (c) serious and individual threat to a civilian's life or person by reason of indiscriminate violence in situations of international or internal armed conflict. (Art. 2(f) and Art. 15 of Directive 2011/95/EC-Recast Qualification Directive).

Refugee: A third-country national who, owing to a well-founded fear of being persecuted for reasons of race, religion, nationality, political opinion or membership of a particular social group, is outside the country of nationality and is unable or, owing to such fear, is unwilling to avail himself or herself of the protection of that country, or a stateless person, who, being outside of the country of former habitual residence for the same reasons as mentioned above, is unable or, owing to such fear, unwilling to return to it (Art. 1A of the Geneva Refugee Convention and Protocol)

Although narrower in scope, the term 'refugee' is used to describe all beneficiaries of international protection for the purposes of this report.

Third country national (TCN): Any person who is not a citizen of the European Union within the meaning of Art. 20(1) of TFEU and who is not a person enjoying the European Union right to free movement, as defined in Schengen Borders Code (Art. 15 of Directive 2011/95/EU-Recast Qualification Directive).

References

Ager, Alastair, and Alison Strang. 2008. Understanding integration: A conceptual framework. *Journal of Refugee Studies* 21, no. 2 (June): 166–191.

Amnesty International. 2019. Greece: Proposed Bill on Asylum Downgrades EU and International Law Standards On Refugees' Protection. 24 October. Accessed 6 April 2022. https://www.amnesty.org/en/documents/eur25/1278/2019/en/

Anagnostou, Dia, Aimilia Kontogianni, Dimitris Skleparis, and Giorgos Tzogopoulos. 2016. *Local Government and Migrant Integration in Greece.* Athens: Hellenic Foundation for European and Foreign Policy (ELIAMEP). DOI: 10.13140/RG.2.2.17310.95046

Bourdaras, Giorgos. Greek PM unveils four-point plan for migration. *E-Kathimerini*, 5 October 2019. https://www.ekathimerini.com/245200/article/ekathimerini/news/greek-pm-unveils-four-point-plan-for-migration

Bryman, Alan. 2012. *Social Research Methods.* 4th ed. Oxford: Oxford University Press.

Ceccorulli, Michela, and Sonia Lucarelli. 2017. Migration and The EU Global Strategy: Narratives And Dilemmas. *The International Spectator* 52, no. 3 (August): 83–102.

Cryer, Robert, Tamara Hervey, and Bal Sokhi-Bulley, with Alexandra Bohm. 2011. *Research Methodologies in EU and International Law*. Oxford and Portland: Hart Publishing.

D'Amato, Silvia, and Sonia Lucarelli. 2019. Talking Migration: Narratives of Migration and Justice Claims in The European Migration System of Governance. *The International Spectator* 54, no. 3 (September): 1–17.

European Commission. 2004. European Website on Integration Migrant Integration Information and good practices: Common Basic Principles for Immigrant Integration Policy in the EU. Accessed 1 April 2021. https://ec.europa.eu/migrant-integration/librarydoc/common-basic-principles-for-immigrant-integration-policy-in-the-eu

European Commission. 2013. Using EU Indicators of Immigrant Integration Final Report for Directorate-General for Home Affairs. Accessed 1 April 2021. https://ec.europa.eu/home-affairs/sites/homeaffairs/files/e-library/documents/policies/legal-migration/general/docs/final_report_on_using_eu_indicators_of_immigrant_integration_june_2013_en.pdf

European Commission. 2014. Migration and Home Affairs: Asylum, Migration and Integration Fund (AMIF). Accessed 3 April 2021. https://ec.europa.eu/home-affairs/financing/fundings/migration-asylum-borders/asylum-migration-integration-fund_en

European Commission 2016. Migration and Home Affairs: Action plan on integration and inclusion. Accessed 3 April 3 2021. https://home-affairs.ec.europa.eu/policies/migration-and-asylum/legal-migration-and-integration/integration/action-plan-integration-and-inclusion_en#:~:text=The%20 2016%20action%20plan%20on,to%20implement%20in%20this%20regard

European Commission. 2017. EU Skills Profile Tool for Third Country Nationals. Accessed 2 April 2021. https://ec.europa.eu/migrantskills/#/

European Commission. 2019a. European Website on Integration Migrant Integration Information and good practices: EU policy framework for migrant integration. Accessed 20 March 2021. https://ec.europa.eu/migrant-integration/main-menu/eus-work/archive/framework

European Commission. 2019b. European Website on Integration Migrant Integration Information and good practices: EU Actions. Accessed 15 March 2021. https://ec.europa.eu/migrant-integration/public/main-menu/eus-work/actions

European Commission. 2020. Action plan on Integration and Inclusion 2021-2027. Accessed 13 March 2021. https://ec.europa.eu/home-affairs/sites/homeaffairs/files/pdf/action_plan_on_integration_and_inclusion_2021-2027.pdf

European Council, Council of the European Union. 2009. European Security Strategy. Accessed 23 March 2021. https://www.consilium.europa.eu/en/documents-publications/publications/european-security-strategy-secure-europe-better-world/

European External Action Service. 2019. EU Global strategy. Accessed 15 March 2021. https://eeas.europa.eu/headquarters/headquarters-homepage_en

European Parliament. 1999. Tampere European Council 15 and 16 October 1999 Presidency Conclusions. Accessed 15 March 2021. https://www.europarl.europa.eu/summits/tam_en.htm

Expert Council on NGO Law. 2020a. Opinion on the compatibility with European standards of recent and planned amendments to the Greek legislation on NGO registration. Accessed 10 March 2021. https://rm.coe.int/expert-council-conf-exp-2020-4-opinion-ngo-registration-greece/16809ee91d

Expert Council on NGO Law. 2020b. Addendum to the opinion on the compatibility with European standards of recent and planned amendments to the Greek legislation on NGO registration. Accessed 10 March 2021. https://rm.coe.int/expert-council-conf-exp-2020-5-addendum-to-the-opinion-on-the-compatib/1680a076f2

Fouskas, Theodoros, Symeon Sidiropoulos, and Athanassios Vozikis. 2019. Leaving no one out? Public health aspects of migration: Health risks, responses and accessibility by asylum seekers, refugees and migrants in Greece. *International Journal of Health Research and Innovation* 7, no.1: 13–28.

Garcés Mascareñas, Blanca, and Rinus Penninx. 2016. *Integration Processes and Policies In Europe: Contexts, Levels And Actors*. IMISCOE Research Series, Springer Open. https://library.oapen.org/bitstream/handle/20.500.12657/28047/1001947.pdf?sequence=1#page=97

Greek Ombudsman. 2019. Observations on the Ministry's Citizen Protection Draft Law on International Protection. Accessed 2 February 2021 (in Greek). https://www.synigoros.gr/?i=kdet.el.news.608123

Hart, H.L.A., and Green Leslie. 2015. *The Concept of Law*. Oxford: Oxford University Press.

Hellenic Ministry of Migration Policy. 2013. National Integration Strategy. Accessed 15 March 2021 (in Greek). https://migration.gov.gr/migration-policy/integration/politiki-entaxis-se-ethniko-epipedo/

Hellenic Ministry of Migration Policy. 2019a. National Integration Strategy for third country nationals. Accessed 20 March 2021 (in Greek). https://migration.gov.gr/migration-policy/integration/politiki-entaxis-se-ethniko-epipedo/

Hellenic Ministry of Migration Policy. 2019b. Report on Public Consultation in the National Integration Strategy. Accessed 15 March 2021 (in Greek). http://www.opengov.gr/immigration/?p=801

International Organization for Migration. 2019. *Glossary on Migration*. Geneva: International Organisation for Migration.

Karamanidou, Lena. 2021. Migration, Asylum Policy and Global Justice in Greece. In Michaela Ceccorulli, Enrico Fassi E, and Sonia Lucarelli, *The EU Migration System of Governance. The European Union in International Affairs* by: 89–117. Palgrave Macmillan, Cham. DOI: 10.1007/978-3-030-53997-9_4

Kentikelenis, Alexander. 2018. Intersecting crises: migration, the economy and the right to health in Europe. *European Journal of Public Health* 28, Supp. 5 (December): 61–62.

Kourachanis, Nikos. 2019. From camps to social integration? Social housing interventions for asylum seekers in Greece. *International Journal of Sociology and Social Policy* 39, no. 3 (April): 221–234.

Kourachanis, Nikos. 2018. Asylum seekers, hotspot approach and anti-social policy responses in Greece. *Journal of International Migration and Integration* 19, no. 4 (June): 1153–1167.

Koutsouraki, Eleni. 2017. The Indefinite Detention of Undesirable and Unreturnable Third-Country Nationals in Greece. *Refugee Survey Quarterly* 36, no. 1 (March): 85–106.

Kovner, Bella, Adar Zehavi, and Daphna Golan. 2021. Unaccompanied asylum-seeking youth in Greece: protection, liberation and criminalization. *The International Journal of Human Rights 25, no.10* (February):1744–1767.

Mavrodi, Georgia. 2005. Europeanising national immigration policy. The case of Greece. *Arbeitspapiere* No. 8, Bielefeld: Centre on Migration, Citizenship and Development.

Ministry of Interior. 2016. "Asylum office data (1.1.2016 - 30.4.2016)." Accessed 5 March 2021 (in Greek). https://migration.gov.gr/en/statistika/

Papadakaki, Maria, Christos Lionis, Aristoula Saridaki, Christopher Dowrick, Tomas de Brú, Mary O'Reilly-de Brún, Catherine A. O'Donnell, Nicola Burns, Evelyn van Weel-Baumgarten, Maria van den Muijsenbergh, Wolfgang Spiegel, and Anne MacFarlane. 2017. Exploring barriers to primary care for migrants in Greece in times of austerity: Perspectives of service providers. *Eur J Gen* Pract. 23, no. 11:128–134.

Rapp, Carolin, Tim Huijts, Terje A. Eikemo, and Theoni Stathopoulou. 2018. Social integration and self-reported health: differences between immigrants and natives in Greece. *European Journal of Public Health* 28, Supp. 5 (December): 48–53.

Robinson, Ian, and Francis Johns. 2007. Legal Research as Qualitative Research". In Mike McConville and Wing Hong Chui, *Research Methods for Law*: 18–47. Edinburgh: Edinburgh University Press.

Scholten, Peter, Han Entzinger, Rinnus Penninx. and Stijn Verbeek (eds). 2015. *Integrating Immigrants in Europe: Research-Policy Dialogues*. IMISCOE Research Series, Springer Open. https://library.oapen.org/ bitstream/handle/20.500.12657/28048/1001946.pdf?sequence=1#page=124

Strumia, Fransesca. 2016. European Citizenship and EU Immigration: A Demoi-cratic Bridge between the Third Country Nationals' Right to Belong and the Member States' Power to Exclude. *European Law Journal* 22, no. 4 (December): 417–447.

Triandafyllidou, Anna. 2001. *Immigrants and National Identity in Europe*. London: Routledge.

Triandafyllidou, Anna. 2009. Greek Immigration Policy at the Turn of the 21st Century. Lack of Political Will or Purposeful Mismanagement? *European Journal of Migration and Law* 11 (January): 159–177.

United Nations High Commissioner for Refugees. 2019. UNHCR urges Greece to strengthen safeguards in the draft asylum law. Accessed 15 March 2021. https://www.unhcr.org/gr/en/13170-unhcr-urges-greece-to-strengthen-safeguards-in-draft-asylum-law.html

United Nations High Commissioner for Refugees. 2020. Towards ESTIA II: UNHCR welcomes Greece's commitment to ensure the continuation of the flagship reception program for asylum-seekers. Accessed 10 March 2021. https://www.unhcr.org/gr/en/15985-towards-estia-ii-unhcr-welcomes-greeces-commitment-to-ensure-the-continuation-of-flagship-reception-programme-for-asylum-seekers.html

Van Aeken, Koen. 2011. Law, sociology and anthropology: a liaison beginning endlessly. In Klink van Bart and Sanne Taekema , *Law and Method: Interdisciplinary Research into Law*: 55–84. Tübingen: Mohr Siebeck.

12

Italy's Mixed Response to the Syrian Refugee Crisis

AUGUSTA NANNERINI

The most evident steps undertaken by Italy to show solidarity with Syrian refugees in the aftermath of the crisis is the resettlement program run by the government and the humanitarian corridors led by civil society, both started in 2015. These programs did not begin as explicit responses to the war in Syria, but most of their beneficiaries were individuals fleeing the Syrian conflict who had found refuge in neighboring countries. In this chapter, I shed light on the context, purpose, and structure of these humanitarian programs. However, as not all the Syrian asylum seekers reach Italy through these means, I begin my discussion by giving an account of other ways through which Italy manages asylum and migration, under a logic influenced by security concerns to protect the borders of the country. By doing so, I also provide the reader with much-needed information about the context of migration and asylum policies in Italy, including the EU influence on them, and I explain the difference between the security and humanitarian logic that shape the Italian response to the Syrian refugee crisis.

In discussing these different logics, the chapter identifies two main forms of governance. The first is influenced by the urge to prevent or stem irregular migratory flows from crossing the borders of the country. To this category belong the bilateral agreements signed with Libya to control migration fluxes, and actions undertaken to stop boats carrying migrants and asylum seekers rescued in the Mediterranean Sea from docking in Italian ports. This form of governance affects the lives of those refugees who arrive in the country without pre-arranged official agreements with Italian organizations, and it materializes a category that I call 'spontaneous arrivals'. The second form of governance, on the other hand, pertains to all the initiatives to bring refugees and asylum seekers to Italy through administratively organized channels. This form includes the Italian resettlement scheme and the initiative of the

Humanitarian Corridors and constitutes a category that I call 'administrative arrivals'. In the rest of this chapter, I focus on elaborating these distinctive forms of governing and responding to migration and asylum, which together illustrate that there is not just one Italian response to the Syrian refugee crisis and that there is internal tension among these different forms of governance and consequent categories.

Methodology

This chapter is based on desk research and semi-structured interviews conducted between September 2020 and February 2021. I completed 12 interviews with representatives of NGOs, an International Organization and Italian government staff, at the Ministry of the Interior and the central service of the 'Associazione Nazionale Comuni Italiani' (ANCI), the Italian National Association for Local Authorities. Interviews were not taped. I took notes and transcribed them before writing my analysis. They took place over the phone or via Zoom calls, and lasted between 45 minutes and 1 hour and 15 minutes. To ensure confidentiality, interviewees are kept anonymous and direct quotations are not attributed. Interviews were used to inform my own understanding and for suggesting additional relevant documents that I could include in my research to consult already existing data.

The Category of Spontaneous Arrivals

By spontaneous arrivals, I address the category of refugees that arrive in Italy without being included in safe and legal pathways to claim asylum. Asylum seekers that belong to this category are subject to different application procedures to assess their claims and, to a certain extent, they enjoy different treatments and access to benefits compared to the ones that arrive in Italy through other means. To be understood, the processes and reasons why this category of refugees materializes need to be explained within the complex political debate around Italian migration and asylum policies, where one of the most divisive and dramatic topics of discussion is the humanitarian crisis taking place at the Italian Southern maritime borders, part of the so-called 'Central Mediterranean Route' to reach Europe. According to official statistics, in 2021 Italy witnessed more than 67,000 arrivals to these areas, and at least 1,552 people died or went missing during the journey along that route (ECRE, 2021).

In this context, one way to respond to this high level of migratory flows includes attempts to prevent migrants and potential asylum seekers from reaching Italian territory. This way of managing migration has historically been part of the Italian Foreign Policy strategy, way before the Syrian war started. It dates to the Italian cooperation with Libyan authorities under Muammar Gaddafi and the bilateral agreements that came with it – the most emblematic being the so-called 'Treaty of Friendship' signed in 2002 (effective in 2008), where Italy agreed to build a motorway in Libya as a compensation for the Italian domination over Libya in its colonial past (Paoletti 2010). As part of the agreement, in addition to economic cooperation, Italy provided Libya with military forces to control sea departure and to construct four migration detention centers. In exchange, Libya committed to accepting Italian-apprehended individuals back into its territory (whether to its soil or territorial waters) intercepted during that country's naval patrolling operations (Paoletti 2010).

Since its inception, bilateral cooperation with Libya has never stopped. Human rights organizations and the UN have documented and criticized the Libyan detention centers' appalling conditions (e.g., Human Rights Watch 2021). Still, their concerns have never shifted Italy's policy of seeking to control its southern borders by recurring to these sorts of bilateral agreements (Easo 2021). In February 2020, the Memorandum of Understanding between Italy and Libya was renewed, even though an Italian Criminal Court ruled that it was not in conformity with the Italian Constitution and international law, and despite the fact that it had been criticized by several organizations including the Association for Juridical Studies on Immigration (ASGI), and the Council of Europe Commissioner for Human Rights (Aida 2021). To justify and contextualize this policy, however, one should also keep in mind that the EU policies towards Libya and migration are also very similar to the Italian agreement (Amnesty International 2022). Part of the refugees that belong to the category of 'spontaneous arrivals,' therefore, are those who manage to go beyond this preventive Italian and EU strategy and reach Italian soil to lodge their asylum claim.

Cooperation between Italy and Libya was heavily affected by the death of Muammar Gaddafi in 2011, and, especially when the number of arrivals and shipwrecks skyrocketed in the aftermath of the political instability in the country. Several Search and Rescue (SAR) operations have since been put in place by Italian institutions and independent civil society organizations. These initiatives are important because they show the different trends in place in the country to respond to migratory crisis, and present initial evidence to explain why the main claim of this chapter is that the Italian response to the Syrian crisis has been 'mixed'.

For example, one of the most noteworthy exceptions in the ways of governing migration and asylum by Italian authorities can be identified in the 2013 decision of the Italian government to launch Mare Nostrum, a humanitarian and military mission aimed at patrolling international waters (i.e., not only within the Italian jurisdiction), to search for, and rescue, migrants and asylum seekers and disembark them on Italian soil. The initiative was launched as the Italian response to the humanitarian crisis following a terrible shipwreck on 3 October 2013, involving migrants coming from Libya that resulted in more than 300 deaths. Operation Mare Nostrum highlights the tensions created between the securitization of borders and the humanitarian imperative of saving lives and shows how the forms of migration governance in Italy has always alternated between security and humanitarian concerns, even before other EU states experienced the consequences of the Syrian refugee crisis. More recently, many other examples of SAR took place in the Mediterranean, but most of them encountered several difficulties in obtaining permission to disembark their passengers in an Italian port.

Another aspect that Operation Mare Nostrum helps to explain is the importance for the Italian government of negotiating cooperation and support with the EU Member States and institutions, both to share the responsibilities towards refugees, under the humanitarian imperative, and to keep the EU borders safe, in line with security concerns. The Prime Minister at the time of Mare Nostrum, Enrico Letta, launched the mission under the expectation that EU institutions or its individual member states would also decide to participate, either by sharing with Italy the financing of the operation or by offering support in processing asylum claims, dealing with the relocation of refugees and repatriation of failed asylum seekers (Fondazione Migrantes 2013). In this sense, Mare Nostrum is a good example of an attempt of 'Europeanisation' of Italian asylum policies.

Europeanization is an important concept through which to consider Italian migration policies. In the academic literature, it is described as a phenomenon that aims at understanding and justifying the 'issues of causes' that connect policy changes at the domestic and European levels. (e.g., Olsen 2002, 291). Since it is a vast category, which is not 'itself a theory' (Bulmer 2007, 47), discussing Europeanisation requires a distinction between a 'top-down and bottom-up' approach (Caporaso 2007). In the top-down version, the analysis starts from the EU level, explaining the consequent adaptation to EU policies at the domestic level. The bottom-up stance starts from the national level, examining domestic policy transfer and influence at the European level. Mare Nostrum was an excellent example of a bottom-up Europeanization attempt, but in this case, one that failed. The EU did not join the mission. The government that proposed the operation fell out of power, and the new Prime Minister, Matteo Renzi, decided to end Mare Nostrum and support a smaller EU-funded mission, called Triton (Caffio 2014).

The concept of Europeanization is of critical analytical importance because Italy remains one of the 'doors' to the EU. How it manages its borders needs to be interpreted within its request for cooperation with the EU to ensure security, fight smuggling and human trafficking, protect the right to asylum, and protect its borders. Failure of extending Mare Nostrum at the EU level sheds light on the repeated, and unanswered, calls by the Italian government for more substantial political and pragmatic support in managing migratory flows. Other attempts include calls by Italy to establish an EU-wide relocation system for asylum seekers and migrants that reach national soil by sea, as well as to reform the Dublin system, particularly by changing the clause of first country arrival, which is perceived as overburdening Italian reception systems (Cheli 2013; Pontieri 2014). Clearly, EU actions (or the lack thereof) keep being a key point of reference that influences the domestic political and policy debate. (Gatta and Teodorescu 2013). The next section of the chapter will explain how, in deciding to join a EU-led scheme for Syrian refugees, Italy chose to take steps towards an approach to manage migration in a EU-coordinated and funded, manner. In this sense, the decision to start the Italian resettlement program and the humanitarian corridors reflected a way of governing migration in light of the humanitarian imperative, and it also strengthened the possibility of keeping negotiation concerning asylum matters with the EU open.

At the same time, as I argue in the chapter, in joining EU actions to resettle refugees, Italy contributed to establishing a system where the way by which refugees arrive in the country determines the procedures through which their applications are processed by authorities. To a certain extent, this also affects the access to services offered by the government and civil society organizations to refugees, to facilitate their integration into Italian society. Even if the UNHCR clearly specifies that 'Article 31 (1) of the 1951 Convention prohibits the penalization of refugees for illegal entry or presence, provided they come directly from countries where their life was threatened and show 'good cause' for violating applicable entry laws' (UNHCR 2000), the ways of managing migratory flows through the lenses of security materializes a category of refugees that get to Italy in the form of spontaneous arrivals. This category is very different from the one of those refugees that arrive to Italy through other institutionalized administrative procedures, according to a humanitarian logic. The rest of this chapter explains the procedures of the Italian resettlement programs and the humanitarian corridors, explaining how through these channels Syrian refugees are welcomed to Italy as a category that I call administrative arrivals.

The Category of Administrative Arrivals: The Italian Resettlement Program

While attempts to prevent asylum seekers and migrants from reaching the Italian territory have historically been part of the Italian migration policies, before 2015, the Italian experience with resettlement was sporadic and *ad hoc*. For example, in 2010, Italy resettled 180 Palestinians in the 'Al Tanf' camp, which used to be located in a border area between Syria and Iraq (UNHCR 2010). However, it is only with the Syrian crisis that Italy undertook substantial steps to institutionalize its resettlement program. Before that, Italy had developed two legal proposals regarding the issue of asylum and humanitarian protection (numbers 2410 and 1390), both including the possibility of resettlement measures, and never endorsed by Parliament (CIR 2007). In policy fora, the idea of an Italian resettlement program was first discussed 2005, when the Ministry of the Interior, in collaboration with the EU Commission, funded a research project conducted by the IOM to analyze the different resettlement experiences of the United States, Sweden, and the United Kingdom, to investigate whether they could be reproduced in Italy. The study proposed establishing an Italian resettlement program called 'Piano Dante' (Di Giacomo 2005). This plan suggested that the 'comuni' (i.e., Italian local authorities), would be responsible for hosting the refugees for one year, collaborating with NGOs in independent facilities managed locally. The study was commissioned when the EU was just beginning to discuss the establishment of a joint resettlement plan and, without any certainty of EU commitment to support resettlement in the future, Piano Dante tentatively indicated that the Interior Ministry should be responsible for bearing the initiative's cost. The proposal was never implemented, due to lack of political will and institutional funding.

When, finally, in 2014 the EU Regulation No 516/2014, by the European Parliament and the EU Council, established the Asylum, Migration and Integration Fund (AMIF or FAMI in Italian) and offered financial incentives for member states to resettle refugees, providing 6,000 or 10,000 euros per refugee resettled, Italy decided to join the program. In the first two years, between 2015 and 2017, Italy pledged 1,989 places and resettled 1,612 persons (UNHCR 2019). In 2016, following the EU-Turkey Statement, Italy decided to use a 'share' of its first pledge to resettle Syrian refugees from Turkey (UNHCR 2019). When, at the beginning of 2017, the EU launched a call for resettlement pledges for 2018, Italy pledged to resettle 1,000 individuals and eventually resettled 871 persons. For the year 2020-2021, Italy pledged 700 places, but has resettled a minimal number (21) due to the COVID-19 pandemic.

When resettlement started to be part of the Italian institutions and supported through AMIF funds, the Ministry of the Interior established a new section to deal with the issue, known as the Department for Resettlement (Interview with staff at department on 23 February 2021). In 2015, this section had a Vice-Prefect, three external consultants, and one consultant seconded by UNHCR. In 2021, the team became more prominent and counted four external consultants, one secondment from UNHCR, and three Interior Ministry staff members. The new section was created because of the lack of internal expertise on the matter, which confirms the little experience that Italy possessed. In addition to having a staff member seconded to the Ministry, UNHCR offices in the field provide the refugee profiles that meet UNHCR resettlement criteria. The department of resettlement of the Ministry of the Interior selects the individuals proposed by UNHCR and then submits their dossiers to the security department. Once applications are approved, IOM and UNHCR are responsible for arranging for pre-departure courses and, ultimately, the journey to Italy. Because security screenings take place before departure and the criteria for assessing the asylum claim are already expected to be fulfilled, this category of administrative arrivals follows quicker and smoother procedures to regularize refugees' status in Italy. This results in a facilitated process, less difficult to navigate and experience for the refugees themselves.

The legal framework currently in use in the resettlement process is Art. 12 Comma 2 of the 'Decreto Procedure'. According to the 1951 Refugee Convention, an asylum seeker needs to be physically inside Italian territory to lodge an asylum claim, so, technically, those who are resettled through the resettlement scheme do not yet have their refugee status at the time of departure. They only have refugee recognition from UNHCR and are granted a visa to travel to Italy by the government. However, once they are accepted into the resettlement program, ahead of the journey, the Ministry of the Interior alerts the Commissione Territoriale di Roma, the entity responsible for assessing asylum claims, and shares the dossiers of the asylum seekers in advance. When the asylum seekers land in Rome, they file a request to claim asylum in Italy officially (called Module C3). At this point, la 'questura di Roma,' the police headquarters, based at Fiumicino airport, notifies the Commissione Territoriale di Roma, which starts processing the dossiers that it had already received in advance from the Ministry. In this way, these resettled refugees, differently from other asylum claims of the spontaneous arrivals, do not have to present themselves at the Commissione Territoriale to introduce their case and have their first interview. They only go in person once the process ends to collect their papers. The speed of the procedure is catalyzed by the fact that security concerns have already been considered at the moment of the selection of the individuals, and therefore are not part of the logic that inform this form of governance, very different from the case of spontaneous arrivals.

The choice of countries from which to resettle is set by the EU Commission's calls, which lists some priority countries, including Lebanon, Jordan, Turkey, and African countries that are points of transit for the so-called Central Mediterranean route. Less significant numbers are refugees from Niger and Libya, resettled to reduce the pressure on states along the Central Mediterranean route. To increase its resettlement quota and take steps to address the humanitarian crisis in the Libya detention centers, in 2017, Italy started to collaborate with UNHCR to evacuate some individuals from the detention centers in Libya. There were six evacuations from Libya to Niger and partially to Rwanda, and two evacuations from Niger to Italy. However, these humanitarian evacuations followed a different procedure than the other resettlement processes, because UNHCR cannot conduct a full security assessment of asylum cases in the detention centers. Therefore, before departure, there are no individuals' dossiers to be shared in advance with the Commissione Territoriale in Rome. In this case, when the refugees arrive at the airport, they undergo the usual procedure to apply for asylum, the same that is applied to spontaneous arrivals. Another option is 'Education Pathways,' based on partnerships with Italian universities, but the program has resettled a limited number of individuals to date (UNHCR 2020b).

Differences in Post-arrival Treatment

When Italy decided to engage in the EU resettlement programs, it chose to include the new resettled refugees in the already existing Italian national system of reception, the so-called 'SAI' system (i.e., Sistema Accoglienza e Integrazione, in English, Welcoming and Integration System). The SAI provides projects for integration for refugees and different forms of assistance for asylum seekers. The decision to include the resettled refugees in this system meant that the EU AMIF fund, a total of 10,000 Euros per resettled individual, is disbursed by EU institutions to the Ministry of the Interior, which then subsequently allocates it to the SAI. Local authorities are part of the SAI system in different Italian regions. The entity that assigns individuals to each local authority and is responsible for disbursing the funds to support their expenses is the 'central service' of the Associazione Nazionale dei Comuni Italiani (ANCI) (i.e., Italian Association of the National Local Authorities). The central service of ANCI connects the Ministry of the Interior and the local authorities.

Local authorities collaborate with NGOs or private entities for the implementation of the program, and the organizations arrange for refugees and asylum seekers to be hosted in common areas, private apartments or partially shared accommodations (including hotels), depending on the availability of their structures. Services provided in these facilities include Italian language, skills training, and cultural awareness. Each implementing organization is reimbursed an average of 35 euros per day for hosting one refugee that belongs to the category of spontaneous arrivals. In the case of the resettled refugees, the total per person per day can reach 80 euros, which is justified by the system because the resettled persons' vulnerabilities might need special care and assistance. The different amount distributed is one of the differences that results from the two different procedures proper to the categories of spontaneous and administrative arrivals.

Once members of a spontaneous arrivals group are in Italy and have manifested a desire to apply for asylum, they are directed to the centers of 'prima accoglienza' ('first welcoming') that is assigned to them by the ANCI central service. To do so, asylum seekers are divided into three categories: 'vulnerable,' 'unaccompanied children,' and 'ordinary' (interview with staff member on 25 February 2021). Within these categories, local authorities can decide to host one of these categories, or also sub-categories, for example accepting only 'vulnerable women'.

The group of refugees that arrive through the administrative arrivals are hosted at the SAI for one year, while refugees who arrive spontaneously can stay for six months. The six months are counted from the day that asylum seekers obtain refugee status. Asylum seekers wait in the SAI while their application is processed and then have six months of 'accoglienza' (i.e., 'welcome period') to find a job and accommodation. Individuals can extend their stays, depending on their asylum application stage (for example, in case of appeal, they can continue staying in the SAI structure). During the period in which they are part of the SAI reception system, the administrative arrivals refugees and the ones who are part of the spontaneous arrivals group enjoy the same treatment and are included in the same projects. However, as mentioned above, what differs is the length of the period they are allowed to stay.

Since 2018, at the end of the SAI period, refugees who arrive as administrative arrivals can choose to join projects carried out by Italian civil society organizations to further facilitate their social and economic integration. The EU funds these projects through the AMIF funding allocated for integration initiatives and resettlement. Two main groups of NGOs implement them, the Associazione Ricreativa e Culturale Italiana (ARCI) (i.e., Italian Association for Cultural and Recreational Activities), and Consorzio Communitas. The projects' selection criteria include being resettled through the Ministry of the Interior program and having already been living in Italy for at least six months. There can be cases of refugees that apply to be included in the projects without having a direct SAI referral, but they all need to be part of the administrative arrivals. Notably, because most resettled refugees live in SAI located in the southern part of the country, some of the entities that work in the North struggle to reach their quota because they do not always find resettled refugees to include as beneficiaries (interview with staff on 15 December 2020). This phenomenon, that comes as a result of the different categories that created the diverse forms of governance to respond to migratory flows, is particularly paradoxical if one considers that the Southern part of the country is also the one with the highest number of spontaneous arrivals.

ARCI is the project lead of Compasso, an acronym that stands for the Italian words 'competencies' (COM-), 'passion' (Pass-) and 'occupation' (O-), and that aims to support refugees' integration into the labor market. The project is active in the region of Lazio, Campania, Basilicata, Calabria, Puglia, Sicilia, and Sardegna. Consorzio Communitas covers the rest of the country, i.e., the north-eastern regions and maintains a similar focus on employment opportunities. Consorzio Communitas counts about 23 entities that work together, and it also collaborates with Caritas. Among other things, Caritas contributes with its network of 230 parishes that have agreed to participate in the initiatives. Each project assumes different nuances in its implementation. Overall, projects can offer vocational training, support for self-employment activities, provision of educational tools, assistance in finding an accommodation that replaces the structure provided by the SAI system, help in getting a driving license and similar services. The implementing entity in the region budgets a total cost of 3.900 euros per individual for the project's duration. These projects fill a substantive gap, because without them, at the end of their time at the SAI, refugees risk encountering homelessness or labor exploitation in the agricultural sector, a very concerning example of modern slavery in the south of the country (Open Society 2018). However – given that even young Italian generations sometimes leave small urban centers in the south to find better economic possibilities elsewhere – at the end of the project, some refugees may decide to do the same and move somewhere else in the country. Families with small children are more likely to stay in the areas that welcome them at first, and in this sense, the interviews carried out for this research also discovered several positive integration experiences (interview with staff on 30 December 2020).

It is important to reiterate that the EU AMIF funding supports these projects only for the group of refugees that arrive to Italy through the administrative procedures of resettlement of the Ministry of the Interior. In practice, this model leaves out the spontaneous arrivals. Hence, as a result of the different structure and *modus operandi* of the different forms of migration and asylum governance of Italian policies, the refugees that belong to the group of the administrative arrivals, the majority of which, as I explained, are Syrians, can benefit from the state or NGOs' assistance for more extended periods than refugees who reached Italy by other means and they can be included in more organic integration projects.

The Category of Administrative Arrival: The Humanitarian Corridors

In addition to the resettlement program run by the Italian Ministry of the Interior in cooperation with UNHCR, refugees can also reach Italy through the so-called Humanitarian Corridors. This initiative represents another channel for the administrative arrival of refugees. The negotiation to establish the humanitarian corridors started around the same time when the Italian government began its engagement with the EU funded resettlement schemes. In 2015, the Ministry of the Interior signed a memorandum of understanding with the Ministry of Foreign Affairs and International Cooperation, the Tavola Valdese (Waldesian Council), the Community of Methodist Churches, the Federation of Protestant Churches in Italy (FCEI) and the Community of St. Egidio to start the first 'humanitarian corridor' (Sigona 2015; Squire 2020). In 2018, the Community of St. Egidio, Caritas, and Fondazione Migrantes started a second humanitarian corridor from Ethiopia to offer safe routes to Sudanese, Eritreans, and Somalis. (Confronti et al. 2020). In a nutshell, the humanitarian corridors are an example of community sponsorship, whereby local Italian communities assume responsibility to welcome and integrate refugees. It is a project that is complementary to the Ministry of the Interior's work for resettlement. Therefore, it is added to the quotas that the Italian government pledges to the EU. This *additionality* criterion (i.e., the fact that the number of refugees brought to the country is 'added' to the one pledged by the government) is crucial for the humanitarian corridors' vision because it shows the desire not to free the state from its moral responsibilities to resettle refugees.

The legal framework of the humanitarian corridors is based on Article 25 of the Codice Visti, (the Italian Visa Code), which envisages the possibility of issuing a visa with the purpose of lodging an asylum claim. The process, starting from the referral from the ground and ending with a flight ticket to get to Italy, usually lasts five months, a much shorter period than other resettlement procedures, that can take up to two years from the moment a person starts the first interview with the UNHCR. The HQs of FCEI and St. Egidio in Rome receive referrals from the country where individuals are staying, assess whether to go forward with the application process, and present on their behalf the visa application to be processed by the relevant Italian authorities at the embassy. Italian authorities carry out security checks and eventually issue the visa that allows the applicant to travel to Italy. Referrals from the ground happen in different ways, depending on the network of the organization responsible for the 'corridor'. Criteria to be selected are set around the issues of vulnerabilities, enabling the organizations to understand a 'need of protection' that is less constraining than the 1951 Refugee Convention (for example, allowing for being considered as part of the category of humanitarian protection).

Most of the organizations that implement humanitarian corridors have a presence in the field to receive applications and select individuals. It is essential to review the applications, interview individuals and carry out pre-departure courses, that describe to refugees what to expect once arrived in Italy. During my interviews, one of my interviewees mentioned that the fact that the humanitarian corridors are implemented by churches, in a shorter time compared to state-led channels, risks amplifying the dynamics where the 'savior' humanitarians working for religious organizations are rescuing the 'victims' refugees to give them a better life in Italy (interview with staff on 19 November 2020). These dynamics translate into the fact that once in Italy, some resettled refugees expect the organization that brought them there look after them in a way that goes beyond the organization's capacity. Part of the pre-departure courses' mission is to explain the individuals' responsibility in undertaking the migratory journey and report all the difficulties that individuals may encounter in the future (Corridoi Umanitari 2020).

Once arrived in Italy, refugees are taken care of in the project for a period that ranges between 18 months to two years. During this time, rent and allowance for basic expenses are provided by the project, along with help with legal paperwork, vocational training, and referrals to organizations that offer Italian lessons. Refugees arrive in Rome and are then distributed to different parts of Italy, depending on the structure and partner organization that can host them. The matching between the place and individuals considers the refugees' needs, particularly their vulnerabilities. For example, in the case of health issues, the organization that sponsors the person makes sure that there are adequate health facilities in the locality where they will be hosted. Often, the organization notifies the hospital of reference in the area in advance. As with any other Italian citizen, refugees have free education for their children and access to the national health system.

The humanitarian corridors' original agreement included Lebanon, Morocco, and Ethiopia, but the project in Morocco never started and the one from Ethiopia counted very few individuals. At a later stage, Caritas also started selecting individuals from Jordan, Ethiopia, and Nigeria. De facto, most individuals that benefited from the projects fled the Syrian crisis. The most common nationalities are Syrians and a smaller number of Iraqi. One reason to explain this trend, as per the fact that most individuals resettled by the Ministry of the Interior are Syrians, is that it is almost inevitable for a Syrian to be granted refugee status in Italy. This certainty about asylum applications' outcomes removes the issues of returns of failed asylum seekers, which would waste the program's resources and overall undermine its main purpose of giving refugees a new beginning in Italy.

In four years, counting from the beginning of the project until March 2020, FCEI reported that 1896 individuals reached Italy through the first humanitarian corridors (Corridoio Umanitari 2020); 94 per cent of them had fled the Syrian crisis. Overall, the refugee portion of this category enjoyed faster resettlement and a longer period of assistance for their integration in Italy, coupled with some very supportive structural facilities to foster their self-reliance and well-being in the country. As such, the humanitarian corridors differ from the treatment for so-called spontaneous arrivals and also from the resettlement programs run by the government.

Conclusions

This chapter has briefly described the different ways by which Italy responded to the Syrian refugee crisis. How refugees arrive in the country (or fail to do so) is the most important factor that determines the set of policies and initiatives put in place to support their stay, or to prevent their arrival in case they decide to attempt the migratory journey through spontaneous migratory routes. In addition, concerning the refugees who arrive by safe and legal pathways, a significant difference materializes depending on who is responsible for their stay, which can be the Italian governmental authorities in the case of the resettlement program or civil society and faith-based organizations in the case of the humanitarian corridors. The variety of the actors, purposes and institutional frameworks that are part of this scenario explain my claim that the overall Italian response to the Syrian refugee crisis has been mixed.

Within the analysis, this chapter has shown that the Italian response to the Syrian refugee crisis has proven to be especially complex because migration and asylum is part of the delicate Italian relations with the EU. The chapter provided a brief background of Italian ties with Libya, the way of protecting the country's sea borders from the threat of irregular crossings and explained the role that Italy's relationship with the EU has exercised in the decisions that have been taken over time. The securitization of migratory flows, embedded in the policies that restrict access to asylum in the Central Mediterranean since the implementation of the Treaty of Friendship, is entangled with the crisis of the shipwrecks that have been occurring there for more than a decade. In turn, the death of those who failed in their crossing of the sea has been co-constituting the issue of migration as a humanitarian emergency that started to be perceived in the country many years before the 2015 refugee crisis. Therefore, the logic of security and humanitarianism are intertwined in the various forms of governance of migration and asylum.

Humanitarian and security concerns have influenced very diverse policy responses, which were also affected by the initiatives of the EU institutions (or lack thereof). Examples of this variety include decisions to launch Mare Nostrum in 2013 to search for, and rescue, individuals drowning in international waters bordering Libya and bring them to Italy, which directly opposes the bilateral agreements still in place with Libya to prevent migrants and asylum seekers from reaching Italian ports. Simultaneously, these decisions were never taken entirely independently from the European Union.

For example, Mare Nostrum started with the expectation that more EU states would join the initiative and ended due to the EU's lack of intervention. With a similar logic that kept the EU in sight, the first plan for an Italian resettlement program, the Piano Dante, did not have enough support to be implemented. Italy started engaging with resettlement initiatives only in 2015, in conjunction with the EU resettlement program and AMIF funding. The renewed interest in resettlement provided the institutional framework that also enabled civil society and faith organizations to play a vital role in offering legal and safe pathways for asylum seekers fleeing the Syrian crisis.

Therefore, to conclude, the Italian response to the Syrian crisis must be understood in light of the complexity that the issues of migration and asylum represent to the country, and the many nuances that it has assumed over time in different scenarios. The research carried out to write this chapter suggests that this mixed context and policy has created the two categories mentioned above; administrative arrivals and spontaneous arrivals. Further research is needed to include the role of domestic political debates in shaping the Italian response, as well as the refugees' perspectives that are part of these two different categories, to inquire how being part of these two groups affect their lives.

References

Amnesty International. 2021. Libya/EU: Conditions remain 'hellish' as EU marks 5 years of cooperation agreements, press release available at https://www.amnesty.org/en/latest/news/2022/01/libya-eu-conditions-remain-hellish-as-eu-marks-5-years-of-cooperation-agreements/

Bulmer, S. 2007. Theorizing Europeanization, in Paolo Graziano and Maarten P. Vink (eds.), *Europeanization: New Research Agendas.* Basingstoke: Palgrave Macmillan, 46–58.

Caffio, F. 2014. L' Europa fra Triton e Mare Nostrum, in *Affari Internazionali*, 11 November 2014. http://www.affarinternazionali.it/articolo.asp?ID=2865

Camera dei Deputati. 2021. Dirittto di asilo e accoglienza dei migranti sul territorio. https://www.camera.it/temiap/documentazione/temi/pdf/1105104.pdf

Caporaso, J. 2007. The Three Worlds of Regional Integration Theory, in Paolo Graziano and Maarten P. Vink (eds.), *Europeanization: New Research Agendas.* Basingstoke: Palgrave Macmillan, 23–45.

Cheli E. 2013. 'Immigrazione: poteri e doveri dell' UE", in *Liberta' Civili, Rivista bimestrale del dipartimento per le liberta' civili e l' immigrazione del Ministero dell,' Interno*, pp. 33–35.

Confronti, Idor, Oxfam, Federation Entraide Protestante. 2020. Sponsoring Integration. Impact Assessment of the Primary Achievements of the humanitarian Corridors Program in Italy and France, edited by Claudio Paravati and Antonio Ricci.

Corridoio Umanitari-Una pratica replicabile. 2020. Atti della Conferenza. Report edited by Confronti, idos, and the Italian Ministry for Foreign Affairs and International Cooperation. https://www.esteri.it/mae/resource/ doc/2020/10/corridoi_umanitari_una_pratica_replicabile._atti_della_ conferenza_-_luglio_2020_def-compresso.pdf

Council of Europe. 2012. Action Plan, Communication from Italy concerning the case of Hirsi Jamaa vs. Italy (Application No. 27765/09).

Di Giacomo. 2005. Uno sguardo verso il futuro: Ipotesi per un Piano Dante. FA.RE. -Studio di fattibilità per un Programma di Reinsediamento in Italia, report funded by Consiglio Italiano per i Rifugiati, Commissione Europea, Ministero dell' Interno.

Easo. 2021. EU-Libya Relations Factsheet, Easo website: https://eeas. europa.eu/headquarters/headquarters-homepage_en/19163/EU-Libya%20 relations

ECRE. 2022. Med: Tragedy Continues as Routes Change and Situation in Libya Deteriorates Even Further, press release. https://ecre.org/med-tragedy-continues-as-routes-changes-and-situation-in-libya-deteriorates-even-further/

European Council. 2013. Conclusion 24 and 25 October 2013, euco 169/13. https://www.consilium.europa.eu/uedocs/cms_data/docs/pressdata/en/ ec/139197.pdf

European Resettlement Network. 2019, Italy, website. https://www. resettlement.eu/country/italy

Fondazione Migrantes. 2013. Interview with Enrico Letta, Non accetteremo compromessi al ribasso, 22 Ottobre 2013. http://banchedati.chiesacattolica.it/ pls/cci_new_v3/v3_s2ew_consultazione.mostra_pagina?id_pagina=51353

Gatta A., Teodorescu L. 2013. Il direttore della Rappresentanza della Commissione Europea in Italia, Lucio Battistotti, sottolinea come lo sviluppo di una politica migratoria dell' Unione Europea sia uno degli obiettivi centrali della presidenza Italiana, in *Liberta' Civili, Rivista bimestrale del dipartimento per le liberta' civili e l' immigrazione del Ministero dell' Interno*, pp. 29–33.

Golini. 2013. Italia e Unione European nel processo di globalizzazione, in *Liberta' Civili, Rivista bimestrale del dipartimento per le liberta' civili e l' immigrazione del Ministero dell' Interno*, pp. 36-41.

Human Rights Watch. 2021. EU: Time to review and remedy cooperation policies facilitating abuse of refugees and migrants in Libya. https://www.hrw.org/news/2020/04/28/eu-time-review-and-remedy-cooperation-policies-facilitating-abuse-refugees-and

Olsen. 2002. The Many Faces of Europeanization, *Journal of Common Market Studies*, 40 (5), pp. 921-52.

Open Society Foundation. 2018. Is Italian Agriculture 'Pull Factor' for Irregular Migration—And, If So, Why? https://www.opensocietyfoundations.org/publications/italian-agriculture-pull-factor-irregular-migration-and-if-so-why

Paoletti, E. 2010. *The Migration of Power and North-South Inequalities. The case of Italy and Libya*, Palgrave Macmillan.

Paolicelli, M. and Vignarca, F. 2009. *Il caro Armato. Spese, Affari e Sprechi delle Forze Armate Italiane*, Milano:Altraeconomia.

Pontieri, M. V. 2014. The ABC of the Dublin regime, in *Liberta' Civili, Rivista bimestrale del dipartimento per le liberta' civili e l' immigrazione del Ministero dell' Interno*, pp. 49–52.

Sigona, N. 2015. Two Bottom-up humanitarian corridors for refugees launched, 31 October 2015. https://nandosigona.wordpress.com/2015/10/31/bottom-up-humanitarian-corridors

Squire, V. 2020. Corridoi Umanitari: Dignity in Motion and a Politics of Welcome. In *Europe's Migration Crisis: Border Deaths and Human Dignity*. Cambridge: Cambridge University Press, 105–133.

UNHCR. 2000. Executive Committee of the High Commissioner's programme,18th Meeting of the Standing Committee (EC/50/SC/CPR.17), 9 June 2000. http://www.unhcr.org/excom/EXCOM/3ae68d144.pdf

UNHCR. 2010. Wim Wenders inspired by integration model. https://www.unhcr.org/news/latest/2010/3/4ba7a0126/wim-wenders-inspired-integration-model-set-idyllic-town-calabria.html

UNHCR. 2019. Resettlement Handbook. Country Chapter: Italy. https://www.unhcr.org/protection/resettlement/5d778f907/unhcr-resettlement-handbook-country-chapter-italy.html

UNHCR. 2020. Complementary Education Pathways, UNHCR website. https://www.unhcr.org/complementary-pathways-through-education.html

13

National Responses to the Syrian Refugee Crisis: The Cases of Libya and Malta

EMMA CASEY AND YANNIS A. STIVACHTIS

Millions of refugees have fled Syria and North Africa since the start of the Syrian Civil War in 2011, moving across the Mediterranean world in all directions. Initially, these people were mostly Syrians fleeing the chaos and terror of their home country. According to the United Nations High Commissioner for Refugees (UNHCR), since the beginning of the Syrian Civil War, more than 6 million Syrians have fled their homeland in search of asylum in neighboring states, North Africa, and the European Union (EU) (UNHCR 2021). However, in addition to the millions fleeing that country, there have been additional millions of people fleeing other conflict zones in regions near the Mediterranean for more than two decades. Afghanistan, for example, has seen 2.5 million individuals depart that nation since the start of the NATO intervention in 2001. Other conflicts in Sub-Saharan Africa, in the Sahel region and others, against Jihadist groups have increased the number of people who have left their homes in the face of violence and dislocation.

The national governments of the receiving states have been facing the pressures associated with this massive dislocation as well as the costs related to economic migration. Indeed, the sheer magnitude of this human stream has made it more difficult for recipient national governments and their citizens to distinguish clearly and carefully between refugees and economic migrants and treat each according to their appropriate legal status.

Irregular migration within the Mediterranean region is not new, but the abnormally large number of refugees, asylum seekers, and economic migrants during recent decades has put increased pressure on states located in the area, especially since the number of incoming migrants and refugees dramatically surged with the Syrian Civil War spurred exodus in 2015. The overwhelming majority of migrants in the Mediterranean region have traveled north to the countries of the European Union, where they have hoped to find more peaceful living conditions and economically fruitful opportunities. Many migrants and refugees from North Africa and the eastern Mediterranean have sought to cross into Europe either via land routes through Turkey and the Balkan states, or by sea via Greece, Italy, Spain, Malta, and other states on the European periphery. This stream of refugees and migrants has created humanitarian crises where they otherwise might not have occurred. The rapid influx of refugees of individuals of different nationalities, religions, and cultures has placed a strain on Mediterranean states that have, by and large, proven to be economically and politically unprepared to address it.

This chapter explores the factors that have affected the treatment of refugees and asylum seekers in Libya and Malta. In both countries, the migrant stream in the last two decades has constituted a challenge for governments ill-equipped to manage it effectively. In the case of Libya, its own civil conflict and lack of institutional capacity have hobbled the development of a coordinated and robust policy response of any kind as warlords, tribes, Islamists, and rival governments have each pressed to protect centers of power in different parts of the country. In the case of Malta, a history of policy already resistant to migrant populations, mounting popular discomfort with immigration and squabbles with the European Union have hampered efforts to respond effectively to refugees.

Libya and the Refugee Crisis

Libya has seen its share of hardship since 2011. After an uprising against the late dictator of the country, Muammar Gaddafi, a NATO-led coalition intervened on the side of the rebels to enforce a ceasefire. Although the intervention was successful, the interim government set up soon after proved weak and the nation slid into civil war in 2014. This fact, coupled with a resurgence of Islamist terrorist groups and the omnipresence of migrants, has encouraged an increase in human trafficking, constant civil strife, and human rights violations of all kinds. Unfortunately, the migrants and refugees detained in Libya are extremely vulnerable to inhumane treatment, as many migrant and refugee detention centers are under militia control (Al-Dayel, Anfinson and Anfinson 2021, 2). That reality has spawned large scale human trafficking in the country, in particular (Al-Dayel, Anfinson and Anfinson 2021, 2).

Though Libya's nominal governments have made some efforts to accommodate refugees and migrants, their relative weakness and the general lack of stability in the country have rendered them unable to address refugees effectively. The EU has offered some assistance via border security programs and through financial support of communities most affected by increased refugee presence. However, the human rights violations and human trafficking occurring in Libya and targeted at refugees continue to be widespread.

The Libyan Civil War and Its effects on Refugee Treatment

Following the overthrow of Gaddafi and the outbreak of the Second Libyan Civil War in 2014, that nation's citizens found themselves governed by a complicated and inefficient tripartite regime created under the terms of the Libyan Political Agreement (LPA) in 2015. This attempt to address the Libyan political crisis aimed to prevent wider conflict and provide a UN-recognized authority with which other states could negotiate. The agreement ultimately failed and there would be two centers of power within Libya until 23 October 2020. One government was located in Tripoli in the western part of the country and was known as the Government of National Accord (GNA) and it served as the official UN-recognized government. A rival faction led by the House of Representatives (HOR) and dominated by the Libyan National Army (LNA) claimed power in Tobruk in the eastern region of the nation (Fitzgerald and Toaldo 2016).

Each government was supported by a variety of militias and armies under the control of local warlords who operated independently and without oversight. These were organized according to a system of benefits and incentives related to tribal status and religious conviction, rather than loyalty to a unified Libyan national identity. Islamist militias, which comprised a good portion of the fighters in the Second Libyan Civil War played especially notable roles. Libyan Islamists, primarily consisting of independent Salafi and Muslim Brotherhood members, frequently assumed responsibility for policing and security during the war, especially in Tripoli and the eastern part of the country (Boukhars, Anouar, and Wehrey 2019, 119). They were consistently among the best armed and most disciplined of the independent militia groups in Libya. Their extensive use during the war by the GNA and LNA made them important participants in the nation's proposed internationally supervised elections in December 2021. But those collapsed, leaving a nation in ongoing crisis. In essence, there were and are no truly reliable Libyan government institutions such as one would expect in a Western country. Instead, there are many separate 'city-states' and autonomous militias that use their power in efforts to attain independently determined ends. There is no true Libyan law enforcement, customs or military personnel. Neither the GNA nor the LNA has managed the nation's refugees in any meaningful sense.

This lack of capacity has only served to increase the danger to migrants and refugees trying to cross or depart from Libya. Specifically, during the height of the Syrian Civil War exodus many refugees from that country's conflict sought to cross Libya, which caused intense stress on the state's already weak institutions. Since the government was unable to manage this influx of humanity, those who could afford it hired smugglers or guides to lead them to known crossing sites to Europe. Since Syrian and Iraqi refugees had greater financial resources, they were able to hire guides and that fact created a $300 million market for transporting migrants and refugees by 2015. After 2015, the surge of migrants and refugees into Libya slowed, and smugglers, militias, and criminal networks began controlling and operating unofficial detention sites (Al-Dayel, Anfinson and Anfinson 2021, 2).

Human trafficking has become pervasive in Libya as authorities lack any ability to slow or reverse its rise. According to the U.S. Department of State (2020), the Libyan criminal justice system lacks specialized courts or administrative units to oversee human trafficking cases. Libya's Ministries of Justice and Interior have failed to prosecute human trafficking cases since 2014 due to a lack of police personnel. As a result, suspects and perpetrators have largely been allowed to continue their activities unabated (Al-Dayel, Anfinson and Anfinson 2021, 5). Given the access these corrupt actors have to vulnerable populations of detained migrants and refugees, the financial gain they can accrue and the lack of government response to their criminal activities, it is no surprise that human trafficking has become pervasive in the nation's many militia-and warlord-operated detention centers.

In addition to political divisions, domestic instability and the lack of institutional capacity, corruption has played an important role in the mismanagement of refugee flows.

Specifically, international observers and NGO representatives have become increasingly frustrated with the inability of Libyan authorities to crack down on corruption among government officials, many of whom have been accused of complicity in human trafficking and refugee and migrant smuggling (Al-Dayel, Anfinson and Anfinson 2021, 5). In fact, the United Nations has imposed sanctions on some of these officials (Al-Dayel, Anfinson and Anfinson 2021, 5). The U.S. Department of State (2020, 72) has argued that this corruption has occurred in part because of the infiltration by militia groups and 'criminal networks' into government agencies that address immigration and defense concerns. To the extent this is in fact occurring, it provides perpetrators with authority to pursue their crimes under cover of official responsibility. There are many reported cases of 'disappearing individuals' once in the custody of Libyan authorities. In some cases, traffickers are reported to have impersonated UN personnel at disembarkation points within Libya, a move that would certainly require institutional corruption (Al-Dayel, Anfinson and Anfinson 2021, 5).

In addition to trafficking, sexual assault and rape of refugees by purported Libyan authorities is common. The U.N. has found that at least half of migrant women reported experiencing sexual violence while being transferred between detention centers by security forces in Libya. In addition, three-quarters of migrant and refugee children reported being harassed or beaten, with girls being especially susceptible to such violence (Al-Dayel, Anfinson and Anfinson 2021, 5). There have also been accounts of racial and religious harassment and violence against Christians and darker-skinned refugees and migrants. By far the greatest examples of the failure of Libyan institutions to address migrant and refugee challenge in recent years are the migrant detention facilities which, as noted above, are often managed unofficially by local militias, traffickers, and smugglers. Although after 2020 many of these centers were returned to official government control, they are still characterized by horrible conditions for the migrant and refugee detainees. This situation is mainly due to the corruption and indifference of the officials tasked to manage them.

A critical factor in understanding the nation's widespread human trafficking is the role that decentralized power structures have played in permitting and perpetuating it. It was common under Gaddafi for officials to intercept refugees at sea in Libyan waters and force them to return to that nation without proper screening to determine their refugee, asylum or other migrant status. These actions violated the principle of nonrefoulement protecting refugees from being expelled or returned to an area where they fear for their lives (Al-Dayel, Anfinson and Anfinson 2021, 4). Some detainees were sold by smugglers into forced labor or prostitution by corrupted security officials when these illegal returns occurred.

Libya included the right to asylum in its constitution following the fall of the Gaddafi regime in 2011. However, that document did not offer a process by which to determine the asylum status of petitioning individuals. Given the involvement of corrupt actors in the operation of detainment centers, these continue to function as small illicit economies within Libyan politics (Al-Dayel, Anfinson and Anfinson 2021). The lack of stable government institutions after the fall of the regime allowed these actors to become entrenched. Today, those who benefit from these illegal micro-economies bend every effort to protect them (Shaw, Mark, & Mangan 2019, 99–110). The drug trade, human trafficking, refugee and migrant smuggling, and slavery all provide steady income and any serious attempt to end their operations risks a return to civil conflict.

Libya has signed several agreements with the EU and other Mediterranean states, including the Malta Declaration of February 2017. That pact sought to reduce irregular migration and human trafficking along the Central Mediterranean route by making EU funds available to affected nations to improve the reception and voluntary return of migrants (Palm 2020, 13). In Libya's case, the agreement aimed to keep migrants in Libyan territory and arrange for their lawful return prior to their arrival in any Union country.

Within Libya, the GNA has sought to use this European Union dependence to its advantage, by preventing asylum seekers and migrants from leaving Libya in exchange for diplomatic concessions. The joint Libyan-EU policy on migration has placed still greater pressure on Libya's detention centers and exacerbated the already dismal conditions present in them.

Beginning in 2017, the EU began to focus its actions on the training of cooperating nation's coast guards, protecting and assisting migrants and refugees, supporting local communities and improving border management (European Council 2021). These actions have been funded through the EU emergency trust for Africa and account for €408 million of the €4.5 billion general budget for the trust (European Council 2021).

While the EU has pledged training and aid to the Libyan Coast Guard in addition to aid to affected coastal communities in that country further to the Malta Declaration, conditions within Libya have not really changed positively for migrants and refugees (European Council 2021). What has changed has been the number of migrants and refugees successfully reaching the European Union. Since 2016, migration to the European Union from Libya has fallen by 95%, suggesting that the EU has assigned priority to stemming the tide of migrants and refugees over improving human rights conditions in Libya.

Malta and the Refugee Crisis

Small EU states, including Malta, have seen their political institutions strained by the Syrian refugee crisis. Malta, an island nation located between the northern coast of Libya and the southern tip of Italy, emerged as prime stop for refugees on their way to Europe in the wake of the Syrian Civil War.

In direct contrast to Libya, Malta is a stable republic with functioning democratic institutions. With a population of a little more than half a million people, it has perhaps been more dramatically affected by the migrant and refugee stream during the last fifteen years than any other country in the EU or along the Mediterranean Sea. According to EU data, Malta has the highest ratio of refugees to resident population in the EU with more than 56.23 such individuals per 1,000 citizens, as of 2019. For reference, large countries, including France and Germany have like ratios of 5.73 and 10.67 per 1,000 inhabitants respectively (European Union 2021). Malta's location, small population and land area dispose it to be affected disproportionately by flows of migrants and refugees from the south. Though this is also a problem for other small EU states, including Luxembourg and Iceland, Malta is unique in that its location makes it an attractive transit location to the continent.

According to a recent report on migration into the European Union, the Central Mediterranean route saw the most significant increase in irregular migration of any such path during 2021 (European Council 2022). The Central Mediterranean route refers to the routes that refugees from North Africa and beyond follow to travel to Malta, Italy and France. Although Malta, in particular, saw a net decrease in migration in 2022, the central Mediterranean route to the EU remains popular, especially with migrants leaving from Libya and Tunisia. As of late September 2021, for example, 54,000 migrants had taken this route to the EU, with 41,000 of those landing in Italy alone. By that same date in 2021, Malta had offered asylum to only 470 migrants, owing to its much harsher policy on migration and its cooperation with Libya's interim government (ECRE 2021).

Malta has been an EU member and a participant in the Schengen area agreement since 2004. This means that if Malta allows entry or asylum to migrants, they can thereafter seek asylum elsewhere in the EU. Thus, Malta has become a prime target for refugees. However, Malta has always had restrictive immigration and asylum policies, which its leaders have maintained even in the face of criticism. In an infamous case in 2002, for example, Malta deported more than 200 asylum-seeking Eritrean migrants who were subsequently tortured, maimed and in some cases killed following their return to their home country (Leone-Ganado 2015).

Main actors and national legal framework

The main actors involved in the management of refugee flows in Malta include the state, the Catholic Church, and various international organizations. Malta's laws that govern migration, asylum and human trafficking are its Immigration Act; Refugees Act, amended in 2015 and 2017; White Slave Traffic (Suppression) and Victims of Crime of the Laws of Malta; Care Orders Act and Prevention of Disease Ordinance. A part of the Maltese Criminal Code is dedicated to human trafficking and the most recent amendment to that statute occurred in 2018. Furthermore, Malta adopted several amendments to its Criminal Code in 2013 to integrate the EU Directive 2011/36/EU on Preventing and Combating Trafficking in Human Beings (Migrants/Refugees 2020).

In terms of international obligations, Malta has ratified the Convention on the Rights of the Child (1990); the ILO Convention on the Worst Forms of Child Labor (2001); the Optional Protocol on the Sale of Children, Child Prostitution and Child Pornography (2002); the Protocol to Prevent, Suppress and Punish Trafficking in Persons, especially Women and Children (known as the Palermo Protocol) (2003); and the Council of Europe Convention on Actions against Trafficking in Human Beings (2008) (Migrants/Refugees 2020).

The main government players responsible for the implementation of laws governing migration, asylum seekers, and human trafficking in Malta are the Ministry for Home Affairs and National Security and the Ministry for Justice and Home Affairs. As far as governmental agencies are concerned, the Office of the Refugee Commissioner (REFCOM), department of the Ministry of Home Affairs, provides information about asylum procedures and statistical data concerning that population. The Agency for the welfare of the asylum seekers (AWAS) provides information about employment, housing, health, education, and welfare, while the *Aġenzija Appoġġ* supports and protects children and youths against exploitation (Migrants/Refugees 2020). Despite these law enforcement measures, the government of Malta does not fully meet the minimum standards for the elimination of trafficking and has received a TIER 2 ranking, which means that it is making significant effort to fill the gaps in its laws and institutions (Migrants/Refugees 2020).

The Catholic Church is deeply involved in caring for refugees through several front-line organizations that help them by providing different services (Migrants/Refugees 2020). Caritas Malta has offered services to vulnerable people since 1968 and was officially registered as *Fondazzjoni Caritas Malta* in 2017. The Malta Emigrants' Commission (established in 1950) provides pastoral care, counselling services and protection to migrants as well as people on the move and itinerant persons. During the current COVID-19 pandemic (2020), the Commission also engaged in the distribution of food and other basic necessities to needy refugee families.

Since 1993, the Jesuit Refugee Service Malta (JRS) has been providing legal assistance and social work services (including healthcare and psychological support) to asylum seekers, while also advocating for just support and protection of the most vulnerable. Through its team of lawyers, social workers, nurses, Jesuit priests and religious, cultural mediators and volunteers, JRS Malta also reaches the local community through awareness raising programs aimed at highlighting the realities that each refugee and migrant experiences.

The John XXIII Peace Lab, founded 30 years ago by a Franciscan friar, promotes a culture of peace and justice through adult education programs based on Christian beliefs. Since 2005, following an agreement with the Ministry for the Family and Social Solidarity, the Peace Lab has been providing accommodation and basic care to asylum seekers.

Working in Malta since 2009, the RENATE project (Religious in Europe Networking Against Trafficking and Exploitation) is part of the *TALITHA KUM* international project created by the International Union Superiors General and helps the victims of human trafficking by offering a variety of services. The Salesians of Don Bosco provide educational and pastoral activities in a number of residential homes, schools, churches, and youth centers. The Diocesan Commissions of the Archdiocese of Malta are deeply involved in the migration issue, while the Order of Malta is particularly involved in the wellness of migrants, especially single migrant mothers and their children.

In this context, and in view of the huge pressures experienced by the country because of the large number of boat arrivals (1,200 in April 2020), Maltese bishops, through the Maltese Episcopal Conference, which is made up of two dioceses: the Island of Malta with its 70 parishes and the Island of Gozo with 15 parishes, have taken very firm positions on defending the rights and dignity of refugees, especially with regard to the phenomenon of the ongoing tragedies in the Mediterranean. They continue to make repeated appeals for concrete, concerted and collaborative action (Migrants/Refugees 2020).

Among the international organizations involved in the management of refugee flows, it is worth mentioning the Platform of Human Rights Organizations in Malta (PHROM) that is a network of NGOs that promotes human rights, and International Organization for Migration (IOM) and the United Nations High Commission for Refugees (UNHCR) that support different projects focused on migrants and asylum seekers. The IOM Office in Malta was established in 2007 and is currently working on several resettlement projects and programs, assistance to refugees and migrants, return, relocation and the fight against human trafficking. IOM also provides a free telephone helpline for migrants and victims of human trafficking while also promoting awareness-raising campaigns for the local population (Migrants/Refugees 2020).

Considering the strengths and weaknesses of the various organizations and entities involved in migration issues raises several concerns. concerns. First, there is a lack of coordination not only among the government ministries, but also between them and the lay and religious associations involved in the care and protection of migrants. Second, the government does not enforce a labor recruitment regulation specific to those sectors most directly involved in human trafficking. Third, there is little accurate and current information about migration and refugee flows.

Asylum seekers and refugees in Malta

In 2019, the total number of asylum seekers arriving in Malta was 3,406. In the first six months of 2020, slightly half that number (1,699) arrived. Until mid-2018, due to an informal agreement between Malta and Italy, all migrants who had been rescued in Maltese territory or in its search and rescue waters were disembarked in Italy. When the Italian government decided to stop those flows in 2018, Malta signed relocation agreements with other EU countries and some 1,000 people who had been rescued at sea were transferred from Malta to France, Germany, Portugal, Spain, Luxembourg, and Ireland.

When asylum seekers arrive in Malta, most are transferred to its Open, Detention and Initial Reception centers. These allow asylum seekers only a certain amount of mobility beyond their confines, which are located far from the nation's urban areas. Consequently, the refugees have almost no interaction with the local population. In June 2020, the Open centers housed 1,490 persons, another 1,653 were in Detention centers and 321 were in Initial Reception centers (Migrants/Refugees 2020). The journey that the refugees endure before their arrival in Malta has a very high level of risk and danger. While in Libya, they run the risk of being tortured or raped. After that, crossing the Mediterranean Sea in often fragile boats represents another high degree of risk. Arriving in Malta, some asylum seekers must wait in Detention centers before they receive a decision about their claims. Others must wait in Open centers, living in crowded containers with little protection in cold and hot weather.

It is important to note that compared to the total number of claims, the percentage of successful claims is very low. Between January and May 2020, Malta saw 777 claims but only 21 per cent of them were recognized. Of those, 5 per cent were given refugee status, 16 per cent were given subsidiary protection and two cases resulted in temporary humanitarian protection. Despite obtaining refugee status or subsidiary protection, those migrants are at significant risk of poverty. This is so in part because asylum seekers in Malta are not entitled to the social welfare benefits designed to help the country's poorer citizens and long-term residents. However, refugees with subsidiary protection status and who live in the Open or Detention centers are eligible to receive basic social assistance.

Human Trafficking

One of the main challenges facing refugees is that they become the subject of human trafficking. In 2017, Maltese police identified 30 victims of human trafficking most of which occurred in urban areas. There is little information about the route or the channels being used by the traffickers while difficulties in accurately identifying the victims can result in them becoming invisible. In 2017 for example, although NGOs reported assisting victims who were children, the government never formally identified them, despite the fact that some minors were eventually accused of prostitution (Migrants/Refugees 2020). The main programs and activities that victims of human trafficking can access include the Program Crime Stop; a phone help line using the number 119. Police also refer victims of trafficking to *Aġenzija Appoġġ* to receive different kinds of support, including shelter. The National Welfare Agency offers medical care, employment services, counselling and additional emergency shelters and staff (Migrants/Refugees 2020). While media tend to look for the more sensational aspects of irregular migration, little coverage is given to human trafficking and its victims. This is consistent with the invisibility that still characterizes this complex issue.

Maltese perceptions of refugees

Maltese perceptions of refugees are very much conditioned by media accounts. Specifically, Maltese media have two different approaches when reporting on forced migrants. On the one hand, some focus on the sensational elements of migration, putting the attention on crisis and invasion and often use inappropriate language in doing so. On the other hand, others focus their reporting on the human rights of these persons and their struggle to reach Malta safely.

Maltese opinion on the matter of migration remains harsh despite public campaigns by NGOs to encourage the opposite. Many Maltese fear that their local culture and heritage will be lost amidst a wave of migrants and refugees, a common sentiment in many EU countries. Indeed, it is not difficult to see why Maltese political and social groups have been successful in securitizing refugees and migrants. Malta's foreign-born population percentage rose from 4.9 per cent in 2011 to more than 23.17 per cent in 2019 (European Union 2021). That growth led to a xenophobic political reaction and Malta adopted a harsher political stance on migration than EU policy recommended. Rising public concern has joined with mounting financial strain, arising from a relative lack of resources and coordinated support from other EU states, to impede Malta's willingness to address the migrant challenge in accord with EU policy.

The large number of migrants moving into and through Malta has heightened widespread anti-migrant sentiments among the local Maltese. Narratives of African and other 'invaders' who purportedly aim to destroy European civilization have circulated widely during the last decade, spiking participation in far-right parties (McAdam and Otto 2020). Maltese public opinion on migration remains generally negative: 63 per cent of the Maltese population identifies migration as a problem and less than one third view it as culturally enriching (Durick 2012). In addition, an overwhelming majority of Maltese believe that migration has worsened crime in the country (McAdam and Otto 2020).

This negative outlook has shaped the Maltese government's migration policies. Often butting heads with the EU over what it considers to be a lack of aid in dealing with migrants and refugees, Malta closed its ports to migrant vessels as well as sent refugees rescued trying to cross from unstable areas back to the ports from which they embarked. In 2018, the Maltese government prohibited a 'Lifeline' ship with more than 200 rescued migrants from docking. This incident occurred just a month after the country had closed its ports to the humanitarian ship MV Aquarius. Both events brought sharp criticism from other EU states, including France, but that outcry did not shift Maltese attitudes (Pullella and Scherer 2018).

In 2020, Amnesty International condemned Malta for its 'illegal tactics' in dealing with refugees. Amnesty highlighted Malta's redirection of ships containing migrants towards Italy, forcible return of refugees to Libya and illegal detention of individuals in ill-equipped ferries off its shores (France-Presse 2020). In addition, Malta has for some time followed a policy of mandatory detention of migrants through which men, women, and children are held for long periods awaiting extradition. This detention policy led to the rioting of detainees in September of 2019, which brought broad attention to their plight. Weathering international criticism from fellow EU member states and a range of NGOs and aid organizations, Malta has failed to shift its policies or harsh treatment of refugees.

The inhumane conditions at the detention centers

The origins of Malta's severe measures lie in the fact that the country found itself completely unprepared when the migrant stream peaked in 2015. As increasingly large numbers of migrants began arriving at once, the nation began to exhaust its already limited resources to address their needs. The surge of migrants in the past few years, when more than 3,500 and 1,200 people entered Malta in 2019 and the first half of 2020 respectively, has been difficult for the nation to manage (ECRE 2021). The three main facilities on the island – Marsa, the Safi Barracks, and the Lyster Barracks – can handle about 2,000 people, which is quite small compared to migrant housing and detention facilities in other EU countries (ECRE 2021). These detention centers have been roundly criticized in the press for their 'prison-like conditions' (Abela 2019). The European Committee for the Prevention of

Torture and Inhuman or Degrading Treatment or Punishment (CPT) published a report in March 2021 noting that 'living conditions in detention are overall deplorable, with migrants deprived of their liberty and kept in overcrowded units, with nothing to do and very minimal contact with the outside world for prolonged periods' (ECRE 2021). Government officials in Malta have denied the reported conditions of the detention facilities even in the face of evidence to the contrary, signaling that they may not see the deplorable conditions as a pressing concern despite the degradation and human rights violations they represent.

The Lack of a comprehensive EU migration Policy

Another factor that influences Malta's restrictive migrant and refugee detention policies is the fact that the European Union has not offered its members a comprehensive strategy concerning migration. There are several reasons for this situation, but most are linked to the recurring debate concerning national sovereignty that arises in any discussion for a unified strategy within the Union. Migration, in particular, has been an especially contentious issue within the EU as it was a key element in the United Kingdom's decision to exit the community in January 2020. Any Union migration strategy must account for the various national policies and demographic realities of each member state. This fact makes it quite difficult for negotiators. For example, in 2019 Germany, France, Malta, and Italy prepared a plan to screen migrants from boats quickly and relocate them to EU members willing to accept them (Cook 2019). That scheme would allay the incidents of humanitarian migrant rescue ships being prohibited from docking in Italy and Malta. Unfortunately, although this plan was devised by countries that typically disagree on EU migration policy, it nevertheless lacked the support of a majority of EU members, with only 7 of 28 member states supporting the initiative (Al Jazeera 2019).

Conclusion

The refugee challenge, which has continued to affect Mediterranean states since its peak in 2015, continues to confound countries around the region. In many cases, it has put great strain on the resources and institutions of governments unprepared to address it. Libya and Malta have been pressed hard in their efforts to meet the needs of those crossing their borders. Both countries have also experienced pressures from internal and external sources that have fostered harsh environments for refugees while also creating impediments to addressing their needs coherently. Both states have failed to address the inhumane conditions and treatment of migrants at their detainment centers. In Libya, detention centers are often the province of corrupt officials and militias and have become a hotspot for human trafficking, torture, and forced labor. Meanwhile, Malta's detainment centers have been criticized for their inhumane conditions and long and uncertain stays. Malta has also forcibly returned refugees without proper screening and acknowledgment of their human rights.

Apart from its governmental divisions and domestic instability, Libya faces the issue of impotent and corrupt institutions that are ill-equipped to address the human rights abuses that are visited daily on migrants across the country. Human trafficking, slavery, and other forms of abuse run rampant and the lack of security along the borders means that the crisis is likely to continue. In addition, the decentralized nature of Libyan society and its corrupt and convoluted power relationships make any reform difficult. Thus, it is a very difficult task for the Libyans to reform these institutions or centralize and legitimize governance. It will undoubtedly be a major challenge for Libya to reform itself internally so as to address its institutional corruption in a competent and holistic way.

Malta is a small island nation with a relative lack of resources and popular disdain for migrants. Given the country's geographical location between Libya and Italy, it experiences a high number of migrants and refugees seeking to travel to the larger EU countries. These factors set the country up to fail in properly handling the refugee influx. Malta's difficulties have also been exacerbated by the lack of a coherent EU migration and asylum policy. This situation has placed Maltese officials in a situation where they have come to perceive that an aggressive anti-migrant posture is their most viable course politically.

References

Abela, Kristina. 2019. 'Living at Safi Barracks Was a Nightmare'. *Times of Malta*, 3September,

2019. https://timesofmalta.com/articles/view/living-at-safi-barracks-was-a-nightmare-migrant.732880

Al Jazeera. 2019. Several EU Countries Refuse to Back Migrant Boat Plan. Humanitarian Crises News, *Al Jazeera*, 8 October 2019. https://www.aljazeera.com/news/2019/10/8/several-eu-countries-refuse-to-back-migrant-boat-plan

Boukhars, Anouar, and Frederic Wehrey. 2019. Chapter 6. In *Salafism in the Maghreb: Politics, Piety, and Militancy*, 119–19. Oxford University Press.

Cook, Lorne. 2019. Several EU Countries Refuse to Back Migrant Boat Plan. ABC News. *ABC*

News Network, 8 October 2019. https://abcnews.go.com/International/ wireStory/eu-migration-chief-urges-support-disembarkation-plan-66127331

Durick, Hannah E. 2012. African Irregular Migrants in Malta: Exploring Perceptions and Renegotiating the Socio-Cultural Siege of Malta, *Pursuit - The Journal of Undergraduate Research at The University of Tennessee*: Vol. 4(1), Article 4.

ECRE—European Council for Refugees and Exiles. 2021. European Council on Refugees and Exiles: Country Report: Malta, May 2021 https:// asylumineurope.org/wp-content/uploads/2021/05/AIDA-MT_2020update.pdf

ECRE—European Council for Refugees and Exiles. 2021. Conditions in Detention Facilities - Asylum Information Database: European Council on Refugees and Exiles. Asylum Information Database, European Council on Refugees and Exiles, 7 May 2021. https://asylumineurope.org/reports/ country/malta/detention-asylum-seekers/detention-conditions/conditions-detention-facilities/

European Council. 2021. Central Mediterranean Route. *Consilium*, 29 April 29 2021. https://www.consilium.europa.eu/en/policies/eu-migration-policy/central-mediterranean-route/

European Council. 2022. Migration Flows: Eastern, Central and Western Routes. *Consilium*, 12 January 2022. https://www.consilium.europa.eu/en/ infographics/migration-flows/#

European Union. 2021. Migration and Migrant Population Statistics. Migration and migrant population statistics—Statistics Explained. https://ec.europa.eu/ eurostat/statistics-explained/index.php?title=Migration_and_migrant_ population_statistics

Fitzgerald, Mary, and Mattia Toaldo. 2016. A Quick Guide to Libya's Main Players. *European Council on Foreign Relations*. https://ecfr.eu/archive/ page/-/Lybias_Main_Players.pdf

France-Presse, Agence. 2020. Amnesty Says Malta Using 'Illegal Tactics' against Migrants. *VOA*. 8 September 2020. https://www.voanews.com/a/ europe_amnesty-says-malta-using-illegal-tactics-against-migrants/6195586. html

Leone-Ganado, Philip. 2015. Eritrean Activist Reflects on Malta's Dark Hour in 2002. *Times of*

Malta, 13 November 2015. https://timesofmalta.com/articles/view/Eritrean-activist-reflects-on-Malta-s-dark-hour-in-2002.591914

McAdam, Mark, and Laura Otto. 2020. Interests Under Construction: Views on Migration from the European Union's Southern External Border. *Political Studies*, (November 2020). https://doi.org/10.1177/0032321720966464.

Migrants/Refugees. 2020. Migration Profile: Malta. https://migrants-refugees.va/it/wp-content/uploads/sites/3/2020/12/2020-CP-Malta-EN.pdf

Nadia Al-Dayel, Aaron Anfinson & Graeme Anfinson. 2021. Captivity, Migration, and Power in Libya. *Journal of Human Trafficking*, DOI: 10.1080/23322705.2021.1908032

Palm, E. 2020. Externalized Migration Governance and the Limits of Sovereignty: The Case of Partnership Agreements between EU and Libya. *Theoria*, 86: 9–27. (2020) https://doi.org/10.1111/theo.12224

Pullella, Philip, and Steve Scherer. 2018. Italy Says Malta Not Taking in Migrant Ship Is 'Inhumane'. *Reuters*. 22 June 2018. https://www.reuters.com/article/us-europe-migrants-italy/italy-says-malta-not-taking-in-migrant-ship-is-inhumane-idUSKBN1JI1FS

Shaw, Mark, and Fiona Mangan. 2015. Enforcing 'Our Law' When the State Breaks down: The Case of Protection Economies in Libya and Their Political Consequences. *Hague Journal on the Rule of Law 7*, no. 1: 99–110. https://doi.org/10.1007/s40803-015-0008-4.

Smits, Rosan, Floor Janssen, Ivan Briscoe, and Terri Beswick. 2013. Revolution and Its Discontents: State, Factions and Violence in the New Libya. *Netherlands Institute of International Relations Clingendael*, September.

UNHCR. 2021. Afghanistan Refugee Crisis Explained. The UN Refugee Agency, 16 August 2021. https://www.unrefugees.org/news/afghanistan-refugee-crisis-explained

UNHCR (United Nations High Commissioner for Refugees). 2022. Syria Emergency. The UN Refugee Agency. https://www.unhcr.org/en-us/syria-emergency.html

U.S. Department of State. 2021. 2020 Trafficking in Persons Report—United States Department of State. June 23. https://www.state.gov/reports/2020-trafficking-in-persons-report/

Youssef Mohammad Sawani. 2012. Post-Qadhafi Libya: interactive dynamics and the political future. *Contemporary Arab Affairs.* 1 January 2012; 5 (1): 1–26. doi: https://doi.org/10.1080/17550912.2012.650007

Zaidy, Zakariya El. 2019. EU Migration Policy towards Libya: A Policy of Conflicting Interests. Friedrich-Ebert-Stiftung, June 2019. https://library.fes.de/pdf-files/bueros/tunesien/15544.pdf

14

Concluding Remarks

MAX O. STEPHENSON JR. AND YANNIS A. STIVACHTIS

Throughout the chapters of this book, several cross-cutting themes or phenomena appear to have played vital, if varying, roles in government and popular responses to the mass displacement and migration prompted by the Syrian Civil War and we emphasize those here. We first highlight the problem of alterity or othering as a central feature of these nations' reactions to the mass migration challenge represented by that conflict. Thereafter, we discuss the intersection of the human tendencies for xenophobia and fear of difference and change as a key force in producing broad popular ill-will and government opposition to assisting the displaced profiled in this volume. Finally, we suggest that these proclivities merged in each of these nations, although at varying speeds and to changing degrees during the decade of the Syrian migration, to generate calls by many individuals within them that migrants and refugees constituted a security threat to be met with demonization and removal and/or with efforts to ensure they were kept 'at bay' at all costs. We suggest that the comprehensive security approach helps analysts identify salient forces and concerns crucial to such public movements and, at least indirectly, can help government leaders marshal efforts to prevent or mitigate their worsening or recurrence.

Perhaps foremost among the phenomena revealed by these chapters is the centrality of alterity as a driver and mediator of responses to the migrants and refugees who fled Syria's conflict. Every case presented in these chapters is underlaid with popular and public policy choices shaped by fear and 'othering'. Primo Levi has described this human proclivity thoughtfully:

> We [humankind] also tend to simplify history; but the patterns within which events are ordered is not always identifiable in a single unequivocal fashion. ... Nevertheless, perhaps for reasons that go back to our origins as social animals, the need to divide the field into 'we' and 'they' is so strong that this bi-

> partition–friend–enemy–prevails over all others. ... This Manichean tendency shuns half-tints and complexities: it is prone to reduce the river of human occurrences to conflicts, and the conflicts to duels... (Levi, 1988, 31–32).

In the present case, this human inclination has translated to vociferous claims within governments among their officials and beyond them in organized groups and parties alike in every country under discussion in this book, that those fleeing the Syrian Civil War were crass interlopers who, if permitted to remain, would usurp employment from existing citizens and would also despoil the existing supposed racial, religious, and ethnic order within those nations' borders. That is, in each country treated here, the migrants and refugees were depicted, to varying degrees in each affected nation across the period of the Syrian migration, and with the initial conspicuous exceptions of Turkey and Jordan, as especial threats because they were foreigners and despicable 'others,' because of their patent need, and because of the color of their skin. In keeping with this trope of the foreigner as racialized intruder, Syria's refugees were met in many instances in the nations investigated here with an abstractly derived hatred. In tandem with that fear and general rancor, many recipient government officials and populations met the Syrian exodus with companion claims that those comprising it were less than human and could and should therefore be treated accordingly, and with impunity. In some cases, as in Greece and Malta, as the relevant chapters here highlight, while for perhaps different reasons, that attitude was realized in public policies in a notably brutal way, as those nations' officials routinely violated European Union and international norms and law as they dealt with Syria's refugees.

In short, these chapters suggest that the large and sudden Syrian migration unleashed a Manichean and xenophobic reaction in many affected nations that intersected with racism, or reflected it, to result in routine violation of international standards of treatment for Syria's externally displaced population. That situation was surely only exacerbated by the sheer magnitude of that country's migrant and refugee stream. These conditions led to flagrant dehumanization claims by officials and representatives of advocacy groups, especially far-right ones, and a popular ill-will in many nations touched by the exodus that was unrelated to any factual analysis of its likely implications.

The general climate of fear and uncertainty unleashed by Syrians' mass departure provided fertile ground for those wishing to weaponize the catastrophe and scapegoat its victims as constituting a security threat to affected countries. As we noted in the introduction, securitization involves claims that a 'threat' – in this case one represented by those displaced by a war, who often espoused different religious beliefs, looked 'different,' and spoke an unfamiliar language or dialect – were depicted as trespassers undeserving of hospitality, let alone of human and civil rights. Many public leaders and advocates suggested that their presence *must* be viewed as a crisis that *must* be interdicted at all costs. In this view, these individuals should not be permitted to remain in targeted countries and if treating them with discriminatory cruelty and callousness could quicken or secure that result, such efforts should be pursued with urgency and alacrity. As we argued:

> Securitization involves four components: first, a securitizing actor/agent (the entity that makes the securitizing statement); second, a proposed existential threat (the object or idea that has been identified as potentially harmful): third, a referent object (the object or idea that is purportedly under threat and needs protection); and finally, an audience (the target population that needs to be persuaded to accept the issue as a security threat) (Waever 1993; Taureck 2006).

Across these chapters, depending on the nation and time-frame on which one focuses, activist groups and political party members as well as government officials were each responsible for securitizing claims concerning displaced Syrians. Those individuals and advocates offered arguments suggesting that any entry of this population constituted an existential threat against which the resident population must be 'protected'. That citizenry merited and required that concern, according to these advocates, because of the conflation of threats the refugees and migrants represented. These actors asserted a variety of arguments aimed at demonstrating that the displaced constituted an existential crisis, including racial and religious claims and slurs of various sorts, assertions of economic and demographic displacement, and what might be dubbed as straightforward xenophobic alterity – they should be rejected out of hand precisely because they 'are not us'. Every government examined in these pages treated the migration Syrian situation as a security crisis at some point in its duration. Those moments and policies might be described as the result of a perfect storm arising from a concatenation of the factors highlighted here, but that cataclysm arose at different times in each nation.

We should be clear. We are not arguing that the Syrian migration scenario could easily or readily have been addressed by any of the affected countries it has touched. Far from it. Nonetheless, the issue is not whether assisting those displaced was simple, but instead why in each of these nations it became, again to shifting degrees at different times, an opportunity for government actors and populations to slip into a speculative Manicheanism built on fear rather than the much more straightforward option of treating those affected with dignity and humanity, even when or if they ultimately could not be accepted for resettlement. All the populations and governments profiled here flunked this test for various periods of time and to varying degrees during the last decade. But they all failed it, and some did so with an egregious and frightening intensity of rancor and cruelty.

This contention raises a deeper question, especially for those nominally democratic governments whose actions are examined in these chapters, of whether such populations can avoid nativism, the claim that current citizenries were always dominant in a territory and any other individuals are illegitimate by definition, even when, as often is the case in historical terms, the present inhabitants are not aboriginal. It likewise prompts the question of whether political xenophobia is inevitable and perhaps even likely in nominally democratic nations in the face of potential significant economic, social, or demographic change. All the countries treated here to which Syrians sought entry experienced an exponential growth in othering sentiments as those fearful, those disdainful of the migrants on racial or social hierarchy grounds, and those aspiring for power reacted with cruel fright to the reality of a steady stream of displaced individuals, especially during the peak years of that flight.

In short, reflecting on the analyses offered here, we have found ourselves pondering how one may protect the rights of vulnerable populations from the phenomena these chapters highlight. We find ourselves recurring to arguments suggesting that governments must work harder to educate their citizenries concerning the inevitability and benefits of pluralism to diminish popular response to the siren calls of those willing to fearmonger and scapegoat and demonize the dispossessed on racial, economic, or other grounds linked to difference. One need not idealize Syria's migrants as angels to contend that none deserved to be treated with contempt for who they are/were or for the situation in which they found themselves. Nevertheless, the evidence suggests that many were, and that fact should prompt sober and continuing consideration.

In keeping with our point that Syrian migrants should not be idealized as a class, we should also say that not everyone in the nations and populations treated here rallied to xenophobic claims and Manichean alterity. That was surely not the case across all these citizenries or within all their governments during the past decade. Indeed, Augusta Nannerini's chapter, particularly, points to the need to approach these questions with a willingness to disaggregate one's analysis as necessary and appropriate from the national level to capture the vicissitudes of government and social action and refugee experience. We think that reminder is an apt one, even as it points once more to the layered social, economic, and political complexity that resulted in national responses to the Syrian migration.

Finally, we take up the question of how the nations in the eastern and central Mediterranean security subcomplexes analyzed in this book reacted to the Syrian Civil War and the mass migration it spawned during the last decade. In comprehensive security terms, these nations saw a sudden rise in economic claims and an implicit challenge to their collective social identities. Together, these twin forces produced a xenophobic backlash among many citizens in the affected nations in this region that saw the Syrian migration recast and redefined from a crisis in which thousands were fleeing persecution and worse to, instead, the onslaught of an alien and alienating force that posed real danger to settled ways of life and understanding of social structures. Advocates and officials espousing the latter claims successfully weaponized them at an increasing pace as the exodus wore on. The result was the securitization of the Syrian immigration itself as a threat to the peoples and governments affected by it in this region.

What this result meant in practice is harsh treatment of many Syrians solely on the basis of their personhood, surely an unchangeable condition. This result was in no way ordained, even as Primo Levi warned of the depth of humanity's proclivity to it. One can readily imagine different scenarios to those that unfolded in the nations examined here. Indeed, securing that alternate outcome seems to be the critical challenge raised by these analyses. Imagining that the growing climate crisis and profound economic dislocation and inequality wrought by neoliberal globalization are unlikely to abate any time soon, how can national leaders interested in democratic realization prepare for future migration-related challenges, large and small, by ensuring that the human rights of those displaced are honored while at the same time not creating conditions that those clamoring for scapegoats and demanding an end to ambiguity and complexity can exploit to undermine their efforts?

In this regard, we are reminded of the ancient Greek myth of Scylla and Charybdis. Scylla was said to be a six-headed monster who inhabited a rock on one side of a narrow strait while Charybdis was a parlous whirlpool on the other side of that narrows. Scylla routinely seized and devoured sailors when their ships passed near her home as they sought to avoid the peril posed by Charybdis. By analogy, government officials who take democratic values and human rights seriously must somehow successfully navigate the metaphoric waters of migration without falling prey to the monster their own populations may become when aroused, fear-filled, and 'threatened,' while also avoiding the very real human crisis represented by failing to honor the rights of the displaced. This is a difficult challenge by any standard of evaluation and many of the governments treated in this volume failed to meet it to greater or lesser degree as the Syrian migration wore on. That fact should not constrain hope that those straits may not be traversed more successfully in the future, and we believe the lessons contained in these chapters will assist government officials in doing so. It is with that possibility that we conclude.

References

Levi, Primo. 1989, 2013. *The Drowned and the Saved*. London: Abacus Publishers.

Taureck, Rita. 2006. Securitization theory and securitization studies. *Journal of International Relations and Development* 9(1), 53–61.

Waever, Ole. 1993. Securitization and Desecuritization. In Ronnie. D. Lipschutz (ed.), *On Security*, 46–86. New York: Columbia University Press.

Note on Indexing

Our books do not have indexes due to the prohibitive cost of assembling them. If you are reading this book in paperback and want to find a particular word or phrase you can do so by downloading a free PDF version of this book from the E-International Relations website. View the e-book in any standard PDF reader and enter your search terms in the search box. You can then navigate through the search results and find what you are looking for. If you are using apps (or devices) to read our e-books, you should also find word search functionality in those.

You can find all of our books at http://www.e-ir.info/publications